Made in Baja

The publisher and the University of California Press Foundation gratefully acknowledge the generous support of the Peter Booth Wiley Endowment Fund in History.

Made in Baja

*The Lives of Farmworkers and Growers behind
Mexico's Transnational Agricultural Boom*

Christian Zlolniski

UNIVERSITY OF CALIFORNIA PRESS

University of California Press, one of the most distinguished university presses in the United States, enriches lives around the world by advancing scholarship in the humanities, social sciences, and natural sciences. Its activities are supported by the UC Press Foundation and by philanthropic contributions from individuals and institutions. For more information, visit www.ucpress.edu.

University of California Press
Oakland, California

© 2019 by Christian Zlolniski

Library of Congress Cataloging-in-Publication Data

Names: Zlolniski, Christian, author.
Title: Made in Baja : the lives of farmworkers and growers behind Mexico's transnational agricultural boom / Christian Zlolniski.
Description: Oakland, California : University of California Press, [2019] Includes bibliographical references and index. |
Identifiers: LCCN 2019018118 (print) | LCCN 2019022006 (ebook)
 ISBN 9780520971936 (ebook and ePDF) | ISBN 9780520300620 (cloth : alk. paper) | ISBN 9780520300637 (pbk : alk. paper)
Subjects: LCSH: Agricultural laborers—Mexico—Baja California (State)—Social conditions.
Classification: LCC HD1531.M6 (ebook) | LCC HD1531.M6 Z56 2019 (print) | DDC 331.7/6309722—dc23
LC record available at https://lccn.loc.gov/2019018118

Manufactured in the United States of America
26 25 24 23 22 21 20 19
10 9 8 7 6 5 4 3 2 1

To the peoples of San Quintín, who with their hard work, care, and perseverance helped to build this beautiful region.

Proceeds from sales of this book will be donated to set up an annual college scholarship for the children of farmworkers in San Quintín.

CONTENTS

List of Illustrations ix
Acknowledgments xi

    Introduction 1

1. The Birth and Development of Export Agriculture in the San Quintín Valley 23
2. Transnational Agribusiness, Local Growers, and Discontents 48
3. Labor Recruitment: From Local to Transnational Labor Contractors 84
4. "They Want First-Class Workers with Third World Wages": The Workplace Regime of Transnational Agriculture 107
5. Resisting the *Carrilla* in the Workplace: Forms of Labor Protests 127
6. Colonizing and Establishing Roots in Arid Lands 153
7. Watercide: Export Agriculture, Water Insecurity, and Social Unrest 186
    Conclusion 207

Appendix: Policy Recommendations 217
Notes 227
References 239
Index 251

ILLUSTRATIONS

MAPS

1. Map of Baja California along the Mexico-U.S. border *xiv*
2. Map of San Quintín region *xv*

FIGURES

1. View of crop fields along the coast in Vicente Guerrero *5*
2. The author talks with a worker while he waits for his contractor to pick him up *18*
3. A.B.C. Farm's old company sign *36*
4. Desalination plants in San Quintín *45*
5. Driscoll's built a cooling and packing plant for berries in 2007 *52*
6. A BerryMex water reservoir *54*
7. One of Joaquín Cuenca's fields. Cuenca is a share grower for BerryMex *64*
8. Esther in her kitchen in Colonia Santa Fe, getting ready to go to work at Monsanto *85*
9. Labor contractors' buses arrive early to pick up workers in the colonias *89*
10. Arcadio Román's bus that transports workers to the fields *94*
11. First H-2A labor recruiting office of Sierra-Cascade Nursery in San Quintín in 2007 *101*
12. Shadehouses and greenhouses have expanded in San Quintín since the early 2000s *110*
13. A female worker inspects raspberries for BerryMex *118*

14. Justina Sánchez's tiendita in Colonia Santa Fe   *136*
15. Justino Herrera, a longtime labor and community leader, at his home in July 2017   *143*
16. Ramón Suárez and his family at their home   *155*
17. Kin and friends at a weekend birthday party in Colonia Santa Fe   *165*
18. A sign outside a farmworker's house in Colonia Arbolitos announces haircuts and sale of sodas   *171*
19. Chickens and pumpkin flowers are common in workers' backyard gardens   *172*
20. A monthly IMSS-Oportunidades health checkup community meeting in Colonia Santa Fe   *174*
21. Community work by farmworkers is often performed by women   *176*
22. Waterscapes: A water reservoir at Rancho Las Palmas in Vicente Guerrero   *194*
23. Aurelia Suárez and a son get water to do laundry   *196*
24. Aridscapes: A man rides his bike in Colonia Arbolitos   *198*
25. With no sewage system, residents in colonias use latrines   *198*

ACKNOWLEDGMENTS

This book would not have been possible without the support and encouragement of many people throughout the long years it took to complete this project. First, my sincere thanks to all the people in San Quintín who patiently shared their time and knowledge with me. Using the pseudonyms employed in the book to protect their privacy, I am particularly grateful to Esther Chávez, Celeste Hernández, Anayeli and Martín Fernández, and Ramón and Aurelia Suárez for sharing their experiences as farmworkers and residents in San Quintín. Thanks also to Agustín Mejía, Antonio Pedroza, Jaime Coronado, Justina Sánchez, Laura and Luis Flores, Josefina Rodríguez, Rodolfo and Adelina Moreno, Elisa and Nicolás Robles, Rafael Montes, Arcadio Román, Manuel Sánchez Ponce de León, and many others who also helped me along the way. They were always eager to talk even after long hours of hard work, opening their homes and introducing me to relatives, friends, and neighbors to facilitate my research. I also thank the growers, farm managers, and agronomists who invited me to tour their ranches and talk about their businesses and facilities and the challenges of growing fresh crops for export markets. My special gratitude to Henry Clark, Martín Fuentes, Jesús Peña, Joaquín Cuenca, Andrés Palma, and Rubén Hidalgo, as well as the representatives of other companies who opened their doors to me.

I am grateful to the public officers in many government institutions in San Quintín and Baja California. First and foremost, my gratitude to the agronomists of the local Secretariat of Agriculture (SAGARPA) office in San Quintín, especially Arturo Ramos and Eusebio Rincón, who every year provided the latest data available about crop production in the region and from whom I learned much. I also thank the public officials at the Comisión Nacional para el Desarrollo de los

Pueblos Indígenas (CDI) in San Quintín and Ensenada, especially Isidro Pérez Hernández for sharing his insightful knowledge about Mexico's agricultural labor laws. My thanks also to the directors of CESPE, the local agency responsible for providing water to residents in the region and to Radio XEQUIN La Voz del Valle (The Voice of the Valley), an indigenous community radio station that helped me during the first stage of my project.

Many friends and colleagues, more than I can remember, read and provided insightful comments on the multiple chapter iterations. My good friend Annegret Staiger provided loyal support and encouragement throughout the years, reading and offering wise comments. I am also indebted to Josiah Heyman, Roberto Álvarez, David Griffith, and Humberto González for their detailed reading of and suggestions on the final manuscript. I also thank Juan Vicente Palerm who read and offered valuable advice on my analysis of Baja's horticultural industry; he remains an inspiration for ethnographic research on farm laborer rural communities in Mexico and the United States. I also thank Teresa Figueroa Sánchez for sharing her knowledge about farmworkers in the strawberry industry in Santa María. My deep gratitude also to my colleague and friend Roberto Treviño who carefully read and helped me edit earlier iterations and the last versions of the manuscript. I also thank Paul Durrenberger and Suzan Erem, who organized a workshop at the University of Iowa on labor unions in neoliberal times, for their comments on my analysis of labor unions in Mexico. I am also grateful to Sharryn Kasmir, Sian Lazar, and the anonymous readers of *Dialectical Anthropology* for their sharp comments and suggestions on two articles about farmworkers' vulnerability and mobilization responses that helped me refine the analysis on these issues in the book. My sincere thanks also to Naomi Schneider and the staff at the University of California Press for their patience while I completed the book.

The book has benefited from collegial support and input from faculty members at the University of Texas at Arlington. I thank Amy Speier and Heather Jacobsen, my colleagues in the Department of Sociology and Anthropology, for reading and providing insightful suggestions on early drafts of several book chapters as part of a writing group. I also thank my colleagues at the Center for Mexican American Studies (CMAS), Cristina Salinas, Ignacio Ruiz-Pérez, Erin Murrah-Mandril, Ana Gregorio Cano, Isabel Montemayor, David LaFevor, and Marcela Gutiérrez, who commented on parts of the manuscript as participants in the CMAS Research Seminar. I am also indebted to my colleague Luis Plascencia for his careful reading and for providing insightful comments and suggestions that helped to improve the manuscript in its last stage.

In Mexico I benefited from the support of several colleagues and institutions. At El Colegio de la Frontera Norte (Colef), I thank Laura Velasco, who read and commented on parts of the manuscript; Hugo Riemann, who generously shared some photos of his research on water in San Quintín; Angélica Zambrano, who drew the maps of the region; and Marie-Laure Coubes, who offered me a room in her home many times on my way to San Quintín. I also thank Abbdel Camargo Martínez at CONACYT-ECOSUR, who accompanied me in the field during the first years and who shared some of his photos for the book. I also benefited from the knowledge of Marcos López (Bowdoin College) with whom I overlapped a few years in the field when he was doing research for his PhD dissertation. Kim Sánchez Saldaña (Universidad Autónoma del Estado de Morelos) graciously read and commented on several chapters and shared her expertise on agricultural labor contractors in Mexico. I am also indebted to Humberto González at the Centro de Investigaciones y Estudios Superiores en Antropología Social (CIESAS) for the opportunity to present my analysis of export agriculture and water at CIESAS and the Universidad de Guadalajara, where I received helpful comments. My thanks also to Hubert de Grammont and Sara Lara Flores at the Universidad Nacional Autónoma de México (UNAM) for inviting me to present my work at the Instituto de Investigaciones Sociales and for their helpful feedback.

Research for the book received funding from different sources. I am grateful for the funding received from the National Science Foundation and the Wenner-Gren Foundation and from the University of Texas at Arlington for the last part of fieldwork in Mexico.

Finally, I both thank and apologize to my wife, Reina, and children, Pablo and Natalia, for their support and tolerance while I worked on this book. Reina has been a steady and loyal supporter, putting up with my absences for fieldwork or when I was glued to my computer and missing some family events over the years as this project developed and came to fruition. My deepest gratitude to her and to our children.

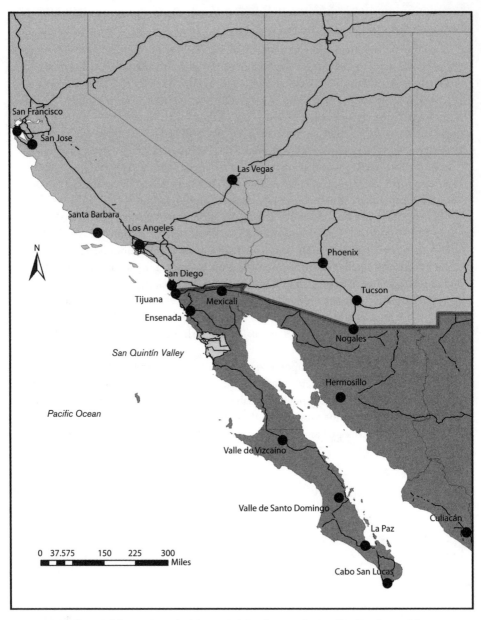

MAP 1. Map of Baja California along the Mexico-U.S. border. Map by Angélica Zambrano Gil. Source: Instituto Nacional de Estadística y Geografía (INEGI), 2017, and U.S. Census Bureau, 2017.

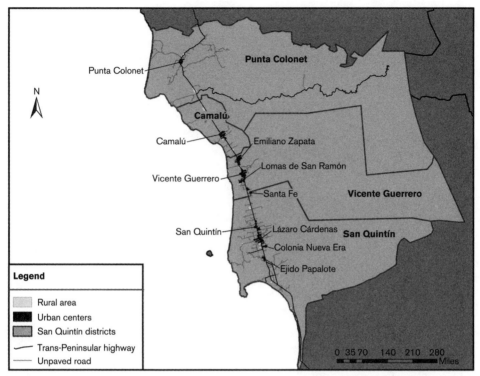

MAP 2. Map of San Quintín region. Map by Angélica Zambrano Gil. Source: Instituto Nacional de Estadística y Geografía (INEGI), 2010, 2018.

Introduction

Export Agriculture and Its Predicaments

It was a placid Saturday in June 2005 when I arrived to interview Jesús Peña, a farm executive at Agrícola San Simón, one of the largest producers of tomatoes for export to the United States located in Baja California's San Quintín Valley. Situated atop a hill in a rural *colonia,* or squatter settlement, in the northern part of the valley, the company's building has an elegant round shape of Mediterranean design with white walls, dark windows, and a large central dome. Surrounded by a well-manicured lawn irrigated by a sprinkler system, this structure contrasts sharply with the shacks and modest homes of the farmworkers who live in the nearby colonias, which lack basic services and are served by dusty, unpaved roads. As I walked into the office and sat in a comfortable air-conditioned waiting area, some farmworkers came to the front desk. One of them, a man in his forties, asked for a "medical pass" to see the company's doctor, but a young secretary behind the counter told him, "The doctor only sees patients on Mondays"; he would have to wait until then. A few minutes later two other field laborers came to pick up their paychecks from the previous week, explaining to the young woman that they could not come the previous Saturday. She replied that they needed to come back on a weekday because Saturday is payday only for the current week.

After a few minutes Jesús Peña, a man in his early forties, arrived and invited me into his private office. Peña's office was neat, clean, and decorated with functional modern furniture and a panoramic bay window from which he could see some of the fields and greenhouses owned by Agrícola San Simón, which extend several miles along the Pacific Ocean. As I looked through the window, he pointed to a big packing plant that stands between two greenhouses from which thousands of tomato boxes are shipped every day north of the border to San Diego and which was built only a few years ago. Peña, who has an accounting degree, was quite attentive and open to talking, exhibiting self-confidence quite different from the more guarded and reticent attitudes I encountered when interviewing older growers with deep roots in the region. He had arrived in the San Quintín Valley in 1987, and, speaking in Spanish, he told me about the changes the company he manages had undergone, from cultivation in open fields to greenhouse production. "Back in the 1980s," he said, "we used to plant thousands of hectares of land and employed thousands of workers who kept coming year after year and anybody could find work immediately.... Everything was massive, and the goal was to produce and export as many boxes of tomatoes as possible. And if we didn't have enough workers we would send a bus [to Oaxaca] to bring more workers, just like that." Then, he continued, things started to change and get more complicated. After years of intensive cultivation on large parcels of land, the aquifer used to irrigate the fields started to dry up, and growers were forced to begin cultivating in smaller areas in green- and shadehouses that required less water. Moreover, American companies that used to buy their tomatoes started to be more restrictive regarding the chemicals and pesticides growers could use and banned several of them. As he explained, "It was in the late 1990s that we started to invest in technology to produce more efficiently, to avoid water evaporation. We became more specialized . . . and started to more carefully plan how much to produce.... We developed a much closer relationship with our American partners as the globalization trend had already arrived.... They began to tell us what they wanted . . . and we realized they didn't care where the tomatoes came from as long as they met certain requirements."

The technological changes Agrícola San Simón introduced to adapt to the new export requirements affected how many workers were hired and what types of farm laborers were needed. As the amount of land planted significantly declined and was gradually replaced with greenhouses, Peña explained, fewer but more skilled workers were needed. Moreover, he added, "many people have settled down here, many workers live here so for many people San Quintín is now their home.... Most of our workers live in the colonias of San Quintín, have their homes, a land lot they own where they started building a home. They are settled down." This more stable and settled labor force affected how Agrícola recruited its workers. Field supervisors, or *mayordomos* as they are known in the valley, were now in charge of recruiting and transporting farm laborers to work, he explained, dramatically reducing the need to bring workers from southern Mexico.

Peña's account of Agrícola San Simón reflects the structural transformation of the fresh-produce industry that started in the early 2000s in San Quintín. Growers shifted from producing a high volume of produce to less quantity but higher-quality products of prime market value. This was a game changer in the region, requiring companies to invest heavily in new production technologies and reorganize the work process to meet the new standards demanded by consumer markets in the United States. Many small local growers were put out of business, while others had to forge commercial partnerships with companies in the United States to access capital to invest in expensive technologies and ensure access to export markets. The new production system also triggered important labor and social changes. Farmworkers' jobs became more specialized, scripted, and monitored to ensure the "product quality" demanded by international markets. Meanwhile farmworkers—most of them indigenous Mixtec, Zapotec, and Triqui immigrants from Oaxaca, Guerrero, and other regions in southern Mexico—began moving in massive numbers from labor camps where they were previously housed by large companies like Agrícola San Simón to makeshift colonias, building shacks in which to live with their children and families. This assured that company managers like Jesús Peña did not need to recruit and transport thousands of indigenous workers from southern Mexico; instead, they could rely on local contractors to hire workers in colonias in San Quintín, bringing labor costs down.

FOCUS OF THE BOOK

This book examines the ecological, social, and human consequences of export agriculture through an ethnographic study of the growers and farmworkers in the San Quintín Valley who produce fresh produce for consumer markets in the United States. Located about 300 kilometers south of the Mexico-U.S. border, San Quintín is one of the most technologically advanced, productive, and economically dynamic agroexport regions in northern Mexico, dominated by companies like Agrícola San Simón. A dormant valley until the 1960s, its population, fueled by the expansion of export agriculture, exploded from 8,600 in 1970 to 38,000 in 1990 and to 93,000 in 2010, the increase largely driven by Mixtec, Triqui, Zapotec, and other indigenous workers. Between 1980 and 2000, thirty-three new colonias were founded by newcomers in the valley. With residents spread around four *delegaciones* (districts)—Colonet, Camalú, Vicente Guerrero, and San Quintín from north to south—the region specializes in the production of fresh fruits and vegetables for North American and other international markets.[1]

Rather than an isolated phenomenon, the agricultural and demographic boom in the San Quintín Valley reflects the consequences of larger structural changes in the agrarian policies in Mexico. Favored by neoliberal principles, export agriculture in Mexico has become a strategy for regional and economic development (Álvarez 2006; Echánove 2001; Sanderson 1986; Lara Flores 1996). These outward-oriented agrarian policies were part of a neoliberal economic reform by the federal government to foster maximum integration into the global market by eliminating barriers to foreign investment and trade (Sanderson 1986). In the process, the Mexican government reduced subsidies for traditional crops such as corn and beans for domestic markets while increasing support to higher-value fruits and vegetables bound for the United States and other international markets (Raynolds 1994; Llambi 1994). The internationalization of fresh fruits and vegetable production led to the weakening of the state in designing food security policies, the concentration of agricultural decision making in the hands of a few transnational corporations, and increasing dependence of Mexican growers on transnational capital for credit, technical assistance, and access to consumer markets in the United States (Sanderson 1986). While the push for export agriculture started in the 1980s, the effective start of the North American Free Trade Agreement (NAFTA) / Tratado de Libre Comercio (TLC) in 1994 made it easier for U.S. agribusinesses, attracted by the ready access to land, lower-cost labor, and lax environmental regulations, to expand in Mexico. NAFTA promoted the notion that Mexico had natural advantages over the United States and Canada for the production of winter fruit and vegetables and that Mexican farmers should turn to these crops to compete successfully in the international market. The Agrarian Reform Law of 1992 further advanced this neoliberal policy change. The reform privatized formerly communal *ejidos*—lands that combine communal ownership with individual use that could not be sold and were ruled by collective councils—giving private investors access to them. The reform enabled international companies to buy or rent land for commercial agriculture, especially in the northern states that could readily export fresh produce to the United States and Canada. In the north, farmers reap the benefits of government programs developed in the 1940s to the 1970s to promote a prosperous export-oriented agricultural sector, paving the way for the emergence of a powerful new class of modern capitalist farmers (Grindle 1995). In the end, commercial agriculture for export markets was expected to generate jobs, reduce rural poverty, and curtail labor migration to the United States.[2]

But the growth of export agriculture in Mexico is also a result of the demand by middle-class consumers in the United States and Canada for fresh vegetables and fruits year-round. More conscious than previous generations about their health and eating habits, Americans' and Canadians' appetite for more green vegetables and fruits, including organically grown crops, has provided an incentive to large U.S. agribusinesses to outsource production to Mexico and other Latin American countries to ensure a continuous supply of fresh crops. In California, horticultural companies sought an opportunity to expand production south of the border to deal with the increased cost of land due to expanding suburbanization and population growth. Droughts, environmental restrictions on pesticides, and water restrictions for irrigation provided additional incentives for U.S. transnational companies to invest in production in Mexico. Other companies developed commercial partnerships with Mexican growers to buy their produce for U.S. markets. As a result, today tons of fresh fruits and vegetables are brought every day by large trucks equipped with the latest cooling technologies to major U.S. nodal

FIGURE 1. View of crop fields along the coast in Vicente Guerrero.

distribution centers, from which they are shipped to supermarkets around the country fast enough to arrive fresh at consumers' dining tables.

Despite these developments, few ethnographic studies have examined the impact of export agriculture on the growers and farmworkers who grow fresh export crops in Baja California. Has employment in the fresh-produce industry enhanced the living standards and opportunities of indigenous laborers who have settled in San Quintín? How has it affected local growers in the region? Did employment in export agriculture reduce their need to migrate to the United States? What are the living conditions in the rural colonias where they have settled? The San Quintín Valley, I argue, is an ideal case to address these questions and examine the economic, social, and ecological effects of export agriculture on the region and the people who produce fresh crops for consumers in the United States. Weaving together ethnographic case stories, I discuss how the development of export agriculture has shaped the lives, challenges, and opportunities of the peoples who have settled in this arid region in Baja. Using an ethnographically grounded approach, I trace the varied social and environmental intersections and their human consequences that the model of transnational agricultural production has brought to the San Quintín Valley. As a new agricultural frontier in the Mexico-U.S. border region, I argue, the fresh-produce industry is predicated on the intense extraction of water as well as new production technologies and forms of labor control to increase worker productivity and meet certification standards required by U.S. markets for imported vegetables and fruits. As the book reveals, the production regime of export agriculture has externalized many of the ecological, labor, and social costs to the indigenous workers and families in San Quintín, who must cope with them in their everyday lives. I unpack the changes that have occurred in the fresh-produce industry and how they have affected growers and farm laborers in the region and discuss the struggles farmworkers confront as they moved from labor camps to their own land lots and homes. Examining farm laborers' lives as workers and settlers, I contend, uncovers the process of social and class transformation that the labor regime of export agriculture has engendered for the farm laborers who live in this region.

DECONSTRUCTING THE WORKPLACE REGIME OF EXPORT AGRICULTURE

The production of fresh fruits and vegetables for international markets is one of the most lucrative sectors in today's global agricultural industry. Generally known as "specialty crops," fresh vegetables and fruits such as strawberries, cucumbers, tomatoes, and table grapes have a high market value and require large capital investments in irrigation systems, pesticides, genetically developed crops, and specialized machinery and equipment. Yet because these crops are perishable, delicate, and difficult to mechanize, they require large contingents of year-round farm laborers in specialized positions such as irrigation, weeding, and soil and crop preparation, as well as hand harvesting and packing. Experts in the study of agrofood systems argue that contemporary capitalist agricultural production is based on a new international division of labor in which the Global South specializes in the production of high market value crops for middle-class consumers in the Global North (Friedland 1994). The result is a system of transnational agriculture in which large agrofood corporations are intermediaries between agricultural producers and food consumers in a global commodity chain in which the most profitable role is distribution rather than the production of crops (McMichael 1994; Friedland 1994; Wright 2005). This production system has generated what A. Haroon Akram-Lodhi and Cristóbal Kay (2010, 274) call the "neoliberal agricultural export bias," a model that promotes the production of nontraditional export fruits and vegetables at the expense of traditional subsistence crops to fuel economic and regional growth in developing countries. Between 1986 and 2007 alone, the share of exports in agricultural output for these countries almost doubled in size, and today fresh produce is processed and packed in countries like Mexico as a means to increase rates of capitalist accumulation (Akram-Lodhi and Kay 2010, 275–76).[3]

But the transnationalization of the fresh-produce industry in Mexico has also transformed the workplace regime in which export crops are produced. At the heart of this change is the homogenization and standardization of planting, picking, and packing practices of fresh fruits and vegetables to meet safety certification requirements for fresh produce for U.S. and other international markets (Phillips 2006, 16; Bonanno and Constance 2001). While food safety regulations existed before, a renewed emphasis began in the late 1990s, when the U.S. Department of Agriculture (USDA) launched the Produce and Imported Food Safety Initiative to enhance hygiene and phytosanitary conditions to prevent food contamination (C. de Grammont and Lara Flores 2010, 235). After September 11, 2001, the U.S. government imposed more regulations under the Bioterrorism Act, requiring growers exporting produce to the United States to register with the USDA and pass tests for phytosanitary control. At the same time, large supermarkets also developed new standards for "food quality" for fresh produce imported from Mexico and other Latin American countries. These norms focus on what Edward Fisher and Peter Benson (2006, 29) call "cosmetic quality," namely, external aesthetic traits such as size, shape, and color of fruits and vegetables arriving on supermarket shelves. The homogenization of "quality standards" by large distribution chains has created a "supermarket governance" (Rogaly 2008), a production regime that has increased the power of large multinationals over the growers of export crops and their workers in Latin America and other developing countries.

In the book, I deconstruct the production model of export agriculture in Baja and discuss how it shapes the experiences and working conditions of farm laborers in the workplace. I pay particular attention to the shift from horticultural production in open fields to cultivation in greenhouses and shadehouses, the epitome of modern capitalist agriculture that seeks to replicate the model of factory production. I also discuss the culture of certification that permeates the fresh-produce industry—the set of technical codes and rules, beliefs, and practices surrounding the production of export crops passed top-down from managers to supervisors—and how it affects the conditions in which farmworkers perform their everyday jobs. The production of fresh produce in Baja, I contend, has generated a workplace environment in which farm labor has become more intensive, regimented, and standardized than ever before. This regime has also created a new class of transnational farmworkers trained in the skills and requirements on which the affluent U.S.-Mexico fresh-produce industry relies as a source of lower-cost and flexible labor.

GROWING WATER-THIRSTY CROPS IN ARID BAJA

The production of water-intensive crops such as tomatoes, berries, and cucumbers in one of the most arid regions in Mexico raises the issue of the ecological logic and social consequences of export agriculture as an engine for economic development. Up until the 1960s, limited water resources and San Quintín's arid climate prevented the development of large-scale agricultural production. The neoliberal agrarian reforms of the 1980s, along with an increasing appetite by U.S. consumers for fresh vegetables and fruits in their daily diets, broke these barriers, unleashing capital investment in water-extraction technologies by transnational corporations to engage in large-scale horticultural production. The arrival of the fresh-produce industry for export markets drastically transformed the political ecology of the region. Unlike other regions along the U.S.-Mexico border that rely on irrigation infrastructure built by the Mexican government since the 1930s (Walsh 2009; Radonic and Sheridan 2017), commercial agriculture in San Quintín mostly depends on underground water, which is tapped by companies and growers with little government oversight. A new water law in Mexico further facilitated the exploitation of the region's aquifer for the development of export agriculture. Amid neoliberal reforms aimed at liberalizing the economy and reducing the role of the government—particularly the regulation of access to land and water—the Mexican government approved the National Water Law in 1992 to decentralize and transfer the administration, distribution, and conservation of water to the private sector (Radonic and Sheridan 2017; Whiteford and Melville 2002; Nash 2007).

The development of the San Quintín Valley as a major agroexport enclave producing water-intensive crops is part of a larger transborder economy marked by transnational capital flows linked to powerful agribusiness interests in the United States. In the 1960s, Mexico launched the Border Industrialization Program to attract foreign investment in the manufacturing sector, generating what is commonly known as the maquiladora program that gave rise to hundreds of assembly plants in major cities along the Mexico-U.S. border. In 1986, the Mexican government extended this program to the agricultural sector to bolster investment in rural areas to foment the development of commercial agriculture and generate employment. As a result, foreign investment engulfed several agricultural regions farther south in Baja, including the San Quintín Valley. This change allowed agribusinesses in California to export farming equipment, seeds, chemicals, and other production technologies to the region free of duties for the production of fresh produce for U.S. markets (Goodman and Lizárraga 1998, 19). After the approval of NAFTA, large U.S. companies began to invest heavily in water-extraction technologies in San Quintín to expand the production of fresh crops, particularly berries, for export markets.

From a political ecology perspective centered on water, I examine the ecological and social effects that the production of fresh vegetables and fruits has had on the local communities and peoples in this region. I analyze the connections between the neoliberal economic policies behind the growth of the fresh produce industry and the ways in which they shape differential access to water along class and ethnic lines. As I show, small growers who cannot afford expensive water extraction and desalination technologies have been displaced by large companies that systematically engage in the overextraction of water from the aquifer. While commercial agriculture has fostered employment opportunities for indigenous farmworkers, I argue, it has also contributed to the overexploitation of underground water resources and a decline of water for the people who have settled in the region. I describe the inequalities generated by this model with regard to the ability by different social groups to access water and the hardships residents endure to have access to this basic resource for their human needs.

SETTLEMENT AND COMMUNITY BUILDING

We are not migrants but indigenous people who live here; we have been living here all our lives and we are [thus] Baja California natives. We are not migrants; the blond-haired men who came here as growers are the ones who are migrants.

—A TRIQUI LEADER AND MEMBER OF THE FRENTE DE UNIFICACIÓN PARA LA LUCHA TRIQUI (FILT) AT A PUBLIC RALLY IN COLONIA NUEVO SAN JUAN COPALA, SAN QUINTÍN, 2005

In spring 2005, shortly before I interviewed Jesús Peña at Agrícola San Simón, I attended a political rally in Nuevo San Juan Copala, a colonia founded in 1997 and named after a town in rural Oaxaca where many Triquis who had settled in the region come from. The rally was organized by several indigenous and political organizations, including the FILT, the Ejército Zapatista de Liberación Nacional (EZLN), and the Ejército Popular Revolucionario (EPR). Officials from the federal, state, and municipal governments and the main delegate of Vicente Guerrero, to which the colonia belongs, had been invited to listen to their demands. Around 150 residents attended the demonstration, including Triqui women in their traditional colorful huipil dresses. Their faces masked like the Zapatistas of the Chiapas revolt of 1994, the leaders of the indigenous organizations presented a list of grievances and demands. It included an end to sexual harassment of Triqui women farmworkers by their mayordomos, a request to pave the rutted and muddy access roads to the colonia, and authorization of a public space where Triqui women could sell handmade crafts to tourists. But the main complaint the leaders presented was that despite the fact that Triquis had lived in the region for many years, often decades, local government officials and the media still portrayed them as seasonal migrant workers rather than local citizens. Addressing this grievance to the government officials attending the meeting, a Triqui leader of the FILT proclaimed forcefully they were tired of racial discrimination that cast them as "migrants," and demanded the right to be treated as full-fledged citizens.

The political rally openly exposed the harsh conditions in which indigenous farm laborers lived and the sharp class and ethnic inequalities that prevailed in the region. The Triquis' public demand to be recognized as full-fledged citizens in Baja also reflected the demographic growth and settlement of indigenous workers and families propelled by the labor requirements of the expanding fresh-produce industry. As this sector developed in the early 1980s, it started to require a more permanent labor force to tend the diversity of fresh crops grown in the valley. This change mirrored a similar trend that had started in California in the late 1970s, when the production of high-value specialty crops such as table grapes, strawberries, melons, and citrus fueled growers' increasing dependence on an immigrant rather than migrant labor force (Palerm 1989, 2002; Du Bry 2007; Santos-Gómez 2014; Hernández-Romero 2012; López 2007).[4] In Baja, farmworker settlements began in the 1980s as the result of more stable, although intermittent, labor demand in export agriculture. The rural sociologist Antonieta Barrón (1999, 273–74) identified the San Quintín Valley as one of the first regions of early settlement, showing that growers openly facilitated land invasion by squatters or even allowed workers to settle on growers' lands to ensure a stable and reliable labor source. A similar trend toward settlement also developed in other regions in Mexico specialized in export agriculture. In Culiacán (Sinaloa), Morelos, and, more recently, Baja California Sur, indigenous farmworkers who in the past lived in labor camps have moved to colonias and built new settlements (Lara Flores and C. de Grammont 2011, 64–65; Sánchez and Saldaña 2011; Saldaña Ramírez 2017; Velasco and Hernández Campos 2018). Despite this trend, horticultural enclaves in Baja and other regions in northern Mexico are commonly conceptualized as "migratory landscapes," spaces for commercial agriculture devoid of social community in which indigenous workers formed a permanently mobile, unattached, and flexible labor force (Lara Flores 2010).

Departing from this approach, an important goal of my analysis is to examine the experience of farmworkers who settled in San Quintín in response to the labor demands of export agriculture. From a diachronic perspective, I discuss the challenges workers confronted as they sought to establish roots in the region and the economic, social, and political strategies they deployed to claim full citizen rights. I describe and analyze this as a process of community formation, paying special attention to how they cope with the economic costs of building their homes, sending their children to school, supporting their families with low wages as farm laborers, and mobilizing to bring basic services such as water to their colonias. I conceptualize this collective experience as a new territorialization, a social and political diachronic process by which farm laborers employed in the agroexport sector collectively claim land and citizenship as settlers in the region. This is a highly creative endeavor in which they have built new rural settlements relying on their ingenuity and mobilizing their social, cultural, and political resources. In so doing they have contributed to populating this arid land on the Mexico-U.S. border, forging a new sense of belonging and identity. The experience of territorialization, however, is a contested political process in which nativist ideologies espoused by many growers and government officials present indigenous workers as either outside migrants or immigrants with backward cultural traditions and values that stand in the way of progress in the region. Contesting this portrayal, indigenous ethnic leaders and organizations have a long history of collective mobilization claiming full-fledged rights as citizens. In this endeavor, I argue, they often rely on political experience and skills they developed contesting ethnic discrimination in their home communities in southern Mexico, using and transforming some of their traditional cultural and political institutions to mobilize for their demands in Baja California.

I also discuss the new forms of labor migration that have emerged in the recent past among farmworkers in the region. As the book reveals, the increasing militarization of the Mexico-U.S. border and new enforcement policies that criminalize undocumented Mexican workers in the United States have fostered the recruitment by U.S. growers of farm laborers in San Quintín under a federal program for seasonal workers. Settlement and migration are thus deeply intertwined in the lives of many farmworkers in the region, shaping their economic, social, and political strategies to capitalize on the opportunities and respond to the challenges entailed in the transnational fresh-produce industry.

RESISTING THE LABOR REGIME OF THE FRESH-PRODUCE INDUSTRY

In the early morning of March 17, 2015, ten years after the rally the Triquis organized in Colonia Nuevo San Juan Copala, thousands of farmworkers in San Quintín launched a massive labor strike to protest their poor wages and treatment in the fields. This was the largest labor protest the region had ever seen, and it was coordinated by a new organization, the Alianza de Organizaciones Nacional, Estatal y Municipal por la Justicia Social. The leaders of the Alianza presented a *pliego petitorio*, a list containing their major demands, including higher wages, inclusion in the Instituto Mexicano del Seguro Social (IMSS), the government agency that provides public health and social security benefits as well as pensions, and an end to the sexual harassment of female field workers. They demanded the approval of an independent labor union to represent the voice of workers and negotiate directly with growers and government officials. To gather the support of sympathizers in Baja and the United States, farmworkers organized a march to the international Tijuana–San Diego border in Playas de Tijuana in coordination with transnational indigenous organizations in California. Unlike previous smaller labor protests, this labor strike attracted national and international attention in the media, with news reports in the United States depicting the harsh working and living conditions of indigenous farmworkers in this border region few people had ever heard of before. The strike revealed the fracture lines that for years had been building in the labor regime of export agriculture in San Quintín. Having witnessed the largest economic growth for agricultural companies in the modern history of the region, field workers employed in this sector felt they had hardly benefited from this bonanza and that their employers were exploiting and putting increasing pressure on them.

The ways in which farmworkers cope with the labor conditions of employment in industrial agriculture occupies a central place in the anthropological scholarship of work and labor resistance. As Miriam Wells (1996, 11) pointed out in her classic study of California's strawberry industry, farmworkers' engagement in different forms of resistance convey an opposition to oppressive forms of labor management and the struggle for "workplace justice." Building on James Scott's study of "everyday forms of labor resistance" by peasants in England, Wells identified different ways by which Mexican immigrant workers opposed labor management methods in California's strawberry fields. She argued for the need to document ethnographically the individual and collective forms of worker resistance that emerge in advanced capitalist agriculture rather than solely analyze the structural changes this sector experiences over time. From this theoretical perspective, more recently a new body of scholarship has emerged that analyzes how farmworkers cope with the requirements of the fresh-produce industry that has expanded throughout the globe. Moving beyond the classic formulation of everyday forms of labor resistance, these studies have uncovered a repertoire of more structured "offensive strategies" that field workers employed in global export agriculture have developed in different countries (Rogaly 2008; Lara Flores and Sánchez Saldaña 2015; Alonso-Fradejas 2015).

Building on this recent scholarship, I discuss the individual and collective resistance strategies farmworkers in San Quintín deploy to address their labor demands and to improve conditions in their colonias. As I show, as transnational companies devised new forms of labor intensification, workers also developed a variety of forms of labor resistance, which provides an analytical window into class politics in today's capitalist agriculture. The study of farmworkers' political mobilization, I contend, requires a theoretical approach that does not simply reduce them to the analytical category of labor, but captures the deep integration between labor and community politics in their everyday lives. As the study reveals, settlement has enabled farmworkers to advance new and more resilient forms of labor resistance and community organization. The push for independent unions articulates a political approach that combines labor demands with community-based claims to improve conditions in their colonias. In this process, the political experience and capital of some indigenous labor and community leaders in their home communities in Oaxaca, Guerrero, and other states in southern Mexico, along with their ability to transform and adapt to the new reality and needs in Baja California, are central resources farmworkers use to mount their demands. Examining farm laborers' lives not only as workers but also as settlers is thus a central research strategy I use to interpret the class transformation and political struggles the production regime of transnational agriculture has elicited in the region.

DISCOVERING THE SAN QUINTÍN VALLEY

This book is the product of a long-term study I conducted in the San Quintín Valley starting in 2005 and continuing on an intermittent basis until 2017. While during the first two years I spent several months at a time in the field, the rest of my fieldwork was conducted in the summers after finishing my teaching assignments. Yet one of my earliest contacts with the region took place earlier, in 1998, when I traveled with my now wife to visit Agustín, one of her uncles from Oaxaca who had been living there since the mid-1980s. Unlike farmworkers in labor camps, Agustín was living in a small colonia in Colonet in a small house made of wood and cardboard he had built himself on a lot he bought after long years of hard work and saving. He was proud of having his own place; he had transformed his arid lot into a beautiful garden by planting tomatoes, chiles, a few fruits, and colorful plants using water from a well he had built.

Later, after starting my field research, I regularly visited with Agustín on numerous occasions until July 2006, when he decided to go back to his hometown, Huajuapan de León in Oaxaca. At the time, he was in his mid-sixties and felt his employer might not give him as much work as in the past. His adult children in Oaxaca convinced him to come back and spend his late years with his family, which he had left more than twenty years before. In preparation for his trip back, Agustín went to the local IMSS office in San Quintín to check his pension benefits. While not expecting a big allotment, he thought it would help him restart his new life in Oaxaca, as he had been working as a farm laborer in San Quintín for more than two decades. I offered to drive and accompany him to the office. After he provided his name and all the information about his employer, the woman at the counter told him that his name had never been registered in the IMSS system, which provides health and pension benefits to workers. Agustín had been working for Agrícola Colonet for the past fourteen years and considered himself a *trabajador de planta*, a permanent worker rather than a seasonal one, because he worked almost twelve months a year. But his employer had never registered him in even one of those years, either as a permanent or a seasonal laborer. With a mixture of resignation and grace, he left the office, telling me that, while disappointed, he was not surprised as it was well known in San Quintín that agricultural companies hardly ever registered their field workers in the Seguro Social, systematically cheating them out of the health, pension, and other benefits mandated by the law. When a few days later I accompanied him to the local bus station for his thirty-six-hour ride to Oaxaca, he only carried a few pesos in his pocket, leaving his home—

his only possession after more than twenty long years of hard work—in the care of a friend while he decided what to do with it. Rather than an anomaly, Agustín's story was common in San Quintín and among many farm laborers in the region. In fact, as the book reveals, the systematic abuse of workers by many companies and local growers was a central grievance that fueled farmworkers' labor and political unrest long after Agustín had left the region.

SAN QUINTÍN AS RESEARCH SITE

My research interest in the San Quintín Valley started in 2003 when, along with two faculty research colleagues at El Colegio de la Frontera Norte in Tijuana, Marie-Laure Coubes, a demographer, and Laura Velasco, a sociologist, we decided to launch a collaborative interdisciplinary research project in the region. Our exploratory field trips revealed major changes in motion: modern greenhouses were expanding and replacing horticultural production in open fields, new state-of-the-art packing and cooling plants were being built, and many companies were installing desalination plants to irrigate the crops after water wells had gone dry from overexploitation of the aquifer. Even more visible was the rapid expansion of new colonias throughout the valley, along with the gradual decline of labor camps that, until the 1990s, housed the majority of farm laborers employed in commercial agriculture. Most workers were now living in small shacks made of cardboard and plastic, often lacking basic services such as electricity, water, and sanitation. Our goal was to document these changes and the settlement experience of indigenous farmworkers who were seeking to put down roots in the region.

To gain access to the colonias where farmworkers lived when I began my fieldwork, I first relied on the support of social workers employed by the Programa Nacional con Jornaleros Agrícolas (PRONJAG), a government agency charged with attending to the needs of migrant farmworkers in Mexico. At the time, this agency was busy responding to the new needs of farm laborers who had settled in colonias and lived in poor housing with few or no public services. This approach allowed me to map out both old and new rural farmworker settlements and strategically choose the colonias where I would conduct in-depth ethnographic fieldwork. In the colonias, I introduced myself as a college professor conducting a study on the economic and social changes that had taken place in the San Quintín Valley in the recent past. At first my white skin, beard, and red hair led some people to believe I was one of the many American missionaries who lived in or periodically came to the region to build houses for poor farmworkers and preach the Bible to local residents. Speaking Spanish (my native language) and being familiar with Mexican culture after having lived in Tijuana for several years helped to dispel the first impression some residents had, allowing me to develop rapport with them. Among people in the community, my position as college professor was generally translated into the cultural category of *maestro* (teacher), which gave me a socially recognized position and created a space to interact and socialize with residents on a regular basis. With time, and after going back to the region almost every summer, my relationships with workers and families evolved, often turning into close friendships, especially with those families I visited more regularly. I was often invited to family and community celebrations such as weddings, *quinceañeras* (fifteenth birthday celebrations), children's birthdays, school graduations, and indigenous patron festivities, allowing me to meet more people in the colonias. I regularly participated in their community meetings, some organized by the colonias' elected committees and others by government programs as well as international nongovernmental organizations (NGOs) that provide assistance for housing, job training, nutrition, and health. My regular involvement in community affairs allowed me to observe farmworkers' social and political lives beyond the workplace, how they negotiated with government institutions to improve conditions in the colonias, and the role of the state in settlement as a political process.

My entrée with growers and horticultural companies was different, demanding a more elaborate and time-consuming approach. This reflected the general suspicion with which many growers saw outsiders, especially journalists and academics. Until the early 2000s, local growers had occasionally attracted negative publicity in the national and international media for labor abuses of indigenous workers. One such report was a Hispanic TV news story broadcast in the United States that showed the use of child labor by Los Pinos, the largest company growing tomatoes in the region. Although the company denied the veracity of the news in the press, the report led numerous supermarkets in the United States and Canada to stop buying produce from the company temporarily. Not surprisingly, when I arrived in the region many growers were suspicious of researchers, especially from the United States, and afraid their public image could be further tarnished.[5]

To overcome this obstacle, I began to reach out to different growers and companies through local government officials as well as agronomists at the Secretariat of Agriculture (SAGARPA), the USDA counterpart in Mexico. At SAGARPA, I accompanied agronomists on their inspection visits to farms across the valley, allowing me to meet with numerous growers and managers. After this initial contact, I generally followed a two-step approach. First, I scheduled an interview with the owner of the company and/or the top manager to gather basic information about the company's history, production, and labor and commercial arrangements. After developing some basic rapport, I followed up with farm visits whenever possible, usually accompanied by head agronomists and supervisors. Most of the time growers responded well and accommodated interviews and guided visits to their production facilities in open fields, greenhouses, and packing plants, which allowed me to observe and talk with on-site managers, supervisors, specialized farm laborers, and field workers. With time, and after spending considerable effort reaching out to and meeting with growers, I was able to cultivate the trust of some important companies, confirming that grounded ethnographic fieldwork is a time-consuming endeavor that hardly allows any shortcuts.

The variety of responses from growers, some more open than others, revealed the power differences within the U.S.-Mexico fresh-produce industry. As I discuss later, rather than a monolithic group, there are significant differences among the companies that operate in the region depending on their size, capital, and commercial links in the United States. Thus, sharing some common interests, growers are segmented by differential access to key resources such as capital, water, technologies, and commercial outlets in the United States. Hence in the field I selected growers to represent this range of companies in regard to company size, type of crops produced, and degree of autonomy, including U.S. and Mexican transnational companies, growers engaged in contract farming arrangements with these firms, and a few independent farmers. As I show, these positional differences translate into different forms of organizing production and the recruitment and control of labor, revealing how companies' differential insertion in the competitive global fresh-produce market has important labor implications at the local level.

From a grounded ethnographic approach, I show the diverse and complex labor arrangements that tie farmworkers and growers together and how the structural position of each of these social actors in the transnational fresh-produce industry shapes and constrains their opportunities. My extended ethnographic study spanning more than a decade was crucial to this endeavor. I was particularly interested in how the production and technological changes that were transforming the agroexport sector and the settlement of workers employed by this industry were reshaping the power relations between companies and farm laborers in the region. To that end, I decided to document how these changes evolved over time, convinced that San Quintín offered an ideal setting to study the key economic, social, and political transformations export agriculture is causing in rural societies throughout Mexico and Latin America. My initial fieldwork plan also changed to capture and analyze some transformations I had not anticipated. Thus, for example, the dissatisfaction and political mobilization around the problem of water scarcity in the region was something that became more prominent over the years, forcing me to pay close attention to this theme and realign my fieldwork plans and theoretical approach, infusing a political ecology dimension in my analysis. This long-term "close-to-the-ground" ethnographic approach, I argue, is best suited to study the way in which everyday people experience and react to local, regional, and transnational forces that impinge on their lives (Wolf, cited in McGuire 2005, 111).

CONDUCTING FIELDWORK IN THE COLONIAS

My fieldwork with farmworkers and their families mostly took place in the colonias where they live. My goal was to observe and document from a diachronic perspective the changes that were taking place in the local communities where farm laborers were settling. While I visited numerous colonias throughout the valley, I focused on two communities to capture in more depth and detail farm laborers' experience of settlement. As a research strategy and for comparative purposes, I selected an old colonia to document the changes it went through since the early pioneer farmworkers began to move there and a newer settlement that was still on its early stage of development. The first was Colonia Santa Fe, which, located in the jurisdiction of the town of Vicente Guerrero, is one of the oldest and most established communities in the valley. With about two thousand inhabitants, it is made up of mestizos, Mixtecs, Triquis, and Zapotecs, reflecting the ethnic diversity that predominates in the region. This colonia is located near the production facilities of large companies such as Driscoll's and Monsanto where many of its residents were employed, providing an opportunity to document their experiences as workers and local residents as well. The second colonia I regularly visited was Tres Arbolitos (hereafter referred to as "Arbolitos"). Located in the southern town of Lázaro Cárdenas, it is a smaller settlement of about six hundred inhabitants that started to develop in the early 2000s and where the majority of residents are field workers, with a large proportion of Zapotecs employed in smaller companies. Compared to Santa Fe, Colonia Arbolitos has a higher concentration of indigenous Zapotec residents, poorer public infrastructure, and less support from state and nongovernmental programs. I was attracted to this colonia by the open and friendly attitude of its residents and the opportunity to observe the experiences of immigrant farm laborers in the early phase of settlement, the challenges they faced, and the individual and collective ways by which they cope with them.

As an ethnographic method, however, participant observation often involves different degrees of involvement, from passive to moderate and from active to complete types of engaged participation (DeWalt and DeWalt 2011, 22–24). In the field I used and adapted each of these modalities, depending on the particular context and tasks at hand. I spent countless hours, usually in the evenings after farm laborers returned home from work, using a "deep hanging out" ethnographic approach through which I regularly interacted with them and their families at their homes and in public spaces like community centers, grocery stores, playgrounds, and churches, as well as by attending community festivities and celebrations. When full-fledged participant observation was not possible, I adopted the role of observer, for instance, in community meetings organized by government programs, where I recorded the interaction between social workers and residents. In addition, I conducted semistructured interviews with farm laborers and other workers focusing on their work, settlement, and migration experiences. The interviews served to gather some systematic quantitative and qualitative information on household demography, settlement history, family budget, workers' labor and migration history, and participation in community and political affairs. Settlement, however, is a

FIGURE 2. The author talks with a worker while he waits for his contractor to pick him up. Photo by Abbdel Camargo Martínez.

social and political process that goes beyond the agency of individuals and families, one that also involves government authorities, community leaders, and civic organizations (Scudder 1985; Oliver-Smith 2010). Thus in addition to local residents, I interviewed other key informants in both colonias, such as school administrators, government officials, social workers, and missionary workers or the heads of NGOs who run community programs in these settlements. I use the information gathered through these varied means to convey the richness and complexity of settlement as a social process shaped by the regional history and political economy of the San Quintín Valley.

ETHICAL CHALLENGES IN THE FIELD

As a research method, ethnographic fieldwork often leads to the development of long-lasting personal relationships and friendships. This is one of the most precious gifts at the heart of the anthropologist's experience in which, as Seth Holmes (2013, 37) puts it, it becomes impossible to "separat[e] research from human relationships." Personally, one of the most valuable rewards of the field research I conducted in San Quintín is the set of relationships and friendships I developed over the years with numerous people, especially farm laborers and their families. In the field they often became advocates of my work, taking the initiative to talk to other people about my study and introduce them to me, directing me to local sources of information, and spending a long time in conversations with me about themes central to my project. Every summer I looked forward to going back to the valley, not just to continue my research, but also to renew my friendships.

But ethnographic fieldwork in situations of significant class, racial, and power differences between ethnographers and the people we study raises important and difficult ethical questions that have led to continuous self-reflection in anthropology. In addition to a common source of joy and self-fulfillment, the ethnographic experience is often a source of uneasiness, introspection, and self-doubt. Anthropologists have addressed and coped with some of the ethical issues raised by power inequalities between the ethnographer and the peoples studied in different fashions, depending on their epistemological and theoretical positioning. When studying the lives of contemporary farmworkers who migrate and travel across the labor circuits of Mexico and the Unites States, "engaged anthropology"—in which the ethnographer puts himself or herself almost literally in the shoes of common field workers and becomes an open advocate for their cause—has been a powerful response, including among medical anthropologists (Holmes 2013; Horton 2016). This move toward a transformative anthropology seeks to have a broader impact, beyond the rather limited circles of academia to mold public opinion and policy making to improve the lives of farm laborers.[6]

While in the field, I sought to deal with those ethical issues and compensate for the significant social and power differences that separated me from farmworkers in San Quintín by practicing different types of reciprocity. Whenever possible, I helped my research participants with everyday needs such as taking them to medical clinics, giving them rides to or from work or shopping, or helping them fill out job applications or bureaucratic paperwork. I served as *padrino* (godfather) for their children at school graduations and other social events or rites of passage and helped some families when they were going through tough economic times. When needed, I engaged in different forms of local advocacy with government officials and institutions on behalf of workers and their families. At the community level, I helped residents in Colonias Santa Fe and Arbolitos write grant applications and secure funds from government agencies and NGOs for job training and improvement of their communities, which was a source of deep personal satisfaction. Finally, the publication of *De jornaleros a colonos: Residencia, trabajo e identidad en el Valle de San Quintín* (Velasco, Zlolniski, and Coubes 2014) provided my colleagues and I with an opportunity to share and discuss the plight of farm laborers in the region in both academic and public circles. Our book came out shortly after the massive labor strike in 2015, attracting considerable public attention that we later used in other formats to amplify awareness of the social injustices migrant and settled farmworkers face in the region (Zlolniski and Velasco 2015; Zlolniski 2015).

In this ethnographic study, I have tried to depict the lives of farmworkers in San Quintín as vividly as possible, relying on their case stories and unfiltered voices. Following a common convention in ethnographic writing, I have changed the names of the farmworkers, growers, and residents to protect their identities, except for some public figures such as government officials, union leaders, and heads of nonprofit organizations. Quotations included in the book come from interviews and conversations I either tape recorded or annotated in my field notes. Many of my informants were Mixtec, Triqui, and Zapotec for whom Spanish is a second language. Because I do not speak any of their native languages, I communicated with them in Spanish; thus sometimes their expressions during our conversations and interviews were truncated. In my rendition of them, I have translated Spanish-language quotations into English, sometimes slightly altering the grammatical structure for the purpose of clarity; I am thus solely responsible for these translations. I have also left in Spanish some folk expressions commonly used by locals in the region to capture important aspects of their lived experience as workers and residents. Overall, I hope my depiction of the workers, growers, and other residents in the book conveys the diversity, richness, and nuanced nature of their experiences and reaches not only scholars in the discipline but also anyone interested in learning about the people who produce the fresh vegetables and fruits in Baja that we consume in the United States.

STRUCTURE OF THE BOOK

The structure of the book reflects the key themes I introduced above. Chapter 1 provides a brief historical account of the development of the San Quintín Valley as a major export hub of fresh crops to the United States and the settlement of indigenous Mixtec, Zapotec, and Triqui workers. I use the case history of the first company that engaged in large-scale horticultural production in the mid-1980s to describe the birth of a transnational agriculture and its impact on farm laborers in the region. From a political economy perspective, the chapter tracks the articulation between regional, national, and international economic actors and policies that led to the production of water-intensive crops in this arid region of the Mexico-U.S. border.

Chapter 2 focuses on the companies and growers that produce these crops in San Quintín. I use the case study of Driscoll's to illustrate the ascendance of powerful transnational corporations that have dominated this lucrative sector since the early 2000s. As I show, Driscoll's operations in Baja represent the most recent stage in the modern history of transnational agribusiness encroachment on the land, water, and labor to grow berries for global markets. Despite this trend, a small group of mid-sized growers strives to escape the control of multinational companies and remain independent. Based on case studies, I analyze how the penetration of transnational corporations has reshaped power relations among growers in the region.

Chapter 3 examines the ways in which farm laborers are recruited to work in San Quintín's commercial agriculture. I discuss the shift from seasonal migrant workers who were recruited long-distance by labor contractors from southern Mexico to local labor contractors who hire settled farmworkers in colonias. Rather than a remnant of the past, I contend, the assemblage of labor intermediaries is a recent development and a vital pillar of the labor regime of export agriculture in Baja. The chapter also depicts the recruitment of farm laborers by U.S. agribusinesses under the H-2A Temporary Agricultural Workers visa program that has expanded in recent years alongside the increasing militarization of the U.S.-Mexico border.

In chapter 4 I focus on the workplace regime of Baja's export agriculture and its effect on farmworkers employed in this sector. I unpack the major changes of the horticultural industry in the recent past, including the shift from cultivation in open fields to indoor agriculture, the transition from day wages to piece rate, the implementation of "good agricultural practices" to meet food safety and quality standards, and norms to control the use of time in the workplace. Examining the labor and working conditions of farm laborers in San Quintín's export agriculture, I contend, allows us to understand how the global trends that dominate the fresh-produce industry penetrate all the way down to the workplace, making farm laborers' jobs highly intensive and regimented.

Chapter 5 discusses the resistance strategies farmworkers have developed to respond to the intensification of work in the agroexport industry. I document work stoppages and other strategies by which laborers seek to negotiate reduction of the workload. I also analyze more structured forms of resistance such as litigation, the labor strike of 2015, and workers' struggles to form independent labor unions. Mapping out different forms of labor resistance from the ground up, I argue, reveals the fissures and vulnerabilities of the production regime of export agriculture that have allowed farmworkers to engage in labor and civil forms of political activism.

Chapter 6 moves away from the workplace to examine the experience of farmworkers as settlers. I discuss how settlement evolved over time, the ways in which farm laborers and their families experienced this change, and the sacrifices and hard work it took for farm laborers to establish roots in the region. With enormous perseverance and ingenuity and mobilizing their social and political resources, farmworkers have reterritorialized these arid lands, succeeding where many past attempts to populate this region failed. Yet settlement has not precluded the development of new forms of labor migration. Thus I also describe the experience of residents who migrate to the United States as H-2A "temporary workers" and/or as seasonal migrants to other agroexport sites in Baja California. As the chapter reveals, settlement and labor migration coexist and reinforce each other in a dynamic fashion fueled by the labor needs of the transnational U.S.-Mexico fresh-produce industry.

In chapter 7 I examine how the production of fresh produce for international markets has affected access to water resources for farmworkers and other local residents in San Quintín. After decades of mining the aquifer to produce fresh crops, horticultural production led to the depletion and salinization of the region's watershed. As I document, the production of water-intensive crops has caused water insecurity for the local population, forcing residents to engage in household coping strategies and leading to social mobilization and political unrest. I use water as a heuristic device to render visible the deep social and ethnic inequalities export agriculture has caused in the region.

In the conclusion I reflect on the new social class of farm laborers that the growth of export agriculture has engendered in northern Mexico. I situate this study in the context of current theoretical debates about the fate of the Mexican and Latin American peasantry, who, displaced from their home communities by neoliberal agrarian policies, are now employed as transnational wage laborers in capitalist agriculture. Rather than a linear transformation from peasant-workers into wage laborers, the class transformation of farmworkers in Baja is more complex and nuanced, involving hybrid economic processes of proletarianization and repeasantization.

In the appendix, I outline a series of policy recommendations to address the most critical problems identified in the book that farmworkers and small-scale growers involved in export agriculture confront.

1

The Birth and Development of Export Agriculture in the San Quintín Valley

All our financing came from the United States. . . . This company [Del Monte] financed the Canelos brothers both in Culiacán and in San Quintín, as well as many other growers in Sinaloa. All the capital came from companies in the United States, and these companies would send their own accounting teams to San Quintín to check the financial reports generated by our own accountants.
—JULIO MENDOZA, FORMER REPRESENTATIVE OF A.B.C. FARM IN SAN QUINTÍN, 2006

The recent transformation of the San Quintín Valley into one of the most productive and technologically advanced agroexport regions in Mexico poses an environmental conundrum. Since the valley's early history, access to water was the most important factor limiting the development of agriculture and settlements. During Baja California's mission period, from 1679 to 1849, for example, the aridity of the territory prevented the establishment of permanent settlements (Wehncke and López-Medellín 2015, 145). Dominican friars established a mission in 1775 at the base of the San Pedro Mártir Sierra, but they abandoned it only twenty years later because water was too scarce to support human life (López 2017, 191). More than 150 years later, in the 1930s, the Mexican government launched a colonization plan for the San Quintín Valley providing ejidos to develop agriculture and populate the territory with a group of Mexican workers who had been deported from the United States during the Great Depression. The arid climate and water scarcity, along with the roughness of the terrain and little government support, however, presented enormous challenges the newcomers could not overcome. Despite the emergence of the first ranches that produced commercial crops and the renewed efforts by the Mexican government to attract settlers, by the 1960s the San Quintín Valley was still sparsely populated, with only four thousand inhabitants (Velasco, Zlolniski, and Coubes 2014, 69).

How then did this formerly isolated valley become one of the most important export horticultural enclaves in Mexico at the turn of the twenty-first century?

What turned an arid region with no irrigation infrastructure into a highly productive and profitable agricultural hub? And who were the people who finally came to live in this valley? In this chapter, I address these questions, discussing the economic development of the San Quintín Valley and the forces that propelled its transformation into an agroexport powerhouse based on the use of a migrant-origin labor force from southern Mexico. From a political economy perspective, I analyze the articulation between regional, national, and international economic actors and policies that implanted a model of capital- and labor-intensive commercial agriculture in this arid region along the Mexico-U.S. border. As I show, technological fetishism—the investment in capital-intensive production technologies to increase economic profit at the expense of environmental and social consequences—has been the underlying logic for economic and population growth in the region. The result is an "agro-dystopia," a production system deeply enmeshed in environmental contradictions and social tensions that raise important questions about the long-term ecological and social sustainability of this model of economic and regional development.

First I describe the early history of the San Quintín Valley, including several failed attempts to develop commercial agriculture and populate the land. Then I focus on the modern history of the region from the 1970s on, explaining its metamorphosis from an inward-looking isolated valley to an outward-oriented transnational agricultural enclave. From an ethnohistorical approach, I detail the rise and fall of A.B.C. Farm, which in the early 1980s became the first company that implemented a system of large-scale agriculture. With close financial and commercial ties to U.S. corporations, as its former representative Julio Mendoza acknowledged, A.B.C. Farm transformed agricultural production and marked a watershed in the history of labor recruitment in the region. I also discuss the technological innovations that since the early 2000s have allowed transnational companies to continue mining the region's aquifer for the production of high-value export-market crops. My critical analysis of San Quintín's model of export agriculture is informed by David Harvey's (2005) interpretation of the role of technology in modern capitalist development, according to which the logic of accumulation provides an incentive to design, develop, and implement technological devices to ensure economic profitability decoupled from their environmental, material, or social consequences.

EARLY COLONIZATION ATTEMPTS: ENVIRONMENTAL CONSTRAINTS

The prehistory of Baja California reveals the harsh environmental conditions native peoples faced to survive in the region. According to archaeological evidence, human occupation of the San Quintín–El Rosario region began prior to

5000 B.C. (Moore 2006, 188). Local peoples practiced a form of "desert adaptation to coastal resources" that consisted of collecting shellfish, harvesting agave, manufacturing stone tools, and living in temporary camps near key ecological resources (Moore 2006, 189). Environmental constraints made agriculture an unappealing option for the local population (Laylander 2006, 13), and foraging groups maintained a simple form of social organization with a few hierarchies based on gender, age, and personal skills (Moore 2006, 192).[1] The arid climate and scarce water kept human settlements small and highly mobile, with small multifamily groups scattered along the Pacific coastal zone (Moore 2006, 192). Dry intervals associated with severe droughts prompted competition for water and terrestrial resources, leading native peoples to rely on the maritime food supplies of the rich beach habitats, a situation that persisted for many centuries (Moore 2006, 184).

The arrival of European settlers in the sixteenth century had a major impact on the region's population and way of life. The first recorded contact between indigenous peoples and Europeans took place in 1542 at the time of Juan Rodríguez Cabrillo's voyage, followed by a short expedition in 1602 by Sebastián Vizcaíno (Moore 2006, 12). It was not until 1769, however, that Franciscans set up missions along the Baja peninsula. In 1774, they passed on the task to the Dominicans, who founded Mission Nuestra Señora del Rosario and Santo Domingo, beginning systematic interaction between native Californians and Europeans.[2] The missions introduced agriculture in the region based on the forced labor of the native population. The Santo Domingo mission, for example, was built near a creek, allowing the production of wheat and, to a lesser extent, corn, figs, pears, and olives, among other crops, covering about 48 hectares (Rangel and Riemann 2015, 39). This disrupted the foraging mode of socioeconomic organization of the native Kiliwa and Cochomí population, dealing them a major blow. Soon after the establishment of Spanish missions, native populations suffered a sharp demographic decline due to infectious diseases, violence, and persecution. In Santo Domingo de la Frontera, for example, the population decreased from 300 inhabitants in 1798 to only 73 by 1829 (Rodríguez Tomp 2002, 215).[3] Because of these early colonization programs and environmental constraints, especially water scarcity, the local population remained small and scattered, preventing the formation of large settlements.

A second major attempt to colonize and populate the San Quintín Valley took place in the late nineteenth century, this time under the guidance of the Mexican government. In 1883, President Porfirio Díaz embarked on an ambitious plan to modernize the economy of the country, launching the Ley de Colonización (Colonization Law) to attract foreign investment, especially in commercial agriculture. In 1887, the first U.S. company—the International Company of Mexico—was granted a license to develop agricultural production in the San Quintín Valley, setting an early precedent for American agribusiness in the region (Velasco, Zlolniski, and Coubes 2014, 66). A few years later, the British Mexican Land and

Colonization Company, known at the time as the "British Company," took over and invested in a plan to grow wheat to export to the United States and other international markets.[4] The company realized that despite its arid climate, the Mediterranean-type region was fertile ground for agricultural production using water wells for irrigation. To overcome the lack of transportation infrastructure, it set up maritime routes linking the ports of San Diego, Ensenada, and San Quintín. It also built a pier in 1890 and a flour mill that at the time was the most technologically advanced in Latin America. To house its workers, British colonizers built the first colonia, consisting of about one hundred homes, one of the earliest settlements in the valley. Envisioning San Quintín as a major wheat exporting region, the British also began building a railroad from San Quintín to Tijuana to ship crops north of the border and connect to the U.S. railroad system.

The British development plans were halted when the Mexican Revolution of 1910 triumphed and Porfirio Díaz was ousted from government. The new Mexican government canceled the contracts with foreign companies, and in 1915 President Venustiano Carranza embarked on agrarian reforms, taking lands from foreign investors to transform them into communal ejidos, including those that had been granted to American and British companies in Baja California. The decision to curtail foreign investment in northern Mexico was driven by the fear that opening up to foreign companies could enhance U.S. expansionist ambitions and make it even more difficult to keep its far northern territories under the control of Mexico City (Velasco, Zlolniski, and Coubes 2014, 67). The British Company stopped the construction of the railroad and even dismantled the sections it had built. Afterward the San Quintín Valley entered a long period of slow economic and population growth but remained isolated because of the lack of transportation infrastructure.

A renewed push to develop the region began in the 1930s, when the Mexican government embarked on a new colonization project to develop agriculture and populate the land. This time the project was a response to the deportation campaign by the U.S. government during the Great Depression that expelled hundreds of thousands Mexican workers south of the border. To cope with the massive flow of people back to the country, the central government granted ejido lands to the repatriates to start a new life in the region. Three ranches that had been abandoned by the British Company were given to Mexican families who returned from the United States (Velasco, Zlolniski, and Coubes 2014, 68). In addition, a group of about thirty farmers from Santa Cruz, Michoacán, many of whom had been deported from the United States, formed an agrarian cooperative to receive ejidos in the region.[5] The Mexican government continued this colonization project through the 1940s by allocating additional ejidos to farmers from Michoacán, Guanajuato, and other regions in western Mexico who had been displaced by the Mexican agrarian reforms.[6]

Despite the state-led colonization plans, the San Quintín Valley experienced little economic and demographic growth due to a combination of paltry investment and environmental constraints. Unlike the Mexicali Valley, where the Mexican government heavily invested in irrigation infrastructure to foster commercial agriculture in the 1940s, especially cotton (Walsh 2009), in San Quintín the amount of land converted into ejidos was comparatively small and there was no investment in irrigation equipment and infrastructure. Only a few farmers set up ranches, which were scattered and far apart, and agricultural production consisted of subsistence crops such as corn, beans, and squash and a few commercial crops including barley, chili, and potatoes, mostly for local and regional markets. Without paved roads, travel from San Quintín to the city of Ensenada, about 112 miles, took about seventeen hours (Velasco, Zlolniski, and Coubes 2014, 69). Many of the early farmers who had migrated to Baja from western Mexico developed a frontier mentality as "self-made" growers, pioneers on rough lands they had tamed on their own to develop agriculture despite the limited interest and support from the federal and state governments. Because agricultural production was limited, the demand for labor was scarce, and most farmers relied on family labor and a few local contracted workers.

FROM PEON TO FARMER: THE TALE OF MIGUEL PÉREZ VACA

While in the field, I met some of the early pioneers who grew up in San Quintín in the 1950s, before it evolved into a modern horticultural enclave. Given the rather thin historiographic record, I was eager to talk to old-timers who could speak about growing up in San Quintín when commercial agriculture was still in its infancy. One such person was Miguel Pérez Vaca, an immigrant from Guanajuato who arrived in the region in the 1950s and whose experience reflects the challenges early ejido farmers confronted. Born in 1915, Don Miguel was ninety-three years old when I interviewed him in 2009, living in a humble house with his daughter's family. At age thirteen, he migrated from Guanajuato to the Mexicali Valley in Baja to work as a peon—landless agricultural worker—in commercial crops that included cotton, beans, and wheat, which at the time attracted thousands of migratory workers. In 1954, along with a group of field workers in Mexicali, he organized a trip to the San Quintín Valley after learning that Braulio Maldonado, the first elected governor of Baja California (1953–59), was distributing land parcels to landless peasants to populate the region. "The governor told us to go and look for vacant land, and if we could find it, he will grant it to us," Miguel recalled. With a group of 102 men, he joined the cooperative Nuevo Baja California, which was originally founded in 1942 in Mexicali. Remembering how he got his first piece of land, he explained, "First a group of fourteen of us came to explore the region, [then] we submitted our petition to the governor for the lands we liked through Via Agraria." Shortly after, by presidential decree, Braulio Maldonado issued

Miguel and his group lots of 20 hectares each as ejidos and additional communal land in the interior of the valley. This was not an isolated case but part of a larger project to populate the region. Thus by late 1950, the state government in Baja had granted about 3,000 hectares of ejido lands in San Quintín.

For Miguel, the change from peon picking cotton in Mexicali to farmer cultivating his own land and crops seemed a dream come true. A few years after he moved with his wife and children to San Quintín to start a new life, however, he realized that earning a living as a farmer in this region was a more complicated endeavor than he had anticipated. With the help of his family and other *ejidatarios* (ejido holders), he had to clear and prepare the land for cultivation, which took considerable time and labor. As Miguel put it, "It was virgin and untamed land full of snakes, hares, wild rabbits, and other animals." He began cultivating rain-fed crops, including beans, barley, and wheat, but because of insufficient water he had to rent much of his land to growers who had their own wells and were producing higher-value irrigated vegetable crops like tomatoes and Brussel sprouts. Unable to make an independent living as a farmer, he also worked as a wage laborer for farmers who had access to water to produce commercial crops. "They paid us only 17 [Mexican] pesos for ten hours of work!" Miguel recalled. To maintain his family, he engaged in other subsistence activities such as catching small fish and collecting clams and other types of shellfish at the beach, a reminder of the rich maritime resources that historically had been used by local peoples in the region.

In the end, however, the arid climate and insufficient access to water became insurmountable constraints for Miguel. A few years later, in light of the limited water resources that prevented them from developing their farms, Miguel and many other ejidatarios of the Nuevo Baja California cooperative petitioned the state government to divide the land into lots to sell. "I asked the government to allow me to divide at least part of my land into lots for sale so I could feed my family.... I requested authorization to start selling lots because there was no water I could use for agriculture," he told me. In the mid-1960s, when the population in the region began to grow, although still at a slow pace, the Baja state government granted his petition and reclassified his land from ejido to *poblado* (urban settlement), which allowed him to sell lots. Over time, he would become the founder of Colonia Arbolitos, a rural settlement for indigenous Zapotec farm laborers from Oaxaca who, as I explain later, settled in the valley in the early 1990s when the region was experiencing a dramatic economic and demographic boom.

PLANTING THE SEEDS OF EXPORT AGRICULTURE: 1973–1981

The regional isolation of the San Quintín Valley's economy that prevailed for much of its history began to change in 1973, when the Trans-Peninsular Highway connecting the region with the Tijuana–San Diego international border (about 190 miles away) was completed. Although it was a narrow road with cheap pavement, the completion of the highway initiated a new chapter in the modern economic history of the region, which became increasingly connected with and dependent on growers and capital investors from the United States, especially California. In this phase local farmers became increasingly articulated with growers and consumer markets in the United States. This early stage also initiated the ascent of the San Quintín Valley as a major production site for export agriculture in northern Mexico, a sector dominated by Sinaloa, which at the time already had a long history of producing tomatoes for U.S. markets. Indeed the early development of San Quintín as a commercial agricultural enclave was closely tied to commercial developments in Sinaloa, as many of the early tomato growers in that state were California growers who had migrated to the region for business after World War II (Lizárraga 1993, 24).[7]

Growers in Southern California capitalized on the paved road to San Quintín and its geographic proximity to San Diego, forging commercial partnerships with local farmers to import their produce to the United States. This was done under a variety of formal and informal systems. One was the "commission system" that prevailed in Baja at the time (Álvarez 2005), in which American growers provided access to markets while Mexican farmers were responsible for organizing production and hiring and managing the labor. The commission system, however, was riddled with problems that reflected the unequal power relations between San Quintín growers and their American brokers and commercial partners. Without a legal mechanism to enforce these early transnational commercial agreements, it relied on what old-time farmers called *confianza* (trust). Trust was the social glue that kept these commercial partnerships together, even though, as many local growers acknowledged, it often worked to their disadvantage as they were paid well below market prices in the United States. Other farmers who did not have the means to produce on their own engaged in what Goodman and Lizárraga (1998, 19) call "silent partnerships," whereby they rented their lands directly to California growers. In other cases, U.S. growers entered into business arrangements with Mexican nationals to "borrow" their names for landownership to grow fresh produce, a common system in Baja known in Mexico as "prestanombres" (Goodman and Lizárraga 1998, 13). While at the time renting ejido land was illegal, it was a common practice; many farmers were too poor to set up production for export markets, and the Mexican government looked the other way to facilitate investment in the region. Silent partnership arrangements provided even less room for legal recourse than the more formal commission system whenever Mexican farmers were not paid according to the verbal agreement with their U.S. business partners.

Luis Ávalos Aviña, a mestizo old-timer in San Quintín, was one farmer working under the commission system growing tomatoes for export to the United States. He arrived in the region in 1945 when he was nine years old, along with his parents and siblings. Like other newcomers at the time, his family came from a small rural town near Zamora in Michoacán along with other migrants from this state who sought to open farms in the region. Upon arriving, his father began working for small farmers in Vicente Guerrero in the central San Quintín Valley who by the late 1940s and early 1950s were producing vegetables such as chiles, tomatoes, and potatoes. A few years later, he obtained ejido land and began producing crops on his own, a business Luis continued after his father died in the early 1970s. In 1972, Luis started selling his crops to the United States through the commission system, which placed him under constant financial strain. When I interviewed him in 2005, he explained how this system worked:

> Commission agents arrived from the United States and we gave them our production, which they brought to Chula Vista. However, we were not paid until the commission agents sold the tomatoes and other vegetables in the United States; only then, they paid us. Some followed the agreement; others would say that the market price [in the United States] was too low and that there weren't any profits that year, and did not pay us. . . . We signed a contract with the agent but with no price attached to the box of tomatoes, because it went on commission under the understanding they would give us a percentage of the sale profits. They used to tell us, "If we do well, you will fare well too, but if it goes bad for us so it would be for you."

The early phase of export agriculture increased the recruitment of indigenous workers from outside the region. In the 1960s, when the production of chilies and potatoes for commercial markets in the United States expanded, growers began hiring the first migrant field workers, many of whom were camped in temporary tents popularly known at the time as "Las Carpas." The growth of tomato production for export markets further fueled a demand for migratory field workers for the harvest. Indigenous Mixtec workers, who had been migrating to work in the tomato industry in Sinaloa since the 1960s (C. de Grammont, Lara Flores, and Sánchez Gómez 2004), were the first group from Oaxaca actively recruited by growers in San Quintín and soon became a visible presence in the region. At this time, the first packing plants for processing the increasing volume of tomatoes were built. Manually operated, these packing plants required additional labor, especially during the summer at the peak of the harvest season. While growers recruited indigenous men from Oaxaca to labor in the fields for planting and harvest jobs, they targeted mestizo women from Sinaloa who were employed in packing plants there as seasonal laborers for the packing plants in San Quintín. Growers' rationale for hiring women for vegetable packing jobs was similar to that used by employers in the *maquila* (manufacturing) industry in Tijuana and other cities along the Mexico-U.S. border since the mid-1960s. With experience in packing in Sinaloa, these women were viewed by farmers as "ideal workers" because of their "manual dexterity," resulting in the segregation of indigenous women from Oaxaca in the lowest-paid jobs in the field. This set up the basis for a segmented labor force along ethnic and gender lines that persisted well into the early 2000s, in which mestizo women from Sinaloa employed in packing jobs earned higher wages and commanded higher social status than indigenous workers employed in the fields at the bottom of the industry's occupational structure.

GOING GLOBAL: EXPORT AGRICULTURE, 1980–1990s

While tomato production for U.S. markets began in the 1970s, it was not until the early 1980s that large-scale commercial agriculture began developing in the San Quintín Valley. This stage, which lasted from the mid-1980s to the late 1990s, initiated the full-fledged globalization of the fresh-produce industry, one that attracted many new investors from California and Sinaloa. Growers began cultivating areas of more than 1,000 hectares, introducing new irrigation and production technologies, and vastly increasing the volume of fresh crops exported to the United States. Former environmental limits that prevented the expansion of commercial agriculture became less restrictive, and in a few decades this arid region with limited water supplies was transformed into a major horticultural export enclave.

Rather than an isolated regional phenomenon, however, the development of large-scale commercial agriculture in Baja in the 1980s was the product of the neoliberal agrarian policies implemented in Mexico at the time. By the early 1980s, Mexico had embarked on the restructuring of the agricultural sector to produce fresh fruits and vegetables for export markets at the expense of traditional subsistence crops for domestic markets. Northwestern regions such as Sinaloa, Sonora, and Baja California, because of climate and geographic proximity to U.S. markets, were considered ideal settings to promote export agriculture. When in 1986 the Mexican government extended the Border Industrialization Program to the agricultural sector in northern Mexico, it provided an important incentive to California growers to engage in agricultural production in Baja. The new legislation authorized Mexican farmers to rent their lands to U.S. growers, replacing the silent partnerships that prevailed in the past with formal agricultural contract partnerships (Goodman and Lizárraga 1998, 19). For California growers, in addition to geographic proximity that reduced transportation expenses, the lower labor and operating costs of growing fresh produce south of the border increased their market competitiveness. By the mid-1980s, for example, the cost for San Diego farmers to produce a carton of tomatoes was about $5.10, while in Baja California it only cost $3.89 (Goodman and Lizárraga 1998, 20). Capitalizing on the new business opportunities and fueled by increasing demand by U.S. consumer markets, U.S. agricultural imports from Mexico jumped by 83 percent between 1983 and 1989, with fresh fruits and vegetables leading this spectacular boom (Goodman and Lizárraga 1998, 18).

Economic and demographic developments in California in the 1980s also contributed to the popularity of San Quintín as an investment site for U.S. growers to produce tomatoes and other fresh vegetables. Population growth in California fueled the rapid expansion of suburbanization, raising the cost of land for growers there and making the San Quintín coastal valley an attractive alternative. The region was considered well suited for fresh-crop cultivation, and its geographic proximity allowed U.S. companies, especially those in Southern California, to closely manage and monitor production (Goodman and Lizárraga 1998, 19; Zabin 1997). The increasing competition for water in California that resulted from intensive farming and population growth also motivated U.S. growers to invest in business partnerships in San Quintín, where water from the aquifer could be used for the production of fresh produce with few if any government limitations. By the early 1980s, the seeds of commercial agriculture for U.S. markets had begun to take hold in the valley. While midsized growers and companies still prevailed, business partnerships with growers in California served as early vehicles for encroachment on San Quintín's land and water resources. Commercial partnerships with local growers in San Quintín enabled U.S. growers and investors to extend the production season of fresh tomatoes in California and reach markets in the off-season. As a result, Baja experienced a rapid increase in fresh vegetable and fruit production for U.S. markets. While in 1980 this region shipped 25 million pounds of tomatoes to the United States, by 1986 shipments soared to 250 million pounds, just when agricultural land in the southern coastal counties of California was rapidly declining (Goodman and Lizárraga 1998, 20). In Mexico, Baja California went from producing only 1.9 percent of the total fresh vegetable crop in the early 1980s to almost 15 percent by the end of the decade (Goodman and Lizárraga 1998, 20).

A GIANT ARRIVES IN TOWN: A.B.C. FARM AND ENCROACHMENT ON LAND, WATER, AND LABOR

No other company better illustrates the shift to large-scale export agriculture in the San Quintín Valley than A.B.C. Farm. Headquartered in Sinaloa, A.B.C. Farm dominated the fresh-produce industry in San Quintín from the early 1980s to the late 1990s. The history of this company serves as a vehicle to explain the consolidation of transnational agricultural production that took hold in the valley since the mid-1980s, a model that drastically transformed the economy and social fabric in the region. By the early 1980s, A.B.C. Farm was one of the largest agricultural companies in Mexico with extensive commercial links to Dole Food Company (formerly known as Castle and Cook), the largest grower-shipper of fresh fruits and vegetables in the United States (Wright 2005, 41). A.B.C. was owned by the Greek-origin Canelos family, which also operated one of the largest Mexican grower-shippers of vegetables in several regions in the country and Central America (Wright 2005, 41; Lizárraga

1993). In Sinaloa, the Canelos family had been growing tomatoes for export since the 1960s, but seeking to expand its reach in the U.S. market, it established an agreement with Dole to produce tomatoes in Baja California (Goodman and Lizárraga 1998, 21). Under the partnership, Dole supplied credit, technological expertise, and access to U.S. markets through its extensive distribution network, and A.B.C. Farm was in charge of organizing production, recruitment and management of labor, and contracting with local growers in San Quintín to produce tomatoes for them. By the mid-1980s, A.B.C. Farm was operating 1,011 to 1,214 hectares in tomato production (Goodman and Lizárraga 1998, 21). This business arrangement was significant because for the first time it introduced a vertically integrated model of transnational agriculture (Echánove 2001), in which A.B.C. acquired and leased large parcels of land to produce fresh tomatoes for export markets.

The model of large-scale agriculture set up by A.B.C. Farm in San Quintín was a novelty at the time, one that crucially advanced the intensive use of the region's land and water resources. When I started fieldwork in 2005, A.B.C. Farm had been closed for several years after a section of the company's packing plant had been burned down in a workers' revolt in 1998. I was fortunate, however, to meet Julio Mendoza, the main administrator who represented the Canelos family and the company in San Quintín since its inception in the early 1980s. Because of the importance of the history of this company in the region, I sought to gather his account of how A.B.C. came to the valley and the business model it brought with it. Indeed, as business and social broker Mendoza played a key role in setting up A.B.C.'s operations in San Quintín, making him a central figure in the company's ability to penetrate the region and articulate production arrangements with local growers.

Born in 1935, Julio grew up in the Guasave region in Sinaloa, which, promoted by U.S. investors, had been growing tomatoes for U.S. markets since the 1910s (Lara Flores and C. de Grammont 2011, 37).[8] As a child, he had seen U.S. growers introduce large-scale tomato production in his hometown and the innovative technologies used at the time to export them to the United States. The production and marketing model the company brought to his town impressed Julio.

> I remember Mr. Santiago Wilson, a North American who arrived in Bamoa in the municipality of Guasave in Sinaloa. He became a powerful producer compared to local growers because [back then] they would cultivate 4, 5, or 6 hectares while, when Wilson arrived, he began cultivating 100 and 200 hectares and brought machinery and equipment nobody had seen before. . . . The company shipped the tomatoes by train to the United States; they were placed in special wagons equipped with compartments called bunkers containing three or four tons of ice to keep the temperature cool so that they would last all the way to Nogales, as it took between two and three days to go from Culiacán [Sinaloa] to Nogales [Arizona]. From there, part of the shipment continued to other cities in the United States, while other boxes were unloaded and sold in Nogales to big supermarkets and food stores.

Julio's early exposure to the transnational production and marketing arrangements in the fresh-produce sector in Sinaloa helped prepare him for his later career as broker for A.B.C. Farm in Baja. In 1956, he began working for the Canelos family, learning the ropes of the tomato-growing business, and in 1965 the company promoted and sent him to Florida to learn about tomato production techniques. In 1980 the company asked him to travel to the San Quintín Valley to explore the possibility of growing tomatoes in that region. At the time, Florida growers were complaining about what they argued was unfair competition and dumping by Sinaloa farmers, prompting companies like A.B.C. Farm to look for other regions in Mexico to grow tomatoes for consumption in the United States. As Julio recalled, San Quintín emerged as an attractive location for several reasons.

> It was then that the idea to produce in San Quintín emerged [and] the Canelos brothers started to put their eyes on that region.... The first reason was that San Quintín was privileged because it has a climate much better than Sinaloa and Florida because here you can produce almost the whole year; in Sinaloa, the production window is shorter. The other reason was that the market is only three to four hours distant. If you pack a tomato today it can arrive fresh in the supermarket shelf in the United States tomorrow early in the morning; it's more competitive. So they told me, "You go to San Quintín; in Tijuana a rental car will be waiting for you.... Go and explore, travel in the region, talk to people, write down what you see and whatever catches your attention in a notebook, whatever interests you." And it was like that that I came here.

Julio's initial exploration of the San Quintín Valley convinced him it was an ideal setting to produce tomatoes on a large scale. The logic and timing of this move reflects what Jane Collins (2003, 12), studying the structural forces that led to the relocation of U.S. garment production facilities to Mexico in the 1980s, calls "regime shopping," in which companies look for advantages in environmental and labor regulation, tax laws, and other incentives. On his first reconnaissance trip, Julio spent two weeks in the region talking to local growers, some from Sinaloa whom he had already met, and taking copious notes to report to his employer. In addition to its location close to the Mexico-U.S. border, the availability of land, "virgin soil not wasted" yet by pesticides and fertilizers, and the possibility of implementing more efficient use of water made him realize the potential the San Quintín Valley offered: "I realized that [unlike Sinaloa], the fields were uncontaminated and free of plagues. Growers here did not use drip irrigation yet but a rudimentary and wasteful system of water pipes so the yields were not good because water just went over the furrows and not the plants."

Julio's reconnaissance trip played an important role in enticing A.B.C. Farm to establish a new production base in the San Quintín Valley. After returning to Sinaloa, he presented his report to A.B.C.'s advisory board, whose members, excited about the prospects San Quintín offered, sent him back for a second and longer trip, this time with the mission of making business arrangements with local growers to rent a few hectares and begin producing tomatoes the following season. In 1981, Julio leased 12 hectares from a local grower he knew from his old days in Guasave. He introduced some of the tomato-growing techniques he had learned in Sinaloa and Florida, including drip irrigation and fertilizers directly applied to the plants through that system, a novelty in the region at the time. After a successful first season, A.B.C. Farm quickly expanded tomato production on a large scale by leasing more land from local growers, and by 1983 it was already cultivating 1,000 hectares, a scale of production never seen before in the region. The company also introduced the first cooling system in the valley and built a large state-of-the-art packing plant that was considered the most technologically advanced in Mexico.[9]

The arrival of A.B.C. Farm in San Quintín implemented a new business model that shocked local companies and growers. With heavy financial support from its U.S. commercial partners, A.B.C. Farm eclipsed most local companies, the largest of which cultivated less than 200 hectares and had only a few rudimentary packing sheds with no cooling technology. Rather than buy land, the company leased it from local farmers, a business strategy that reduced costs and lowered risks. Julio recalled how A.B.C. Farm was able to lease vast stretches of ejido land—which at the time was banned by law—with the silent acquiescence of Mexico's government authorities. His testimony offers an opening to understanding how the use of large swaths of land dedicated to the production of water-intensive vegetables emerged in the region.

> All our land was rented; A.B.C. did not buy any land back then. It was not until 1995 that it started to buy some land . . . and that only happened when President Salinas authorized the sale of ejido land. . . . Before then government authorities looked the other way because they knew it was illegal to rent ejido land. They could use their power to prohibit it, but if they did, it would hamper the economic development of the region, so they had to be flexible. Sometimes a delegate of the agrarian reform of the state would come to find out how much the ejido owners were receiving, how they were benefiting from the rental agreement. He would not approve it but did not prohibit it either. We all understood it was fine and continued the practice.

During the second half of the 1980s, A.B.C. Farm aggressively expanded the leasing of land under cultivation, leading to big increases in the volume of tomatoes for export markets. The company built a distribution center in Chula Vista south of San Diego, adding to another center it operated in Nogales. By the late 1980s, it had 1,500 hectares in San Quintín exclusively dedicated to tomato production, allowing the company to reach consumer markets in the United States and Canada. As Julio proudly explained to me, "From the distribution center in Chula Vista a sales team sold our tomatoes to whoever they could; they sent shipments all over the place, even Canada, and all the way to New York."

FIGURE 3. A.B.C. Farm's old company sign.

The new model of large-scale production A.B.C. Farm introduced in San Quintín, however, placed enormous pressure on the region's delicate aquifer system. To sustain a high volume of production, the company actively engaged in the continuous search for water sources. While at first it relied on water from the Santo Domingo stream –one of the few water sources that run through the valley– once the size of land under cultivation expanded, it began tapping water from other streams. In addition, it rented plots on ejido lands not for cultivation but to mine underground water and shifted production to new fields with wells, exacerbating the competition for water among growers in the region. An agronomist from the local office of the Secretariat of Agriculture commented on the critical impact A.B.C. Farm had at the time on irrigation technologies, organization of labor, and water resources:

> A.B.C. was the company that revolutionized agriculture in the valley. For example, it introduced drip irrigation, the use of *tomate de vara* rather than ground-sown tomatoes. Even how field workers were transported changed because A.B.C. started to drive them in micros and buses [rather than pickups], and also increased a bit workers' wages because of the huge labor needs of the company. The push for the production of tomatoes for export markets led to a more efficient but less ecologically friendly or sustainable use of water with the adoption of drip irrigation that allowed increasing the size of cultivated land by big leaps.

A.B.C. Farm's early financial success radically transformed the nature of commercial agriculture in the region. As the first large transnational company, it was a game changer that signaled the transition to a new production system predicated on the intensive use of land and water to increase the total volume of fresh produce for international markets. The implementation of a model of horticultural production transplanted from Sinaloa also fostered the massive use of fertilizers and pesticides, exposing farmworkers to new occupational health hazards uncommon until then but which with time became increasingly prevalent (Wright 2005).

Dissent and the Demise of Small-Scale Farmers

The new model of large-scale agriculture significantly reshaped power relations among growers in the region, revealing its larger economic and social consequences. Many local farmers did not welcome the arrival of investors and farmers from the United States and Sinaloa. A.B.C. Farm received heavy financial support from the Dole Food Company and later from other U.S. agribusinesses such as Del Monte with which it maintained commercial partnerships over time. This system allowed large U.S. shipper-brokers to exercise close control over agricultural operations in San Quintín, which local growers did not like. Access to technological expertise, financial investment, and consumer markets in the United States gave A.B.C. Farm a clear competitive advantage over local growers.[10] Its success provoked a backlash from local growers, who felt the Sinaloa-based company was driving them out of business and exhausting the region's water supplies. To remain in business, local companies began forging new alliances with commercial distributing partners in California to obtain additional capital and have better access to U.S. consumer markets. With financial investment from abroad, many growers upgraded their infrastructure and expanded the amount of land under production. In contrast, ejidatarios and small farmers cultivating between 10 and 20 hectares were gradually pushed out of business, contributing to a new class divide between small ejidatarios and farmers on the one hand and growers with business arrangements with large U.S. brokers on the other. Luis Ávalos, an old-time ejidatario in San Quintín, recalled the fate that growers like him confronted after A.B.C. Farm and other companies began producing on a large scale and exploiting the water resources in the valley.

> Before the big companies set foot here, we could easily sell our tomatoes and chiles because there was little competition. When the big companies arrived, competition became harsher and small farmers like me had great difficulties exporting because the big companies produced in high quantities to sell both in the United States and in Mexico.... The big companies arrived in 1982–83 and were represented by families like the Rodríguez in Santa María and the García in Camalú.... We [small farmers] had only land lots of 20 hectares and could only produce when and if it rained. In contrast, the big companies can afford to bring water from 20 or 40 kilometers if needed; they have many water pipes, powerful engines to pump the water from far away, and the financial power to do so. Little by little, we were pushed away. "Move away, move away," we were told, because there is enough production by the big companies already; it's the logic of market competition.

The demise of small farmers in San Quintín was facilitated by the neoliberal agrarian reform the Mexican government had launched in the country in the 1980s. A key component of such reform was the denial of credit by Mexican banks for small-scale farmers and ejidatarios producing subsistence crops for local and other domestic markets (Myhre 1998). This was part of a larger process of agrarian reform in Mexico that entailed the elimination of subsidized loans, the dismantling of government-run agricultural marketing entities, and the eradication of the government-operated seed company (Pechlaner and Otero 2010, 195). In the past, ejidatarios and small farmers in San Quintín received loans from a rural bank with a local office in the valley and technical support from agronomist personnel from SAGARPA. Luis Ávalos was a member of the Confederación Nacional de Campesinos (CNC), an organization that represented the interests of local growers. As Ávalos recalled, the neoliberal agrarian reforms under President Carlos Salinas de Gortari critically undermined the support farmers like him received.

> Back then we received economic support from the government to buy a tractor, to plow for sowing, to buy a water pump, fertilizers, for all that was required, so we could produce. . . . Then, no more. If there aren't any means to prepare the land, there is no harvest. . . . With the government of Carlos Salinas de Gortari, Article 27 of the Mexican Constitution was changed [allowing sale of ejido land], and from then on the banks did not lend us money anymore. They did not help us; they would lend only to the big companies who had enough assets [as collateral].

Luis's words echoed what I often heard from other old-time growers who after years of making a living as independent farmers gave up agriculture because they were unable to compete with large agribusinesses. When talking to them I perceived they had lost their identity as independent farmers, which had previously given them a sense of pride and place. Forced to retire, Luis shared that sense of loss, although he still proudly considered himself among the group of early pioneers who developed agriculture in the region at a time when few growers were attempting to cultivate the arid lands. During my fieldwork, I encountered several old-time growers critical of the profit motives and irresponsible use of land, pesticides, and water by outside growers at the expense of local farmers. They pejoratively refer to outside companies as *compañías golondrinas* (swallow companies), those that arrive in search of a quick profit but are not socially invested in the region and leave when producing is no longer profitable. In the end, the increasing power of large transnational companies, along with water scarcity and new agrarian policies that drastically curtailed access to credit by ejidatarios and small-scale growers, led to the latter's gradual but irreversible demise. Local farmers who could not invest in new production technologies were not able to compete with giant companies like A.B.C. Farm. Others were pressured into business partnerships with U.S. grower-shippers to have access to capital and modernize their equipment, packing plants, and increase production. By the late 1990s, the model of large-scale transnational horticultural production was firmly in place, locating this region in the wider circuit of the global fresh-food industry with increasing pressure on its limited water resources.

Labor Camps and Indentured Labor

In addition to affecting land and water, the model of large-scale production transformed the system of labor recruitment by agricultural companies in San Quintín. Until the early 1980s most local growers cultivated small and medium-sized lots and relied on local workers and small groups of migratory laborers from southern Mexico for the harvest season in the summer. When A.B.C. Farm began producing on 1,500 hectares, however, it bumped up the recruitment of migratory workers from outside the region. Copying the system of long-distance labor recruitment in which *enganchadores* (labor recruiters) recruited and transported indigenous workers from Oaxaca to Sinaloa, they expanded this practice to Baja. In so doing, San Quintín became an important site in a labor circuit in which indigenous Mixtec, and later Triqui and Zapotec, workers followed a circular migratory pattern from Oaxaca to the fields of Sinaloa and then Baja California.[11] Julio Mendoza was responsible for organizing the recruitment of migrant workers to San Quintín, including forging arrangements with enganchadores in rural communities in Oaxaca. As he described it to me, the system involved the transportation of hundreds of seasonal workers for the harvest.

> We recruited our workforce from other parts of the country. There were many people from Oaxaca who arrived long ago and were familiarized with farm work; they themselves offered to go to Oaxaca and bring 500, 600, or even 1,000 workers. "I can bring them," they would tell me; and [I said,] "OK but with the condition they return home after the harvest is over." We paid for the trip, fed the workers during the trip from Oaxaca, and when agricultural activities were over, we returned them by bus under the same conditions. That's how we did it.

A.B.C. Farm also introduced labor camps to house indigenous migrant field laborers who came to work in the valley. Using the same model from Sinaloa, workers were housed in small rooms for a fee. The labor camp consisted of about fifty *galerones*, wooden sheds with metal roofs, each with twenty rooms that housed one or more families. Labor camps created a new system of "controlled residency," a type of spatially segregated pool of labor in which field workers were obligated to work for the company for the duration of their contracts (Velasco, Zlolniski, and Coubes 2014, 78). Labor camps were designed to house hundreds of field workers during the peak season, keeping them under tight surveillance to prevent them from leaving to work for other companies. At the core of this system were the *camperos,* employees hired by the company to enforce a strict code of rules for workers living in its camps. Camperos kept the schedule in the camps, turned off the lights at night, intervened in any disputes that emerged among workers, and ensured that all tenants went to work for the company rather than for other employers, among other responsibilities (Camargo Martínez 2015).[12] At the time, labor camps represented a novelty and even an improvement in the region, as before field workers generally slept out in the open (Velasco, Zlolniski, and Coubes 2014, 236). Julio was proud of the labor camp model A.B.C. Farm had brought to San Quintín.

> We were the first company to build galerones to house our workers. When I first arrived in San Quintín, workers from Oaxaca lived under the trees next to the Santo Domingo stream. They worked for local growers who did not provide them housing.... Then when we arrived, we began building labor camps like those we used in Sinaloa. Then little by little, we brought social workers, doctors, and we even made an agreement with the Seguro Social so they could come and treat sick people with infectious diseases to avoid infecting other people.

Julio's testimony speaks of the important labor transformations that large-scale agriculture brought to the region. The San Quintín Valley became what Collins (2003, 13) calls "greenfields locations," referring to the penetration of capital into new locales where workers either have little labor market experience or are exposed to new labor practices and norms. The model of large-scale agricultural production not only included the intensive use of its land and water resources, but more intensive use of labor, setting in motion the massive recruitment of indigenous workers from southern Mexico for decades to come. Labor camps became the new norm, over time creating a highly coercive and exploitative system of indentured labor that lasted until the early 2000s.

The End of an Era: Workers' Revolt and A.B.C. Farm's Collapse

Despite all the technological innovations, the old curse of water scarcity that had prevented the expansion of commercial agriculture in the San Quintín Valley returned to haunt A.B.C. Farm in the end. After more than a decade of rapid growth and economic success, by the mid-1990s A.B.C. Farm entered a period of rapid decline as it encountered increasing difficulties securing water to keep up with the high level of tomato production. Without enough water, the company had to curtail the expansion of land under production. By 1997, it had declined from 1,000 hectares the previous year to only 400 hectares. To compound the problem, many of the tomato boxes shipped to the United States were returned because the distribution center in San Diego could not find buyers; of approximately one million boxes exported that year, about 300,000 were sent back to San Quintín. As a result, A.B.C. Farm lost support from its U.S. commercial partner that had financed its rapid and aggressive expansion since the early 1980s. The company experienced serious liquidity problems, delaying payments to its workers, service providers, and contractors. By 1998, workers at A.B.C. Farm reached a critical point when, accustomed to being paid on a weekly basis, they went without pay for several weeks. A group of workers organized and met with Julio to demand their overdue wages. About a month and several meetings later, field workers organized a collective protest that became one of the most traumatic episodes of labor unrest in the modern history of the San Quintín Valley.

The protest that took place on December 11, 1998, illuminates the social consequences that the model of intensive commercial agriculture brought to this region. While the details of exactly what happened in this famous labor revolt are still murky, when I interviewed Julio he vividly remembered the date that ultimately precipitated the end of his post at A.B.C. Farm. While the Canelos family owned A.B.C. Farm, the company operated under different names to reduce taxes and legal responsibilities, including Frutas y Vegetales del Valle, Ludovica, and Cecilio Espinoza, among others. Throughout it all, Julio was the public face of the company directly negotiating with workers and contractors and running everyday operations. When the labor protests erupted, he recalled the stress he experienced being an intermediary between his boss in Sinaloa and the workers in San Quintín.

> They [workers] knew I was not the owner, and that the only thing I could do was to mediate and try to find a solution. They would ask me, "What is going on? When are they going to pay us? When are they sending the money? What is happening?" In Sinaloa [my boss] would tell me over the phone, "Yes, we will send you the money to pay them; tomorrow we will send it." However, the money never arrived and workers kept coming back to my office to protest and the whole thing would repeat itself.... Then it happened. They set the packing plant on fire. It wasn't the workers at the packing plant but the farmworkers who did it. That day there were about five or six buses of farmworkers who decided to block the highway to protest, but the police told them they should take the protest to A.B.C. Workers started coming, around two hundred people, . . . but later more people joined. As it was always the case in the region, a handful of leaders were in charge of organizing workers' protests, about ten to twelve leaders who were always meddling to obtain an economic profit.... The leaders arrived in the buses, and it was they who broke the fence to get into the packing plant and broke the windows; it was in revenge because they did not get any money from us.... [Meanwhile] in my office I was talking on the phone to my boss in Sinaloa telling him what was going on: "This is what is happening," I kept informing him, and I would say, "I can see smoke coming from the packing plant," but he would just reply, "I don't believe you."

Julio's recollection reflects the consequences of the social distancing involved in the system of contract agriculture. This model allows transnational companies to maintain geographic distance from its workers in order to avoid involvement in labor disputes and divest themselves from the region and local community. Julio's portrayal of the workers' leaders, often indigenous, who serve as social and cultural brokers between indigenous workers and employers and/or government officials, resonates with a commonly held perspective among many growers and government officials I met in San Quintín. People in positions of power, mostly whites and mestizos, often distinguish between docile, well-behaved indigenous workers and a small group of "selfish and corrupt" indigenous leaders who take advantage of labor conflicts to advance their own economic and political interests. This political discourse infantilizes farmworkers and seeks to delegitimize indigenous leaders, casting them as outside agitators who take advantage of their coethnics. It also obscures the fact that many of the ethnic leaders in San Quintín were former field workers who became politicized after years of harsh treatment and abuse by large horticultural companies and repression in the labor camps.

After this episode, A.B.C. Farm never resumed operations and, according to local rumors, used the incident as a pretext to close down and claim insurance benefits. The workers' protest also marked the end of Julio's employment at the company; shortly afterward he retired with a bitter feeling after having worked forty-three years for the Canelos family. A few years after I interviewed him, he died in the modest home he shared with his wife that was bought with the savings he accrued while employed by the Canelos family. Despite its abrupt end, A.B.C. Farm drastically transformed agricultural production in the valley, leaving a lasting legacy that reverberated for decades.

AGRICULTURAL RESTRUCTURING AND THE EMERGENCE OF TECHNOSCAPES

In *A Brief History of Neoliberalism,* David Harvey argues that capitalism tends to develop technological devices to respond to structural crises of models of accumulation not to solve them but to circumvent the very roots that caused them in the first place. The drive for technological innovation, he writes, "becomes so deeply embedded in entrepreneurial common sense, however, that it becomes a fetish belief: that there is a technological fix for each and every problem" (Harvey 2005, 68). Harvey's critical analysis of technological development under the guise of a neoliberal capitalist logic provides a useful framework to interpret the economic restructuring of San Quintín's agroexport sector that began in the late 1990s. The model of large-scale horticultural production introduced by A.B.C. Farm in the early 1980s reached an ecological limit point when the underground water supplies were severely depleted after years of intensive and uncontrolled exploitation by this and other large companies. In the 1990s, commercial agriculture was extracting six times more groundwater than the recharge rate of the watersheds, depleting many water wells used for irrigation (Aguirre-Muñoz et al. 2001, 145). In response, growers had to curtail drastically the amount of land under cultivation. While in 1998 about 10,000 hectares were cultivated to grow fresh produce—setting the record in the history of the region—by the year 2000 water shortages led to an almost 50 percent reduction, with 5,100 hectares in open fields (Gallardo 2010).[13]

The water crisis of the late 1990s fueled a major restructuring of the fresh-produce industry that was built on intensive capital and technological investment. The restructuring consisted of the transition from a high-volume production model aimed at exporting as many tons of tomatoes and other fresh vegetables as possible to a new paradigm of producing a smaller volume but "higher-quality" crops with greater market value. This change was carried out by investing in two new technologies. First, beginning in the early 2000s, the largest transnational firms began building desalination plants to produce water to irrigate their crops. From 2000 to 2009, 25 desalination plants for horticultural production were built in the region; by 2014, the number increased to 52 facilities, and by 2017 there were 62 plants. This technology is commonly used in eastern and southern Spain for the production of fresh Mediterranean crops (Aznar-Sánchez, Belmonte-Ureña, and Tapia León 2014). Unlike Spain, however, where desalinated water comes from the ocean, in San Quintín companies treated well water because it was a less costly option. Second, there was a shift from cultivation in open fields to production in greenhouses and shadehouses to optimize the use of water and yield more homogeneous and higher-quality crops. Production in sheltered environments allowed growers to use water more efficiently and produce crops almost year-round, beyond the natural seasonal limits in open fields.[14] As the number of hectares dedicated to open field production gradually declined, agroexport companies heavily invested in "indoor agriculture" to compensate for the loss. By 2009, production in open fields decreased to only 3,500 hectares; meanwhile, greenhouse production, which accounted for just 1 percent of total surface in 2001, increased to 35 percent by 2008 (Velasco, Zlolniski, and Coubes 2014, 74).

Indoor agriculture significantly contributed to a rise in productivity. By 2008, after several years of experience cultivating in protected environments, tomatoes produced in greenhouses yielded 102 tons per hectare, compared to 49 tons in open fields, while for cucumbers, another popular export crop, productivity was 50 tons per hectare in greenhouses and only 36 in open fields (Gallardo 2010, 58). "With less surface you can obtain higher and better quality yields," commented SAGARPA's agronomist Eusebio Rincón, who had witnessed the technological transformations in the region since the early 2000s. Producing fresh produce off-season also increased profits. For example, Tomás López, a local grower producing cucumbers for the United States, proudly explained to me that while in the winter the volume of cucumbers he exports is significantly lower than in the summer, the market price of each box of cucumbers soars: "While in summer we sell a box of 10 kilograms for $4 apiece, in the winter they reach $16 and even $20 per box!"

The shift from cultivation in open fields to protected agriculture, however, was a costly investment only possible for affluent companies and growers. The estimated cost per hectare for a shadehouse in 2006 was $80,000, while for a greenhouse it was $1,204,098 (SAGARPA, pers. comm., July 14, 2009), an investment well beyond the means of many midsized growers in the region. With neoliberal agrarian policies restricting access to credit, local growers became increasingly dependent on and indebted to U.S. agribusiness as well as Spanish firms to obtain credit for investing in these new technologies. With shrinking water resources, growers who wanted to stay in business but did not have the means to finance their own desalination plants had little choice but to establish commercial partnerships with U.S. grower-shippers to restructure their production facilities.

In addition to the twin technological assemblage of desalination plants and indoor agriculture, the restructuring of export agriculture involved the diversification of fresh produce to reach a larger market. While tomatoes had dominated export crops since the mid-1970s, by the late 1990s growers began producing other fresh vegetables and fruits such as strawberries, cucumbers, onions, celery, and broccoli as a means to reduce risks and capitalize on other market niche opportunities. The most dramatic change was the expansion of strawberry production, which since the early 2000s grew steadily from 643 hectares in 2001 to 1,900 hectares in 2018, a 195 percent increase.[15] In addition, growers began cultivating raspberries, blueberries, and blackberries. From 2012 to 2018, the production of raspberries increased from 220 hectares to 770 hectares, while blueberry production also increased from 80 to 225 hectares in the same time period (SAGARPA, pers. comm., March 5, 2019).[16] The ascendance of different types of berries—crops that require more and better quality water than tomatoes—was accompanied by the arrival of new U.S. companies in the region. Fueled by NAFTA, which allowed foreign companies to buy or rent land and engage in production in Mexico, transnational companies like Driscoll's, Andrew and Williamson, Seminis, and Monsanto set up operations in San Quintín. Mexican companies with transnational capital such as Los Pinos, Agrícola Camalú, and Agrícola Colonet also joined the race to invest in desalination plants and shadehouse production with little regard for the environmental impacts of such a strategy.[17]

The new agricultural technologies significantly altered the rural topography of the valley, leading to what, following Arjun Appadurai's (1990) critical analysis of the technological transformations of the capitalist global economy, can be described as "technoscapes." This refers to the assemblage of capital-intensive water desalination plants and greenhouse or shadehouse facilities to produce high-value crops for international markets. Technoscapes are visual signifiers of the capitalist fetish belief that every ecological crisis that arises as a barrier for industrial agriculture can be fixed with new technological devices. This techno-

FIGURE 4. Desalination plants in San Quintín. Photo by Hugo Riemann.

cratic approach is often taken without considering the question of long-term sustainability and depends on the criterion of return to investments in the short and medium time frame rather than longer ecological time horizons. In San Quintín, water produced by desalination technologies led to the formation of "water reservoirs," artificial ponds of water for crop irrigation. Strategically located near the main fields and production facilities, these artificial oases are covered with plastic and protected with fences to prevent trespassing to steal or contaminate the precious liquid. As investment in desalination technologies increased, so did the number of water reservoirs, punctuating an otherwise arid landscape. At the same time, shade and greenhouse production rapidly spread, covering hundreds of hectares at a time and replacing the older model of open-field production. The water reservoirs that mark the arid landscape of the San Quintín Valley symbolize the privileged access to scarce water resources by large agribusinesses to produce crops at the expense of water for the local population. Every year I returned to the region, I noticed the rapid growth of greenhouses and shadehouses and water reservoirs, the latter offering a striking contrast to many rural colonias that suffer from chronic water shortage to meet the needs of the farmworkers who produce the fresh crops.

CONCLUSION

For much if its history, environmental limitations prevented the development of commercial agriculture as a viable economic option in the San Quintín Valley. The dearth of water for irrigation and alternative rich maritime resources kept the expansion of agriculture in check and precluded the formation of large human settlements. Rather than the result of endogenous forces propelled by local farmers, the emergence and consolidation of export agriculture in the region is the product of transnational companies and capital investment attracted by its benign climate, availability of land, and strategic geographic location near the Mexico-U.S. border. The model of large-scale commercial agriculture that A.B.C. Farm brought to the region was based on the intense exploitation of land, water, and labor. In this regime, environmental and labor costs of producing water- and labor-intensive crops are externalized to the region at the expense of the ecological and social impact the model has engendered. After the demise of A.B.C. Farm, this model of capital- and labor-intensive horticultural production further expanded at the hands of even larger U.S. and Mexican transnational companies with long-lasting environmental, social, and demographic consequences that can still be felt.

The transformation of San Quintín into a major agroexport enclave in the Mexico-U.S. border region rests on what I have called technological fetishism, a blind faith in technology to increase horticultural production and profits at the expense of collateral environmental and social damage. In the early 2000s, in the midst of the region's most severe water crisis in recent history, transnational agribusinesses heavily invested in expensive water-extractive technologies to expand the production cycle of fresh crops to capitalize on international market-niche opportunities with little consideration for its regional effects. Ejido lands that in the past were used for rain-fed agriculture are now covered with hundreds of shadehouses and strawberry fields punctuated by oases of water provided by desalination plants run by sophisticated computer technologies. San Quintín's technoscapes mirror the capitalist logic of the global fresh-produce industry, whereby the decision-making process about what crops to produce and how to produce them has become increasingly deterritorialized and removed from local economic and social actors, making the search for profit the sole engine for agricultural development. The result is an agro-dystopia, a horticultural production regime based on the intense extraction of water from the aquifer at the expense of the availability of water for the farmworkers and residents who live in the valley. In an agro-dystopia, capitalist accumulation based on water exploitation through technological development for global markets becomes uncoupled from the ecological and social effects at the local level. In this system, the production of high-value market crops is an imperative that takes priority over any other goal, shaping the distribution of scarce water resources and political decisions on where to invest public resources.

Production technologies, however, do not operate in a social vacuum but are the product of economic interests of particular industries and actors that transform the social fabric of a region. In San Quintín, the model of export agriculture generated a massive demand for field workers to tend the crops and for laborers to work in the packing plants. Large companies embarked on the systematic recruitment of thousands of indigenous farm laborers from rural villages in Oaxaca and Guerrero who had suffered the worst effects of the neoliberal agrarian policies that undermined traditional agriculture in their home communities. For the first time large, permanent rural settlements of farmworkers expanded throughout the region, prompting an unprecedented population explosion. In an ironic historical twist, the settlement of indigenous Mixtec, Triqui, and Zapotec farmworkers led to a "reindigenization" of the local population after European settlers displaced the Kiliwa and Cochomí peoples who originally inhabited the valley in the late 1500s. The economic, labor, and social effects of the production regime of export agriculture on the growers and the workers who settled in the region is the focus of the rest of the book.

2

Transnational Agribusiness, Local Growers, and Discontents

> *The company has its eyes fixed on Mexico. The company's owners are investing in Mexico because they understand future growth is here and because of all the problems they face in California—the competition for land due to population growth there, regulatory constraints in agriculture, and many other difficulties they confront in California.*
> —HENRY CLARK, A BERRYMEX VICE PRESIDENT
> IN BAJA CALIFORNIA, 2005

It was 8:30 in the morning on a sunny day in May 2005 when I went to meet Henry Clark, vice president of BerryMex, the Mexican subsidiary of Driscoll's, one of the largest producers of berries in the world. I had first met Henry—tall, affable, and conversant—the previous summer when Marcos López, a rural sociologist who was doing field research in the region, and I went to a local office Driscoll's had recently opened in San Quintín. As he explained to us at the time, Driscoll's began producing strawberries in San Quintín in 2004 after he, along with other Mexican collaborators, persuaded the company to come to the region to take advantage of its mild climate, land availability, and close proximity to the border, providing a good alternative to the high cost of winter production in California. One year later, after interviewing him again about the first two seasons of the company in San Quintín, I set up a day for a guided tour to visit some fields where Driscoll's was growing berries. As we drove north along the coast near the town of Vicente Guerrero heading to the first field, it was clear to me that Henry was a different type of grower from many of the old-time farmers I had previously met in the valley. In his early forties, he was younger, had an academic degree in agronomy, spoke Spanish and English fluently, and was open and straightforward in his answers to my questions. His persona reflected his stated goal of bringing fresh air to the region by implementing a modern labor managerial style different from the old patron-client authoritarian model that many ranchers used in the region and that, in his view, was the reason for the animosity between growers and workers there.

As we drove on the Trans-Peninsular Highway in his SUV, his cell phone rang several times with calls from office and field employees asking for instructions, to which he replied with short and clear commands. He carried a digital recorder, which he used to tape work-related memos on his morning drives to inspect the fields to make sure everything was in order.

A few minutes later, we arrived at the first of the two fields we were visiting that morning. It was a 42-hectare raspberry field where a crew of four workers was injecting gas underneath the soil to sterilize it before planting started in late May. "We are sterilizing the soil spraying *bromuro de metilo* to later build the planting beds," Henry explained to me. Then, pointing to a tractor, he continued, "This machine is injecting the gas and covering the soil with plastic to prevent gas evaporation. The gas lasts about three days and kills the seeds of weeds and pathogen fungus on the ground so that they don't damage the plants once they are planted." As we talked, he noticed that none of the four workers was wearing a protective mask, including the tractor driver. Surprised and slightly embarrassed, he reached for his cell phone and called John, the agronomist in charge of the field and his right-hand man, telling him to send masks to the workers right away. Though at first I did not smell any gas, after a few minutes and as the wind blew in our direction I developed a slight headache that lasted for a few more minutes after we left the place, a reminder of the dangers field workers in San Quintín confront when exposed to chemicals for which they have little protection and training.

After leaving this field and visiting a desalination plant Driscoll's had recently built to supply water to produce strawberries, Henry drove me to a second production site, this one exclusively dedicated to growing organic raspberries. He was especially proud of this organic field because it showed San Quintín was at the cutting edge of organic berry production, responding to the changing consumer demands in the United States. When I asked him what drove Driscoll's to produce organic berries in Baja, he responded that whereas in the United States "it takes three years to get a field approved for organic production and demonstrate there are no toxic residues left from previous nonorganic production," in San Quintín it only takes three to four months. As we talked, a group of workers, many of them indigenous women, were picking raspberries and packing them in square plastic boxes with the Driscoll's label that read "Product of Mexico." Grabbing a box of berries, Henry pointed to a number that identifies the box. This number, he explained, allows tracking to the field where the fruits were harvested, the workers who picked them, and even the individual worker who harvested each basket of raspberries. As I listened to him, I reflected on the power traceability technologies confers on big companies, rendering farm workers visible who, for most other purposes, remain invisible and reduced to identification numbers. Afterward, as we were ready to go back to his office at lunchtime, I asked Henry if I could take a picture of him in this organic field. He asked me to wait a moment so he could walk to his SUV to pick up and wear his Driscoll's cap to show the company's logo because, as he put it, "it is more representative" of who he is and what he is doing in San Quintín. His gesture reinforced my impression that Henry was proud of helping bring Driscoll's to the San Quintín Valley, a company that in his view not only was fostering technological and economic progress but also helping to change what he considered the "provincial and backward mentality" that prevailed among many growers and developing a new labor management style.

This chapter focuses on the last wave of U.S. agribusiness penetration into the San Quintín Valley in the 2000s and the responses it has generated from local growers. As I show, the arrival of Driscoll's in Baja represents the most recent stage in the modern history of transnational agribusiness encroachment on land, water, and labor resources to provide fresh produce for global markets. The surge of strawberries as the golden crop has brought a new production regime based on the combination of intensive water-mining technologies and labor management methods to increase production, enhance labor productivity, and exert control over local companies and growers. The pressure of increasing business costs in California provided a further impetus to begin production in Baja close to the U.S.-Mexico border, as Henry Clark pointed out. Despite this trend, a small group of midsized growers strives to escape the control of multinational companies and remain independent. Using the case studies of different growers, I discuss the types of local-global articulation that prevail in the strawberry industry and how the penetration of transnational corporations has reshaped power relations among growers in the region. Export agriculture, I argue, resembles a vertical global commodity chain with power concentrated in a handful of transnational companies that maintain a form of "tutelage farming" with a segment of subordinated local growers.[1] The chapter also reveals a production regime based on the encroachment on land and water resources and critical dependence on indigenous workers as a source of flexible and disciplined labor.

A NEW GIANT ARRIVES IN TOWN: DRISCOLL'S NEW PRODUCTION AND LABOR REGIME

As in the case of A.B.C. Farm in the early 1980s, the arrival of Driscoll's in the early 2000s drastically transformed the nature of agricultural production in the San Quintín Valley. Based in Watsonville, California, Driscoll's is the state's largest grower-shipper and the industry leader in strawberry production (Wells 1996, 126; López 2011, 78). As a global company, it produces strawberries, blackberries, blueberries, and raspberries, as well as organic berries in several U.S. regions and in countries around the world, including Australia, Portugal, and Morocco, among others, with markets around the world (López 2011, 78). The company was attracted to San Quintín because of its ideal soil and climate for berry production, geographic proximity to the border, and large labor pool of settled farmworkers. But as in the case of A.B.C. Farm, U.S. investors and Mexican business brokers were instrumental in bringing Driscoll's to Baja. As Robert Álvarez argues (1988, 72), as capitalist corporations penetrate the production of fresh produce in Mexico, it is crucial to understand how they interact with local-level actors and the role the latter play in navigating conflicting ideologies and behaviors. The development of commercial agriculture in San Quintín shows the interstitial role Mexican ethnic entrepreneurs play in connecting local farmers with large agribusiness and wholesalers in California.

In San Quintín's strawberry industry, Henry Clark was one of the key agents who served as a business and cultural broker for Driscoll's, helping this company navigate the differences in the business and political cultures of Mexico and the United States. Henry's mother was native to the region, and his grandparents had a ranch there that combined dry-land agriculture with livestock farming, a common economic activity until the 1970s. With an Anglo-Mexican heritage and a middle-class upbringing, Henry studied in a public university in Mexicali in Baja, graduating in agronomy in the late 1980s. He spent the next ten years working in the city of Guadalajara for a company that provided irrigation equipment and consultation services to horticultural companies. One of his client companies was Driscoll's, which had recently started growing strawberries in Jalisco. According to Henry, the company tried to recruit him as head of its irrigation operations in Jalisco but instead of accepting the offer, he talked the Driscoll's representatives into considering the San Quintín Valley as a site to produce strawberries for U.S. markets, praising the bounties of its coastal climate, land and labor availability, and proximity to the U.S.-Mexican border. Proudly recounting this episode of his life, Henry commented, "I proposed to them that they come to produce here. They did not know the region, and [I told them] it was close to the border where the transportation logistics for crops was much easier than in Jalisco. I informed them that strawberries were produced in San Quintín and that it was an attractive region. I brought them here and they were impressed; that was back in 1999, and one year later we were already cultivating strawberries here."

After a visit to the valley guided by Clark in 1999, Driscoll's began producing strawberries in 2000 on an experimental basis on 6 hectares. After initial success, it expanded to 68 hectares three years later, and by 2005 it had reached 248 hectares. From the beginning, the company's goal was to grow not only strawberries but also two types of berries it produced in California, blueberries and blackberries, as well as organic berries, an emergent and highly profitable market at the time. Driscoll's' business decision to invest in San Quintín, however, was driven not only by the opportunities presented by this region but also by a concerted effort to expand operations in Mexico in light of the difficulties the company was facing in California regarding the availability and cost of land, as well as new

FIGURE 5. Driscoll's built a cooling and packing plant for berries in 2007.

pesticide regulations. In addition, compared to California, the waiting time and bureaucratic process to have a land parcel receive approval for organic production in San Quintín was shorter, as Henry explained to me. Moreover, in California agribusiness faced increasing competition for land due to population growth and urbanization, forcing growers to follow regulations regarding the use of pesticides near human settlements. The San Quintín Valley, with plenty of land and fewer regulations, offered an attractive alternative. "A year's rent for a field in California costs the equivalent to renting a field in San Quintín for four years," Henry commented, highlighting the fact that Driscoll's had long-term business plans for this region. In addition, unlike other companies that grow berries for export and domestic markets, from the start Driscoll's business plan was to concentrate on international markets alone, banning local growers producing berries for this company from selling them in Mexico. Explaining the rationale for this business model, Henry pointed out the economic costs of producing berries for Mexico's domestic market.

> Other growers here have developed a domestic market in Mexico for second-class quality berries so that what they can't ship to the United States is sold in the domestic market. We haven't entered the national market because our focus is to export; our goal is to export 100 percent of our production. We realized there're problems when you try producing berries for two different markets, having labels for first- and second-class berries, because instead of concentrating on ensuring the quality of your first label, you have to ensure that workers don't pack first-class berries in second-class label boxes [for domestic markets].... You lose a large percentage of fruit on the second-class batch that could have been used for first-class export fruit boxes.

An integral component of Driscoll's business plan in Baja also included building a state-of-the-art cooling and packing plant. Inaugurated in 2007, the plant was conceived to attract local growers to produce berries for this company. The largest of its kind in Baja, the plant grades, cools, and packs the fruit produced by Driscoll's Mexican subsidiary, BerryMex, and all local growers who produce berries for this company, serving as a central gateway for most export berries grown in the region. Explaining the logic of this business strategy, Clark told me that the large investment in this cooling and packing plant allowed local growers to concentrate solely on "production, liberating them from postproduction tasks" such as transportation, cooling, and packing. The plant allowed Driscoll's to establish a quasi-monopoly over strawberries grown in the region. As an agronomist employed by SAGARPA in San Quintín told me, with this cooling plant Driscoll's sought "to close all loopholes of strawberries that leave the region to the United States and have control over the strawberry sector." Driscoll's significantly transformed the transnational geography of strawberry production in the U.S.-Mexico borderlands, making San Quintín the new epicenter for export-oriented production (López 2011, 38).[2]

Mining Local Water to Produce Export Crops

Although the availability of abundant land was a central incentive for Driscoll's move to the San Quintín Valley, the company faced the perennial problem of water scarcity, which in the late 1990s threatened the collapse of large-scale agriculture. The way in which this company addressed this problem was a reiteration of the technological fetishism that first brought large-scale agriculture to the region in the 1980s. From the start, the company decided to confront the problem of water scarcity from a different angle than most other growers. Instead of building channels to bring irrigation water from the mountain streams, Driscoll's was one of the first companies to build desalination plants. As Henry Clark explained to me:

> When we arrived in San Quintín, we immediately identified water [scarcity] as the key problem. "What is everybody doing to have water to cultivate?," we asked. We saw that everybody was going to the river basins to drill water wells and that some companies were going closer to the water stream to drill wells, taking water away from those who were trying to get it from below them. At that point we thought that we either compete in the same [water] race game or take a different approach. We decided to go in the opposite direction, [closer] to the ocean to build desalination plants to deal with water insecurity, periodic draughts, and water fluctuations.... That's why we decided to invest in the technology of reverse osmosis, and now all our growth is based on this technology.

Driscoll's technocratic approach, which reduced water to an input cost for the production of export berries isolated from the region's ecological context, became clear to me during a field visit to one of the numerous desalination plants the company owns. The plant was enclosed in a midsized facility and consisted of a series of twelve large tubes through which water is treated, several electric control panels on the walls with switches to control the process, myriad tubes for water that goes

FIGURE 6. A BerryMex water reservoir.

through the filtering membranes, a high-pressure water pump, and several large barrels connected to intake tubes. Desalination technology is based on reverse osmosis to reduce salinity of brackish water, which requires less energy and therefore is less costly than desalinating seawater. After brackish water is desalinated, the liquid is separated into two types, "product water," which is good-quality water to irrigate the plants, and "rejected water," which is deemed unfit for irrigation because of its high salinity. Product water is stored in a large tank, while wastewater is poured into a container and deposited by electric pumps about 3 kilometers into the ocean. The whole process can be costly, ranging between 60 cents and $1.20 per gallon of desalinated water, depending on the number of gallons produced a day (the higher the number, the lower the cost because of economies of scale). Outside the building was a reservoir, a large pond of desalinated water encircled by black plastic walls to protect against dust. Describing the key role water reservoirs play for the steady production of berries, Henry explained, "Why do we keep water in the pond? Because these [desalination] plants have a lot of delicate electronic components, and if and when one of them fails, then we have a water bank here we can rely on to irrigate our field for fifteen days while the machine is being repaired. It's only reserve water."

Desalination technologies, however, do not operate in an ecological and social vacuum and need to be examined in the larger historical and political ecology in which they are deployed. As Marcos López has shown analyzing what he describes as "the art of manufacturing water," strawberry plants are intrinsically thirsty, requiring twenty gallons of water to produce one ton of fruit (López 2017, 194). Driscoll's decision to invest in this technology was driven by a cost-benefit analysis that would provide an edge over other companies in the region but largely decoupled from considerations about its ecological impact and long-term sustainability. In fact, Driscoll's' investment in capital-intensive water-mining technologies has had a major effect in the region, pushing other large companies to follow suit, an approach with high ecological and social collateral costs. As a business and cultural broker, Henry regarded the desalination technologies Driscoll's had brought to San Quintín as a step toward the modernization of agriculture in the region. But as I witnessed the gradual expansion of these artificial oases in the region, I could not help but think about the gross inequity between the power of large companies to siphon underground water to irrigate their berries and the difficulties the very farmworkers who tend these fruits confronted to access water in their households, as there was not a single desalination plant for human use in the entire region.

Building a "Loyal" Labor Force

The success of export agriculture in Baja not only rests on genetically transformed seeds, modern irrigation technologies, and high-tech cooling and packing plants, but also on labor management methods to enhance productivity. For delicate strawberries, having a well-trained workforce is especially critical. In the strawberry industry in California, the single most important factor determining market value is the quality of harvest labor, including how workers select, handle, and pack the delicate fruits (Wells 1996, 49). Not surprisingly, when Driscoll's arrived in San Quintín, it implemented a new labor management approach to reduce labor turnover, increase workers' productivity, and enhance the quality of the harvest. Mirroring the labor management strategies used in California, the company wanted to create what Henry Clark described as a "new work culture" aimed at instilling loyalty among its workers and building a stable workforce. With no labor contracts, low wages, and few if any labor benefits, farmworkers in San Quintín move frequently among employers, a strategy to cope with seasonal layoffs and optimize their earnings. Seeking to change this behavior and stabilize its workforce, Driscoll's developed a labor management approach to, as Henry described it, "improve dialogue and communication" between the company and its workers. The importance of transforming indigenous workers into a stable and dedicated farm labor force became evident to me during my conversations with Henry shortly after Driscoll's arrived in San Quintín. In contrast to the confident tone with which he described the new desalination technologies the company had brought to the region, when talking about labor-related issues he adopted a more somber tone: "One of the most difficult issues we face here with our workforce is the lack of responsibility. Workers don't have any sense of work responsibility, and they could not care less whenever they don't show up for work or when they don't show up three of four days in a row! More than labor turnover, Christian, the main problem we have is labor absenteeism, which is the main challenge we need to overcome. We try to promote a comfortable and friendly labor environment, but workers do not appreciate it."

Henry's words convey the problem of labor turnover many companies experienced in the region, which he interpreted as a lack of workers' "commitment and loyalty." He considered it his task to transform the work culture and habits of indigenous workers by deploying a more "humane labor management" style that would eventually make them stay with the company. The goal was to have his workers "ponerse la camiseta de la compañía" (wear the company's T-shirt), a figurative expression used in Mexico that refers to workers identifying with the company's goals and developing a strong work ethic. Henry stressed the need to build a new work culture fostering the values of commitment and loyalty.

> There is a very serious problem having a high labor turnover, and that is what we have to address. We need to have much better communication with our workers, to incentivize them so they want to come to work for us, not just three days a week and then rest the remaining days of the week, because when they do that it affects us a lot.... That is part of what we want to change because labor turnover is a serious problem.... We want workers to choose us as their favorite employer. It's a difficult process, not something you can change in two months, but a long process on which we have to work.

Rather than cite factors like low wages or lack of other labor benefits, he explained the problem of labor turnover in cultural terms, as the result of "workers' lack of ambition." When I asked him to elaborate on this point, with a mixture of frustration and surprise about workers' behavior, he commented:

> I believe there is a great deal of *conformismo* among workers, a lack of ambition perhaps. I do not understand it well, but, for example, we know for a fact that Mondays are a difficult day for us [because] many workers don't show up.... We also have noticed that when we pay workers by piece rate, if they earn in one day what would otherwise take them three days, then they decide not to come the next two days because they have already earned what otherwise would take them three days. They should have more ambition and say, "I made three days' wages, and if I keep working all week, I could almost make as much as in one month of work!"

Henry's explanation of worker turnover and absenteeism reflects the "cultural deficiency" model that historically has permeated the public discourse about indigenous farmworkers among white and mestizo growers in Baja. According to this discourse, indigenous workers from poor regions in southern Mexico arrive in Baja with a "backward" mentality and cultural values that prevent them from capitalizing on the employment and economic opportunities capitalist agriculture brings to the region (Martínez Novo 2006). The solution is to "modernize" them by changing their culture and values and fostering a strong work ethic attuned to the good opportunities offered in northern Mexico. This approach, however, does not consider two important factors that often shape farm laborers' decisions about when and for whom to work. As the economic anthropologist Sutti Ortiz (2002) has shown, labor turnover in agriculture is often associated with the piece rate system that pays laborers per unit harvested. This system is advantageous to growers because it keeps costs for a specific task constant and stimulates productivity. The downside is that it enhances labor absenteeism and shifts in employment (Ortiz 2002, 404). In turn, laborers often prefer piece rate despite fluctuating incomes because they can control how much they can earn, they have greater freedom to decide when to come and go, and it provides an option to enhance their earnings using family labor (Ortiz 2002, 404). In San Quintín, field workers with no specialized occupations employed on a temporary basis with few or no labor benefits have no incentives other than wages to stay with a single employer. Instead, they use their contacts and social connections to identify the best job opportunities based on wage levels, type of payments (piece rate, day wage), length of the workday, employer's reputation, and the length of the work offer. This is especially important during the harvest season in the spring when labor demand peaks, providing workers with some leverage to choose among employers and job offers. From this perspective, labor turnover and absenteeism are forms of resistance to low rates and piece rate contracts designed to increase productivity.

In addition, farmworkers in San Quintín consider the drudgery and physical toll of work. With the freedom of living in their own homes rather than in labor camps run by their employers, workers have more latitude to choose not to work if they feel the drudgery of a particular job is not worth their time. In this case, many prefer to allocate their time and energy to nonwage household work or casual jobs in the informal economy. Rather than lack of ambition, labor allocation decisions at the household level reveal a calculation of "opportunity costs," the monetary returns of paid work versus other alternatives (Chibnik 2011, 166; Chayanov 1966). During my fieldwork, I found it intriguing that large companies like Driscoll's were puzzled by worker turnover and wanted to experiment with new labor management methods to "motivate" workers to stay with them rather than simply raise wages and provide good labor benefits to decrease absenteeism and achieve a more stable labor force. Only when workers mobilized in labor strikes did Driscoll's and other companies feel compelled to raise wages, as I discuss later in the book.

Technologizing Labor Control

Driscoll's goal to modernize labor management also included the use of new technologies for labor control. From the beginning, the company wanted "to rationalize the work process," as Henry Clark put it, and increase worker productivity. To that end, it implemented a scientific management approach to reduce the time workers spend at specific tasks and speed up the work process. One such change consisted of reducing the "idle time" of harvest workers in the fields. Accordingly, Henry developed a plan to decrease the distance they had to walk from the rows where they pick the fruits to the checking station by repositioning the stations and the paths workers have to walk to reach them, reducing workers' walking distance from 84 to 42 meters. The new system also reduced the "idle time" workers spent waiting in line for their fruits to be inspected from an average of ten minutes to only about two minutes. More important, as Henry told me, the new system allowed the company to reduce the number of workers and work crews for the harvest. "We have achieved reducing the number of workers required per area of work; while in the past we needed 2.0 workers per acre we now need only 1.5," he proudly commented. In his view, the new system benefited not only the company but also its workers as they could harvest more fruit and thus increase their earnings.

Driscoll's also introduced a new technological device, an electronic card to track harvest workers' productivity and enhance their accountability. The card allows companies to keep count of the number of fruit boxes each worker harvests every day and is commonly used in the strawberry industry in California as part of a broader "biometric job quality control program" for labor control and discipline (Figueroa Sánchez 2013).[3] Imported from the company's headquarters in California, the new system changed the way in which workers' performance was assessed from a manual punch card to an electronic card. In the old system, both the company and the workers kept duplicates of the punch cards, while with the electronic card system only the employer can read the digital information recorded on the cards. If workers wanted to preserve the data, they would have to either memorize or record it on their own. According to Henry, one of the main advantages of the electronic cards is that it allows for recording detailed data such as workers' speed, performance by work task, and changes in workers' productivity over time, identifying areas where worker productivity can be enhanced.

To his surprise, however, the new card system encountered resistance from farmworkers. Workers complained that under the new system, they had lost control of keeping count of the fruit boxes they harvested and the ability to contest the company's record if they believed it was mistaken. Explaining workers' reaction, he acknowledged that many expressed their "inconformity," an expression commonly used in Mexico to refer to a form of soft labor resistance by which workers express dislike for particular labor practices without recurring to collective protest. Sharing his surprise and disappointment about workers' reaction to the new card system, Henry said:

> All workers were against it. It's surprising because we started with the new system a year ago, and we took all the needed precautions to show workers that the new system was as reliable as the old punch cards. We even ran both systems [simultane-

ously] for one week to do that and workers did not experience any problem with the new electronic system. This system provides us with much more information than the old one, and at the end of a day's work we can print a sheet with data for every single worker for each work crew including how many boxes he harvested, what time each worker completed each box, the average number of boxes per worker and hour, and even rank workers in descending order from the most productive to the least, all of which allows us to do a fine analysis. . . . Three weeks ago some new workers who just started to work for us complained about the system . . ., but our response was, "OK, just because you have doubts about the system we are not going to change it; we are not going to step down from an airplane to get on a horse."

Henry's words reflect the consequences of using tracking technologies to collect individual workers' data and for disciplining purposes (Hernández Romero, 2012). In San Quintín, many growers portray indigenous workers as backward and unwilling to embrace technological innovation and progress. From this perspective, workers are cast as too "conformist" or "unconformist," depending on the circumstances. When I gently pressed Henry in order to better understand the source of workers' resistance to the new technology it became apparent that while it provided rich data for the company, workers experienced the opposite effect and were left with less information than with the former "antiquated" punch cards. Unlike the latter, which they could read and check at any time during the workday, the electronic cards did not generate a printed record workers could check and take home after a day's work, making them feel they had lost power. As Henry explained:

[The electronic card system] is different. When the harvest day is over, we print a results sheet and show it to workers the next morning when they come to work. [To overcome their distrust] we suggest they bring a handful of beans and use one bean per box they harvest during the day so they can check the accuracy of the new system the next morning when they come to work. . . . They complain, "The new system does not keep track of all the boxes I pack and it is stealing money away from me," but they say that speculatively without any proof.

Workers' resistance to the electronic cards can be interpreted as a rational reaction to losing the ability to track their productivity and contest the company's record when they felt it was inaccurate. Indeed similar reactions have been observed in other regional contexts with farmworkers in the United States (Figueroa Sánchez 2002; Madrigal 2017). In San Quintín the new card system disempowered harvest workers who in the past could dispute any discrepancies in their punch cards at the end of the workday if they felt there was a factual error. Like other labor management technologies, the new device increased the power gap between employers and farm laborers, leaving workers powerless to contest this change. Henry's suggestion that workers use beans to keep track of their productivity reflects growers' infantilization of indigenous laborers, who are portrayed as distrustful of modern technologies because of 'cultural backwardness.'

In addition, Driscoll's implemented other tracking technologies, including a system to track the berries packed by field workers. Known as a food traceability system (Hsien-Tang et al. 2014), this technology has become a staple in the fresh-produce industry that allows tracking the source of bacteria-contaminated fruits and vegetables to help prevent public health problems.[4] Usually portrayed as a tool for risk management and food safety, traceability technologies, however, are also used as tools for labor control and discipline. One of its key functions is "control and verification," which enables the tracking and identification of the "responsible actors" when something goes wrong (Coff, Korthals, and Barling 2008, 5). As such, the different uses of traceability make it "a potential battlefield" and source of conflict (Coff, Korthals, and Barling 2008, 7). In San Quintín, Driscoll's deployed this system to enhance workers' accountability and to track and discipline "bad" workers. During one of my field visits Henry explained that all the company's berry boxes have a sequence of digits that allows tracking the field where the fruit of each box is harvested and the workers who picked them. When deemed necessary, Driscoll's uses this technology to identify and discipline groups or individual workers. As he explained, "Each box has a number that identifies the worker who harvested it, so if we find a box that is filled with bad fruits, we can track the employee's number and know in which crew he or she is. Then we talk to the mayordomo and tell him, 'This person is not doing a good job,' and he is in charge of addressing the problem and talking to the worker."

In the field, traceability is used as a labor-disciplining tool to demand workers repack fruit boxes when they do not pass the quality-check points at Driscoll's cooling plant. To be paid, workers have to pick berries to replace the "wrong" ones and repack them. Rather than a "neutral technology," traceability is inscribed in the neoliberal language of individual responsibility and accountability, allowing companies like Driscoll's to use it as a tool for labor discipline. The introduction of new technologies to "rationalize" the work process has led to a reintensification of work, where farmworkers have to work harder and faster and are held accountable for the quality of the fruits they pick and pack.

Despite these changes, many farmworkers in San Quintín prefer working for Driscoll's over Mexican companies and growers, especially large firms that have a reputation for exploiting their workers and paying low wages. This preference is the result of several factors. First, unlike many of the latter, Driscoll's regularly registers its workers in the health security system and pays other benefits such as sick leave, pension, and housing. It also has a reputation for treating its workers better than many large Mexican transnational companies such as, for example, Los Pinos, which employs thousands of field workers and has one of the worst reputations among workers in San Quintín. Unlike Los Pinos, some U.S. companies like

Driscoll's lack domestic political connections and are more careful not to openly violate basic labor laws. Driscoll's also landed in Baja with higher labor standards than many of its Mexican counterparts, something that workers and some labor leaders acknowledge. This represents what Ong and Collier (2005) call the "curious problems" posed by globalization, in which rather than a uniform field there exist multiple layers of markets, ethics, and cultures. In this case, the corporate culture this company brought to San Quintín aligned better with labor laws in Mexico than that of Mexican transnational firms. At the same time, however, the company's management approach entails a hyper-intense labor-disciplining regime with multiple checking points to ensure the "quality and excellence" the company uses to promote its fruits. As such, it mirrors a broader trend in the global fresh-produce industry to use quality control checks for "corrective and disciplinary purposes" (Hernández Romero 2012, 79).

TUTELAGE FARMING: JOAQUÍN CUENCA AS A CONTRACT GROWER

When Driscoll's arrived in San Quintín, it transformed power relations among berry growers. From California, the company transplanted a business model in which local farmers are recruited as "share growers" to produce berries for the Driscoll's label, an arrangement known as contract farming, which is a common practice in the United States. The plan was to become the dominant player in the production of berries and transform the region into a key platform to supplement berry production for U.S. commercial markets. One such contract grower was Joaquín Cuenca, who had farmed in the region where his parents arrived in the 1960s. I first met Joaquín in 2010, during a visit to one of his fields accompanying a SAGARPA officer who knew I was looking for local growers producing for Driscoll's. As a contract grower, Joaquín is one of the dozens of local growers in San Quintín who produce different types of berries for Driscoll's BerryMex.[5] Compared to Henry Clark, Joaquín Cuenca was more reserved and guarded when talking about the details of his farm business, which as I explain later reflects the confidential nature of the commercial agreements contract farming often entails. As a business arrangement, contract farming linking local farmers to national and international markets has significantly expanded since the late 1980s, and is considered a central mechanism for the industrialization of commercial agriculture under neoliberal agrarian principles (Echánove and Steffen 2005, 167; Little and Dolan 2000; Raynolds 2000; Narotzky 2016; McMichael 1994). This arrangement allows multinational corporations to access agricultural products without having to obtain land, offering a buffer from labor unions as contracted local growers are responsible for labor recruitment and management (Echánove and Steffen 2005, 166). It also gives large companies the ability to impose a very strict production script that contract growers must follow, qualifying their fields and packing facilities for USDA certification. In the fresh-produce industry, the expansion of contract farming has been linked to the quality standards required for horticultural products such as texture, color, shape, and weight. Because the production of delicate fruits and vegetables is difficult to mechanize and has to meet specific technical standards, it generates high levels of risk for producers, who pass them on to local growers through contract farming arrangements (Echánove and Steffen 2005). Thus in contract farming growers must follow the production script and practices established by the purchaser company in exchange for access to markets and the purchaser normally provides technical assistance, supplies, and services while growers provide access to land and labor (Raynolds 2000, 442).

Not surprisingly, contract farming is a controversial arrangement that has fueled considerable debate among scholars in the field. The central theoretical discussion hinges on whether it is a form of disguised wage labor or independent family farming (Raynolds 2000). In a study of the growth of contract farming in Mexico, Echánove (2001, 19–20) argues that grounded case studies show that local growers assume the market risks when large agribusinesses become saturated and use "quality" as an excuse not to accept their produce, a common practice in agribusiness. Behind the image of a dynamic partnership, she contends, lies a mode of production in which contractors obtain a continuous supply of high-quality produce by placing the risks of production almost entirely in the hands of growers.[6] As in other regions in Mexico, in San Quintín Driscoll's relies on its Mexican subsidiary BerryMex as a direct source of production and a large network of midsized contract growers, which it calls share growers.[7] Business contracts with its "associate growers" give Driscoll's exclusive access to their berries with sole rights to market them. But how does this type of partnership agreement transform the way in which local growers run their farms? How do local farmers evaluate the effect of contract farming on their lives? And how does it affect the way in which they organize production and recruit and manage their workers? I focus on Joaquín Cuenca's case to address these questions and analyze the economic and social transformation that contract agriculture in the berry sector brought to local farmers in the region, their identity, and labor management.

Independent Grower or Maquila Farmer?

Born in Tijuana in 1972, Joaquín Cuenca is one of three children of immigrant parents from the western Mexican state of Zacatecas who settled in the San Quintín Valley in the late 1960s. His parents were farmers who, like many others in the region at the time, went from growing corn, potatoes, and chiles in the 1970s to producing tomatoes in the 1980s and expanded to other export crops such as cucumbers, squash, and peas in the early 2000s. After growing up in the valley, Joaquín went to study in Tijuana, graduating as an agronomist at a public university in Mexicali. Based on his own farming experience, he wrote a thesis about the process of growing cucumbers in shadehouses in San Quintín, illustrating the experience of a new generation of growers who, while having grown up in the region on their parents' farms, have professional training and learned new farming technologies. After graduating, he decided to go back to San Quintín to work on the family farm. By then his parents' farm had been in decline for several years, going from a harvest of 600 hectares a year in the early 1990s to 300 hectares in 2003 and only 40 hectares two years later. The uneven competitive environment fueled by NAFTA opened the doors for large U.S. grower-shipper companies to set up production in San Quintín, driving many local growers out of business. Facing the possible extinction of the family farm, Joaquín decided they had to engage in partnership agreements with large companies to remain in farming. Recalling the changes in the local agricultural industry that his parents confronted and that had driven many growers he knew out of business since the early 2000s, he recounted:

> For the former generation of growers like my parents, it was easy to make tons of money, but then things changed. If you look at the generation of growers and families who started producing horticultural crops in San Quintín, there are only a few who are still in business. Most are now bankrupt and do not produce any longer; they cannot compete with the market or with us, the new generation of growers. . . . In my family, for example, the relatives of both my father and mother were driven out of the market.

Realizing that "lenders and economic problems" were eroding the family business, Joaquín decided to go to California in search of work as an agronomist. It was there he met "the Reiter Brothers," as he calls them, the owners of Reiter Affiliated Companies, Driscoll's' parent company. At that point, Joaquín proudly recalled, people in the company "invited" him to learn about strawberry production in California to set up production in Baja under a business partnership with Driscoll's. Thrilled by the opportunity, he spent more than a year in Oxnard, California, learning about the business of growing strawberries and meeting with technicians, producers, and personnel from "the Driscoll's family." After completing his training, he was offered support to start producing strawberries for the company on his family's land in San Quintín. "Because I had land, water, and some farm equipment, I was offered an opportunity to grow strawberries for Driscoll's," he recalled. In 2003, he began planting 8 hectares of family land that were idle, introducing strawberries for the first time; with time the farm prospered, and when I met him in 2010, he had expanded to 36 hectares, growing not only strawberries but raspberries for export as well.

Like Henry Clark, Joaquín's identity is that of an innovator, part of a new generation of young growers who are modernizing agricultural production in Mexico

FIGURE 7. One of Joaquín Cuenca's fields. Cuenca is a share grower for BerryMex.

and continuing the family farming tradition. To him this change not only entailed switching from tomatoes to strawberries, but also how to run the family farm. As a college-educated agronomist with Driscoll's training in California, he is proud of bringing a new form of business management and changing "the old ways" by which his father ran the farm in the past. In contrast to the reserved mood he adopted whenever I inquired about the details of his business partnership with Driscoll's, Joaquín was eager to talk about the generational change of which he was a part. Comparing generations, he emphasized the role of "professional training" to properly run family farms in today's times.

CZ: How has your approach to farming changed with respect to that of your parents?

EA: They were empiricists [who learned by experience]; we are professionals. We still benefit from the farming experience of their generation, their traditions, and we apply them, but I think we bring a different vision because we are better prepared and have academic training. Some of us have *licenciaturas* [BAs], others MAs, and a few even doctorates. My generation has BAs; the new generation that comes after me, like my cousins' children, is graduating with MAs, and that is a good change

CZ: And do you think that academic training has opened doors for people like you?

EA: Very much so, because you can see that American growers are also entrepreneurs and well prepared to run the farming business. [In contrast], Mexican strawberry farmers [in California] are not the same because they started as farmworkers and then became independent farmers but based on their own work experience, not professional training; yes, they are very good, but it isn't the same.

Joaquín's comments signal a generational identity change from farmer to "professional" grower. What defines a grower is not so much working directly on the farm but having professional training and using it to run it as an enterprise with modern production technologies, carefully designed business plans, and professional office management methods. It also entails being open to and embracing business opportunities with transnational corporations to have access to wider international markets rather than protecting the autonomy of the family farm. This generational change needs to be situated in the larger historical and structural context of the ascendance of large transnational corporations that since the early 2000s have dominated the business of export agriculture in San Quintín. While allowing Joaquín to revamp the family farm, the concentration on producing berries for Driscoll's for export markets placed him in a subordinate status. The new model of contract farming imported by this company from California to Baja drastically altered the business partnerships of local berry growers. Growers like Joaquín who become Driscoll's "business associates" must meet strict requirements regarding what type of berries they can grow and when and how they plant and harvest them, as well as postharvest protocols for handling the fruits until they deliver them to the company's packing and cooling center in San Quintín, severely limiting their autonomy.

Joaquín renews his partnership contract with Driscoll's on a yearly basis, a contract that spells out in detail the amount of land to be planted, the percentages of investments for each partner, and each party's responsibilities. Share growers can have up to 50 percent of investment in any given field; in Joaquín's case, he invests 40 percent and BerryMex covers the remaining 60 percent, with profits split accordingly. As a contract grower, he pays a commission fee of 18 percent for each fruit box he delivers to Driscoll's, and the company has the exclusive right to sell his produce. While highly dependent on Driscoll's for capital and access to export markets, Joaquín is grateful to this company for the opportunity to preserve the family farm and make a living as a grower. For him, working under a "business partnership" with Driscoll's has provided one of the few avenues to access the lucrative export strawberry business, even though under the company's tutelage. Aware of how the power landscape has shifted in the region since the arrival of large U.S. grower-shipper companies, Joaquín sees that the option is no longer whether to operate as an independent farmer but to choose which company he wants to work for as a contract grower. Reflecting on the changes in the agricultural sector in San Quintín and the options he faces as a grower, he concluded:

> Well, I think that the most important thing we need to do is to choose the right broker or distributor. You have to be with the big companies because midsized growers cannot compete [any longer].... I see that today there is a different type of monopoly with strawberries. If you decide to produce them and choose a distributor who does not have access to the right market, it will not give you a good price and will run you out of business.... But if you work with the right distributor who has a monopoly or has good control of all aspects of the berry business, has supplies all year long, and an ensured quality for its clients [you are in good shape]. In my personal experience I am happy working with this company. That is how I was able to sell for $8 or $10 or $7.75, while I hear that some other growers here only receive $6 per box.

Insufficient water and access to desalinated water to irrigate his berries was another key factor that pushed Joaquín to forge a business partnership with Driscoll's. Like many other growers in the region, Joaquín could no longer use underground water on his farm because it was too salty. Without the means to finance his own desalination plant, he contracted with Driscoll's to use water produced by one of the company's desalination plants near his farm to grow berries. "The plant that you see behind us and which you can now hear running as we speak is Driscoll's property, and it's for my exclusive use!," he emphatically told me with pride one morning at his house. In fact, Driscoll's often funded not only the construction of the desalination plants but also the infrastructure to bring electricity to power them.

Joaquín's assessment of the advantages of working in partnership with Driscoll's reveals the predicaments faced by former independent growers who do not have the same financial and technical support from the government they once had. As a grower with limited financial means, he found Driscoll's' business partnership model attractive. He considered particularly important the ability to concentrate on production alone, letting Driscoll's deal with transportation, distribution, and marketing of his produce. He was also relieved not to have to spend time on those business issues and thinks that the company's cooling plant has benefited him. Comparing his situation with the former generation of growers, he commented:

> Back then my uncles here in San Quintín had to have their own cooling room and maintain it year-round. They were also responsible for having their own trucks to bring their produce to the border and [sometimes] for contracting out additional trucks; they also had to do all the paperwork and so on. In my case, in contrast, my job and responsibility ends when I deliver the product to the cooling plant and then I can go home.... You take some responsibilities off our shoulders so that we can be growers rather than entrepreneurs.... I don't mind paying a bit more, and I have peace of mind.

While ensuring easy access to export markets, however, growing berries for Driscoll's has reduced Joaquín's autonomy compared to the time when his father ran the farm. This loss of autonomy and the shift from independent farmers to growers producing for large transnational agribusinesses is often described in folk parlance in pejorative terms in the region as maquila, or factory, growers. As a contract grower, Joaquín acknowledged his subordinate position but blamed the Mexican government for the lack of access to credit in Mexico for small growers: "In the past growers relied on their own capital or borrowed money from Mexican banks; credit back then was easy. . . . When access to credit dried up, they started to rely on credit from their brokers in the United States. It wasn't any longer our own capital; we were no longer [independent] farmers but became *maquiladores* for U.S. broker companies and distributors, and we were part of the distributor's payroll. That is how I always saw it."

Joaquín's comments capture the structural effects of neoliberal agrarian policies in Mexico that made it difficult for small and medium-sized growers to obtain credit and technical support to produce export crops on their own. This policy shift, along with the approval of NAFTA in the mid-1990s, created the space for large grower-shipper companies to penetrate Baja and other regions in Mexico to engage in business partnerships with local growers in a vertically integrated production chain. In talking with Joaquín, I sensed a mixture of resignation to the almost complete control Driscoll's has over the commercialization of berries produced in San Quintín and renewed hope to continue in the farming business as a grower. Compared to the commission system that prevailed before, he feels that the rules of the game for Driscoll's contract growers—while strict and involving a high fee (close to 20 percent plus supply costs provided by the company)—are more transparent than those his parents confronted doing business with smaller American brokers in the past. His case reveals the rearticulation between local growers and transnational companies that since the early 2000s has reshaped the business landscape of export agriculture in Baja. In this process the power gap and social distance between transnational companies and local growers has significantly broadened, reducing farmers like him to tutelage growers under the control of large transnational corporations.

Employing Seasonal Field Workers

Contract farming in San Quintín is not solely a matter of financial, production, and marketing business arrangements. Externalizing the responsibility, costs, and risks of the hiring and management of workers is also a central feature. For local growers, the profitability of contract farming critically depends on their ability to control and reduce labor costs, including wages and the payment of benefits such as health insurance and paid leave. In exchange for access to capital, technology, and export markets, local growers like Joaquín are in charge of recruiting and managing their labor force; the economic success of their farms rests heavily on maintaining reliable, cheap, and flexible labor. To this end, Joaquín maintains a small group of about fifteen permanent workers with specialized occupations, including field and office employees who are registered in the Mexican health insurance system. These include, among others, two mayordomos—one for growing strawberries and another for raspberries—a chief irrigator and two to three irrigation operators under his command, two truck drivers, an accountant, an agronomist technician, and a handful of *surqueros,* those in charge of supervising work crews under the command of the mayordomos in the field. The bulk of the farm's workforce consists of between seventy and eighty field workers, most of them treated as "contingent and casual labor" employed during the harvest in the summer. These workers are recruited by word of mouth, often by the company's mayordomos, while others arrive directly after prompting by relatives, friends, and neighbors who work on the farm.

To keep labor costs low, Joaquín usually pays his workers in cash, which leaves no record of their employment and lets him avoid paying health insurance as well as any work benefits and taxes. Having grown up in the region, he has the local connections to recruit field workers when needed, usually from the surrounding colonias in Vicente Guerrero where his farm is located. As in the case of other growers I met in San Quintín, he rationalizes paying his workers cash as being their preferred form of payment, because that way "they make more money." As he explained to me, workers "do not care about those benefits and prefer to receive the money in cash every day." His words are similar to those of many other growers who blame the low number of farmworkers receiving health insurance and other labor benefits on workers themselves, who supposedly prefer cash. He also faults the government for the poor health services provided in the region, a rationale many other growers use to justify their aversion to registering their employees in the Seguro Social.

As a contract grower, Joaquín is aware that he is competing in a transnational market with other growers both in Baja and in California who source berries to Driscoll's, placing additional pressure on him to keep labor costs low. With previous experience in the strawberry industry in California, he developed a transnational comparative perspective that seeks to capitalize on access to a low-cost labor pool to compete with contract growers in California. When I asked him to elaborate on the advantages of being a berry grower in Baja, he pointed to the labor disruptions growers in California confronted because of anti-immigrant policies in the United States: "For starters the *migra* [Immigration officials] does not come here. It is mainly the lower cost of labor. Labor is cheaper, land is cheaper, and rent too; they are all strong advantages."

His words reveal that the status of the labor force, legal versus undocumented, is an important factor that gives him an advantage over his competitors north of the border. Comparing himself to growers in Watsonville, California, he emphatically pointed out the differential labor cost that gives him an edge.

> It allows me to stay in the market longer and continue producing even when market prices drop. I can still make a profit when the market cost for a strawberry box is $8, while growers in California cannot compete when market price is less than $12. . . . We spend here an average of $2 per box, from planting to harvest and transportation, while there [Watsonville] it costs them at least $4.50 or more. I am not sure, but what I can tell you is that overall they cannot produce if the market price is lower than $12. It is not profitable for them, while we here can remain in the market when prices go down to $6.

Joaquín's comments show the elaborate financial calculations that growers embedded in the competitive transnational fresh-produce market must consider. Transnational companies like Driscoll's use contract growers to maintain a constant supply of high-quality berries throughout the year across the Mexico-U.S. border. For contract growers like Joaquín, locality matters, shaping the opportunities and constraints they confront in the global strawberry industry and exerting considerable pressure to reduce labor costs as the single most important factor in remaining competitive. This confirms that, as Miriam Wells (1996) argued, the political-economic configuration of the labor market at a regional level thus critically shapes the labor regime under which business links between share growers and large agribusiness are forged.

Joaquín embodies a new type of contract grower who emerged in San Quintín since the early 2000s at a time when berries had become the new golden crop in the valley. Contract farming allowed a new generation of local growers with access to land and water, who were actively recruited and trained by Driscoll's, to grow berries for the company. The asymmetrical power relations of contract farming are manifested in the fact that Driscoll's has a great deal of control over the types of berries associate growers like Joaquín can produce; how and when they can produce them; the seeds, plants, and materials they must use; and the extraction of rent after the berries are sold in the market. Joaquín is also the face of a new generation of growers with professional education and training more attuned than their parents to the complex world of market regulations that the globalization of horticultural production has brought to this region. The generational shift from inward-looking farmer to outside-oriented grower did not go unnoticed by him. During an interview at his home, he told me with a mixture of nostalgia and sarcasm that as a contemporary grower in San Quintín he needs to multitask to "deal with banks, providers, and now even with writers," meaning researchers like me. The last wave of agricultural globalization has pushed him to interface with the outside world in ways he had not anticipated, making him uneasy and nostalgic for the more secluded, protected, and private life he had growing up on his parents' farm.

STRUGGLING FOR AUTONOMY: RANCHO LAS PALMAS AND THE QUARRELS OF LOCAL GROWERS

The transformation of the berry industry in San Quintín into a system dominated by a few large transnational companies and contracted growers did not go unopposed. Instead, it elicited the response of a few dissenting growers who wanted to participate in this lucrative sector on their own terms. While people like Joaquín Cuenca accepted the role of contract growers for the income security it provided, others were eager to resist the control of large firms and strive to preserve the autonomy of their farms. This is the case of Andrés Palma's family farm, which after years of working in partnership with several U.S. brokers regained its autonomy and began selling strawberries under its own brand. This ranch specializes in the production of strawberries for international and domestic markets and is one of a small number of medium-scale companies in the region run as independent businesses. While the academic literature on contract farming in Mexico points out the advantages and disadvantages that growers of fresh-produce encounter under this production model, few studies have looked at farmers who have escaped this arrangement to operate on their own selling produce to international markets. As Steven Sanderson (1986, 54) observed when the internationalization of agricultural production in Mexico was in an early phase, few farmers evolve as agricultural entrepreneurs in a "vertically organized food chain" made up of producers, intermediaries, and processors across national boundaries entangled in a truly transnational network. Given that statistics on the consequences of contract farming for growers in Mexico are not available (Echánove and Steffen 2005, 167), grounded case studies provide a close picture of this arrangement's implications for local growers and the strategies some follow to preserve their autonomy in the business of export agriculture. I decided to study Rancho Las Palmas to represent the resistance I found among some old-time farmers in San Quintín to the increasing power and control of large transnational companies since the early 2000s. I was interested not only in the business strategies that allowed this company to escape the tentacles of large firms but also the views of local farmers who rejected working as contract farmers. As I show, examining cases of "independent" farmers reveals the varied local-global articulation in Baja's strawberry industry and how the transnationalization of this sector in the Mexico-U.S. border region shapes power relations and labor management in San Quintín.

From Local Farmer to Global Grower

My first visit to Rancho Las Palmas took place in the summer of 2010. Accompanied by one of SAGARPA's agronomists who offered to take me, we arrived one morning in his pickup at the company office. Like most other ranches in the region, entering Rancho Las Palmas was not easy. Its office is surrounded by high walls with a huge door through which cars and trucks must pass and mounted TV cameras that monitor people entering and leaving. After we were let in, a young mestiza secretary led us to an office where Andrés Palma, one of the two brothers who run the company, received us. While not big, Andrés's office was well equipped with computers, phones, a fax machine, and other electronic devices. After the initial greeting, he kindly invited us to sit in front of his desk to chat with him. An outgoing and affable person, he explained that they had 30 hectares of strawberries under cultivation and that they had been expanding fast since they became independent growers. Achieving independence from large American brokers, he added, was a central goal for the Palma family soon after they began to produce strawberries for the United States. After developing some rapport with him, Andrés and I talked extensively during two subsequent interviews and a farm visit. During these encounters, he shared the history of his family farm, how they were able to achieve independence from broker firms with whom they worked in the past, and the main advantages and challenges of being an independent company.

Andrés's parents were born and raised in the northern state of Chihuahua and moved to the San Quintín Valley in the late 1970s, where Andrés and his two siblings were born. His father, Vicente Palma, was a former employee in a Mexican government agrarian bank who in the early 1990s decided to venture out as a grower to produce fresh crops for U.S. markets. At first he grew tomatoes, chiles, and watermelons for export. In the late 1990s, he began experimenting with strawberries on 1.5 hectares of his own land. As in the case of Joaquín Cuenca and other growers I met in San Quintín, Vicente Palma's interest in the strawberry business began with an American grower in California who "invited" him to grow strawberries because "his company needed more growers in Baja to produce for him." The grower offered Vicente financial help to capitalize on the market opportunities in the United States and the geographic proximity to the Mexico-U.S. border. In 1998, the Las Palmas family farm ended this partnership and began growing strawberries for a Japanese distributor based in Southern California who offered Vicente a better deal and had partnerships with other local growers in San Quintín. The farm prospered, and in 2001 Sunrise, a large American agribusiness, offered Rancho Las Palmas an opportunity to produce and sell strawberries exclusively for this company for a better profit margin than its former Japanese distributor.

For the next few years, the farm produced berries for Sunrise. But the family dreamed of becoming an independent company and achieving better profit margins. The main barrier the farm confronted at the time was not having its own water supply. Water from its well was too salty for growing berries, and it had to rely on desalinated water provided by another ranch. For the next two years, while growing berries for Sunrise, the Palma family saved part of its profits to build its own infrastructure. In 2004, after successfully growing strawberries for five consecutive years and with a loan from an American bank, the farm was able to build its own water desalination facility and a cooling plant. "The desalination plant is the heart of the farm," Andrés proudly told me during one of my visits with him, by which he meant that it provided the means and opportunity to finally operate as an independent company. In the following years, the farm invested its profits to acquire a second desalination plant and expand the volume of production. It also started to rent land from small growers who could not afford to keep up with the growing demand for strawberry production for international markets. While in 1997 the Palma family farm started cultivating 1.5 hectares of berries, by 2010 it was producing on 35 hectares, 10 of which were their own land and the rest on rented property, and growing berries almost year-round in three cycles.

But the shift from contract farmer to independent grower was not an easy one. Andrés, who along with his brother Carlos was running the company after his father retired, had firsthand experience of many of the challenges independent growers confronted in San Quintín. Among them were the high financial costs of growing berries for international markets, the difficulties of accessing credit, and the higher risks independent growers undertake compared to contract growers who receive financial and technical assistance from large U.S. companies. He explained:

> Overall it's a very painful and difficult process; it isn't easy when you want to become independent. You go against the tide 100 percent to find your place and be able to sell your strawberries directly because nobody knows you and because the cost of producing strawberries per hectare is very high. That's why many farmers here choose to work with American distributors, because they have everything secured; they don't struggle to produce because the distributors provide them with all the supplies needed. But when you become independent you have to get bank loans and buy your own supplies and all the risks fall on you.

In addition, Rancho Las Palmas needed to meet the certification standards for exporting berries to the United States and find their own suppliers. Developing the professional expertise to grow berries to meet the certification requirements necessitated significant changes in the farm. After reaching adulthood, Andrés and Carlos—both of whom had grown up in San Quintín and graduated from public universities in Baja California with degrees in agronomy and business administration, respectively—made a concerted effort to "professionalize" the family business. Together they brought a new set of skills to run the company and a more sophisticated understanding of the certification regulations required by the USDA. In addition, unlike contract growers who receive seeds, plants, fertilizers, and other supplies from companies like Driscoll's as part of a "technological package" stipulated by the grower-shippers, Andrés and Carlos had to build their own network of suppliers for the transportation, marketing, and commercialization of the farm's strawberries. To this end, they affiliated as independent growers with the University of California, Davis, from which they buy berry plants. Every year they travel to California to acquire new technical information, stay abreast of developments in the strawberry sector, and buy new seeds to experiment with on their farm in San Quintín. Explaining the importance of plant experimentation and innovation, Andrés commented:

> You see, every year we go to the University of California in Davis and they tell us about new varieties. Because we are affiliated as growers, we have the right not only to buy the plants but also the right to try them; if we like a particular variety, we test it here and if it works, we buy it. This year we planted three different types of berries. . . . [Also] when I buy the plant, I have the ability to sell the strawberries I produce to whomever I want. It's better that way and much less rigid than working with American distributors.

Andrés and Carlos's management approach corresponds to what the agricultural anthropologist Miriam Wells (1996, 131–33) calls "building business," a strategy that relies on innovation and risk-taking to compete and grow an agribusiness in a transnational market. To revitalize the family farm and enhance its competitiveness, they implemented structural changes after taking over the business once their father retired. They reduced operating costs and invested in a new accounting software program to become self-sufficient instead of relying on outside accountants. They also instituted a new family division of labor in which Carlos is in the field in charge of supervising the day-to-day operations with the help of his assistants and technicians, while Andrés is responsible for the administration and marketing side of the business, in constant search of buyers and distributors. In turn, their father, Vicente, despite having relinquished control of the farm, is still involved in public relations, often using his social connections with other growers and local government officials to learn about occasional programs and funding opportunities from the Secretariat of Agriculture for farmers in the region.

The Pride of Running an Independent Farm

From the time I met Andrés, he was openly proud of running an independent family farm business. Despite the numerous obstacles it had to overcome, the transition from a subordinated to an independent horticultural company brought important benefits. Among the most significant advantages was the ability to sell their crops in the open market rather than tied to a particular broker. Unlike contract growers like Joaquín Cuenca who must sell their produce exclusively to Driscoll's, as an independent business Rancho Las Palmas also sells strawberries to domestic markets in Mexico. When prices for strawberries in the United States get too low because of oversupply, he looks for buyers in Mexico's domestic markets. Thus the company produces two types of strawberries it calls "first" and "second" quality berries, which are packed in three types of boxes for different markets. The first type contains first-quality strawberries for international exports; the second type contains of "first-quality" strawberries destined for Mexico's national market when prices in the United States drop to a point deemed unprofitable; and the third type contains "second grade" strawberries for domestic markets only. Not having commercial obligations to large brokers gives Rancho Las Palmas greater market flexibility. Explaining the benefits of operating as an autonomous firm, Andrés identified this flexibility, higher profits, and lack of commission fees, all of which make him "feel liberated" from exploitative business partnerships with U.S. companies.

> Before [with Sunrise] all our production had to go to them, 100 percent regardless of whether the market price in the United States was good or not.... And for each box of strawberries they sold, they charged us 10 or 15 percent commission! Moreover, they discounted all the costs of the supplies provided, like the boxes they sent us to pack the strawberries. When you work with a distributor... you don't have the freedom to contract with a cheaper transportation company; you have to do everything with them. All your production also has to go to them, and at the end, they charge you for transportation costs, customs inspection, supplies, and so on, plus a commission. To the point that sometimes we were producing strawberries and instead of making a profit, we were in the red.

To operate as an independent business, however, Andrés had to concentrate on market niches not exploited by large transnational corporations. These are small niches and opportunities in which small farms can respond quickly and have a competitive edge. Describing this business approach, he emphasized not only the importance of finding the right market opportunities but also "keeping a low profile" when selling to big retailers like Costco to avoid being perceived as a threat by large companies that dominate the market.

> We optimize direct sales whenever we can, direct sales with large supermarket chains that usually buy from big distributors.... For example, Costco: we sell to them directly without intermediaries.... Sometimes when they need more strawberries they call me. Also some distributors contact me if they run short of produce and say, "I have a client who needs strawberries and I want you to service him so that he doesn't go to a rival company." They don't see us as a threat because we are a small company and they aren't afraid that we can compete with them selling to giant buyers like Driscoll's or Gigante [large supermarket chain in Mexico]. They rely on small companies like ours that are not going to hurt their business.

Independence from the control of large American brokers has allowed Rancho Las Palmas to sell strawberries not only in Mexico but also in international markets other than the United States. Between 2007 and 2010, for example, the bulk of the company's strawberries exported north of the border went to Canada, using a Canadian distributing firm that paid a higher price than U.S. distributors with whom it did business in 2006. Later Rancho Las Palmas began selling strawberries to a buyer in Taiwan, expanding its international reach to avoid concentrating on a single market. Describing the economic benefits of dealing with a buyer in

Canada as compared to California-based brokers, Andrés said, "Over the last years, all my exports have gone to Canada. I have an agreement with that company in which I pay 10 percent sales commission, but this company only sells our crops and does not impose on us any [technological] packages like U.S. companies; it's just sales. The agreement doesn't come with additional stipulations like those we used to have with California companies.... They have now offered me the option to sell in Japan because it pays well, although it requires high standards."

The ability to capitalize on small market opportunities and the economic advantages of operating outside the control of powerful U.S. brokers allowed Las Palmas to prosper. "We never let a company or distributor monopolize us; we always look to have several options and to sell at the best price possible," Andrés remarked, expressing pride in being an independent farm. To him, the higher profit margins spoke loudly:

> Before when we worked with US distributors, on a scale of one to ten dollars a box, we were paid $4; now we can sell at $10 a box! ... We can now make a minimum of 200 percent profit for each box, up to 500 percent; that is the difference between now and before when we worked with distributors.... When the market is hot and prices are high, I can sell my strawberries directly and instead of earning $10 per box as before, I can sell them at $30 or even $40. Distributing companies only pay you $20 per box at best.

Andrés's comments convey a feeling I observed among other independent midsized growers in Baja who believed that California-based brokers and companies were taking advantage of them. For Andrés, the allure of running an independent farm is predicated on reaping higher profits and constructing an identity as an independent grower who successfully contests the intrusive power that large U.S. agribusinesses have in his native region. "It's better to be alone than in bad company," he told me good-naturedly. While the literature on export agriculture does not say much about the segment of growers who resist being engulfed in contract farming arrangements, the pride of maintaining independence appears an important incentive, aside from the economic payoffs. To Andrés, running an independent company was a central ingredient of his identity as grower, a sign of pride in a region where most midsized growers produce crops under contract farming agreements. Unlike small growers in other regions near the Mexico-U.S. border who grow fresh vegetables such as chiles and tomatoes for U.S. markets and speak with pride about the "quality" of the vegetables they produce (Álvarez 2005), the pride I observed among growers like Andrés in San Quintín seems to come from their positioning in the industry as independent producers. This language of autonomy, choice, and individual accomplishment reflects the neoliberal ideology of entrepreneurship as an avenue for economic mobility and success, a discourse with deep roots in northern Mexico.

The Role of Rebranding: From "Rancho Las Palmas" to "Las Palmas Strawberries"

Despite the economic benefits, Rancho Las Palmas' transition from contract farming to an independent company was more challenging than Andrés and Carlos had anticipated. As they soon realized, running an independent farm not only required finding credit, building its own desalination, cooling, and packing facilities, and restructuring its internal operations to increase business efficiency but also retooling the branding and marketing sides of the business. The central role branding plays in marketing food commodities to global capitalist markets has been well documented in ethnographic studies. William Roseberry's (1966) study of the cultural logic of capitalist reinvention of coffee as a stylish beverage for the professional and middle classes showed that companies spent considerable resources creating logos and brands to connect to the class sensitivities of consumers. Branding is commonly used by commercial food companies to sell "authenticity" and to carve special market niches by appealing to consumers' cultural sensitivities along class, ethnic, race, and ideological cleavages (Cavanaugh and Shankar 2014). In this context brands function as a "social contract," seals of ownership relaying information about the origin of a commodity to consumers (Thomas 2013, 148). In turn, logos operate as "signatures of authenticity" connecting corporations and consumers through webs of affect and meaning, as well as symbols that convey a sense of global modernity (Thomas 2013, 145).

The transformation of the Palma family brand illuminates the importance of branding in the global strawberry market. After becoming an independent business, Rancho Las Palmas faced the challenge of finding a market niche for its berries and developing a brand to attract consumers in the United States. From the beginning, Andrés realized the importance of developing an attractive label to penetrate the competitive U.S. market. Relying on the social contacts he had developed in college, he began working with firms in Ensenada to redesign the old family farm's boxes and come up with a name and logo attractive to international buyers. The input he received from potential U.S. brokers while attending an annual international meeting of producers and clients in the United States was crucial to how he rebranded the farm's name. American distributors advised him to change the firm's name from Spanish to English and to identify Baja California as the region where the berries were grown. He explained the logic behind such changes.

> We used to have our old logo, but when I went to one of those international meetings that bring together producers and clients, the brokers suggested I change the name of the farm. "Your boxes have a Rancho Las Palmas logo, why?" they asked me. "Because we are Rancho Las Palmas," I replied. "What do you produce?," they asked. "Strawberries," I answered. "Where do they come from, Michoacán?" "No, from Baja California," I replied. Then if I wanted them to buy strawberries from me, they said,

I would need to change my logo and have more information on my boxes about the origin of the strawberries. And that's how we came up with our new logo "Palmas Strawberries" stamped on our boxes, which also indicate "Baja California" as the source.

Andrés's recollection provides clues to the cultural logic of branding in the U.S.-Mexico fresh-produce industry. The change of the company's name from Spanish to English denotes a de-Mexicanization of the produce to increase consumers' connection to and trust in the producer of the berries. Marking the region's source as Baja California can be read as an effort to appease U.S. consumers, evoking Baja as a natural and safe geographic extension of U.S. California where many of the berries sold in this country originate. The accommodation business strategy by the Palma family reflects the power of U.S. distributors and brokers to shape the options of Mexican producers south of the border. At the same time, the rebranding of the family company reflects Andrés's own notion of what it means to run a "modern" Mexican company, one that uses English rather than Spanish and modern designs and logos to appeal to middle-class American consumers.

Finding buyers for the rebranded "Palmas Strawberries," however, required ingenuity and entrepreneurial skills. Unlike his father, who conducted business face-to-face or by phone, Andrés uses social media and other modern communication tools to look for market opportunities, reach out to potential buyers, and promote the family brand. Familiar with these technologies, he relies heavily on the internet to search for market opportunities when they arise and pursue "just-in-time" sales with buyers like Costco when they fall short of supplies and need additional batches of strawberry boxes. "I am constantly glued to my laptop," Andrés explained, describing how he keeps a constant eye on evolving market opportunities in Mexico and international markets. His approach to marketing consists of what has been termed "niche advertising" in which independent firms present themselves to corporate clients as being best able to reach specific (minority) audiences and markets (Cavanaugh and Shankar 2014, 55). Speaking about this facet of the business, Andrés explained the importance of raising the international visibility of the company and his role in achieving this goal: "We began producing brochures and other promotional materials and created a Hotmail account and website. They [buyers in the United States] wanted us to have a more visible and formal firm presentation. So when I came back to work on the family farm, I implemented all these marketing changes.... Unlike my father, who still calls people by phone and goes to the bank in person, I do many business transactions such as sales online."

Andrés was proud of the new markets this approach has brought to the business and how it has helped rejuvenate the family farm. The generational changes young people like him brought to family businesses reflect a common trend

I noticed among other family-run farms in San Quintín, where a second generation of growers has replaced their fathers at the helm. Young growers like Andrés see themselves as grower-entrepreneurs unafraid of the outside world, in contrast to their parents who they often portray as inward-looking regional farmers who did not like interacting with the outside world. A "building business" approach that favors innovation, risk taking, and an entrepreneurial attitude is permeated by the neoliberal flavor that penetrated the region in the early 2000s and is predicated on the values of individualism and competition. Rather than an isolated phenomenon, this seems common among growers invested in export agriculture in Latin America. As Fisher and Benson (2006, 43) have shown, Maya farmers in Guatemala growing broccoli for U.S. consumers frequently talk about exporting to the United States not only as a good opportunity to earn more money than they can as subsistence peasants but also for the pride of competing with California's producers. The ability to compete with powerful U.S. corporations and find market niches on his own is a source of personal pride for Andrés and an intrinsic component of the rebranded identity of the family farm in Baja.

Building a Dual Labor Force

While for Andrés running an independent family farm injected a sense of entrepreneurship and pride, his approach to the recruitment and management of labor was similar and almost undistinguishable to most contract growers I met in San Quintín. In fact, the restructuring of the company led to a new division of labor and dual workforce. The introduction of new production technologies generated a demand for workers with specialized occupations, while the decision to run the administrative side of the business in-house created openings for office personnel. The company employs ten full-time administrative employees, including accountants, electronic engineers in charge of the cooling and desalination plants, business administrators, and an agronomist who assists Carlos. As Andrés told me, they are all considered *personal de planta*, full-time employees with benefits such as health insurance, sick leave, pension, paid vacation, and Infonavit, an employer-funded housing allowance. At the same time, the push to produce berries almost year-round reinvigorated a demand for a more stable labor force on the farm but one in which field workers are still treated as seasonal workers. As Andrés explained to me, the bulk of the labor force employed by his company consists of between 150 and 200 farmworkers, depending on the growing season, who are employed for planting, cleaning, and harvesting. Most field workers live in colonias near the farm, providing a steady supply of cheap and flexible labor. Some come looking for work on their own as "walk-ins," while others are recruited by the company's mayordomos and by word of mouth by other workers, a typical arrangement among midsized growers in the strawberry industry (Wells 1996, 163–64).

Like its contract grower counterparts, Las Palmas's ability to operate as an independent strawberry firm thus critically relies on maintaining a large contingent of flexible workers, many of whom are paid cash to avoid registering them in the social security system and paying health and other labor benefits mandated by law. To that end, Andrés uses a series of practices "to incentivize" his workers. For example, instead of paying field workers once a week (Fridays or Saturdays) as is customary among most companies in the region, he developed pay options to keep them attached and reduce labor turnover. He elaborated on this topic during one of our conversations.

AS: Workers come to work for us on their own. I pay them cash every day after work or three times a week; they like it. As long as workers are happy they do a good job; you are giving them a benefit, and they come on their own to the farm. We don't force them to work for us.

CZ: I see. What do you mean by "benefit"?

AS: A benefit such as paying them cash or to paying them every day they work. And we pay them according to what they produce [piece rate].... When you pay them daily, workers come to you.

Enticing poor workers by paying them in cash on the days they work allows his company to reduce labor turnover and avoid paying benefits for most of its workers. By reducing the number of workers officially registered in the IMSS, Andrés is able to offer higher wages to the field workers and attract them to the farm. Aware that this system allowed him to reduce labor costs and improve the farm's competitiveness, he still refers to its workers as *trabajadores temporales*, casual and temporary laborers, despite the fact that, as he proudly recognized, many of them lived in the region and had worked for the company for several years in a row. This symbolic construction of indigenous farmworkers as "temporary" justifies treating them as "casual labor," despite the fact that many of them have been living in the region before many of their own employers arrived in the valley.

THE CULTURAL MATRIX OF RACISM AND NATIVISM

The combination of a business philosophy predicated on innovation and embracing international markets along with a labor management regime that treats workers as temporary, embraced by both large transnational companies and independent growers, is not a recent development in San Quintín. Instead, this labor regime is rooted in the long history of racism in Mexico that forms the cultural matrix within which modern agribusiness operates in the region. The history of racial discrimination against indigenous workers in the valley goes back at least to the 1970s, when the first large number of farm laborers from Oaxaca began arriving after being recruited by local growers engaged in commercial agriculture.

Reflecting the historical subordination of indigenous people in Mexico's colonial and postcolonial eras, immigrant workers were expected to accept lower wages than mestizos (Martínez Novo 2006, 34). Indigenous laborers from Oaxaca were constructed as a more docile, patient, and frugal population, providing growers with a rationale for the bad labor and living conditions they endured, including those in the labor camps that prevailed until the 1990s. Some employers argued that Indians were accustomed to living in small and crowded quarters in their home communities and that the living conditions in the labor camps were not that different (Martínez Novo 2006, 34). Indigenous farmworkers were also represented as a migrant and transient population that moved back and forth between San Quintín and their communities in southern Mexico, thus not needing the same accommodations and benefits as local mestizo workers. The "seasonal" nature of work done by indigenous people has been traditionally used as a justification not to provide health and labor benefits to them. In the field Mexican growers often told me that farmworkers were not interested in having health coverage, as they prefer to have money in their pockets and to send to their families in Oaxaca, an observation that ignores the fact that many of these workers have been living in San Quintín for decades and that their children were born there.

By 2010, when it became evident that many indigenous workers were not "migrants" but permanent residents, the elite of Mexican growers and professional middle-class workers used a different discourse that couched racial discrimination in cultural terms. In this discourse, indigenous peoples are portrayed as a distinct and self-contained social group who, because of their own cultural customs and values, choose to live together in extended families and are not interested in the labor benefits that other workers value, preferring to keep the money for their families. Growers also referred to indigenous laborers as docile and noble, yet easy prey for manipulation by outside agitators who take advantage of their naïveté and ignorance for their own political aims. Labor protests and strikes are often explained as the result of outsiders who come to the region to promote their own political agendas, a perspective that negates indigenous peoples' political agency. The notion that indigenous workers are "childish and naive, lovable but definitively not equal," embodies a form of "benevolent despotism" that, as Martínez Novo (2006, 11) has shown, is common in northern Mexico.

In addition, old-time growers often espouse a nativist ideology according to which they are the true pioneers of the region while indigenous peoples are the newcomers. In this discourse, growers who came from central and western Mexico in the 1940 and 1950s "arrived first" and through their hard work and entrepreneurship made possible the development of agriculture in this frontier region, despite the lack of interest and support from the government. This sense of having arrived first brings together a nativist elite of growers, middle-class professionals, merchants, and government officials who portray indigenous workers as having benefited and prospered thanks to the economic opportunities and vision brought by the early pioneers (Velasco, Zlolniski, and Coubes 2014, 292–308).[8] This image of self-made men fits the myth of the Mexican north that presents the region as a democratic land of opportunities for hardworking self-made men, in contrast to the interior of the country where class lines and prejudices are the norm (Martínez Novo 2006, 53). When confronted with the poor conditions in which many farmworkers live, growers often argue that they generate much needed jobs for indigenous peoples who otherwise would be worse off and poorer, blaming the government for not investing enough to provide the education, health, housing, and public services needed in the region.

Growers who embrace a nativist ideology often relate to their workers through paternalist ties as the preferred form of labor management. When personal and paternalistic relations are not enough to prevent labor strikes and protests, they deploy other forms of social and political control. During the 1980s and 1990s, for example, some of the most powerful regional barons used "guardias blancas" (armed guards) to inflict violence on leaders of indigenous workers who threatened the status quo and were trying to mobilize them. The shift to a more technological and standardized production process since the early 2000s, however, along with the need to meet new certification requirements to export their produce to the United States, forced many companies to adopt more "scientific" forms of labor control to discipline their workers. As companies grew in size, the push to increase workers' productivity and comply with certification regulations brought new forms of labor control that have affected farm laborers' experience in the workplace as well as the ways in which they contest them, as I discuss later.

CONCLUSION

The emergence of berries as the new golden export crop marked a critical transition in the history of modern agriculture in San Quintín, reshaping the power balance between U.S. agribusinesses and local growers. The production of berries— a prime crop that requires even more and better quality water than tomatoes— meant that growers became increasingly dependent on foreign capital to finance expensive desalination technologies to stay in business. The arrival of Driscoll's in the San Quintín Valley was a game changer. By investing in desalination technology and a large cooling and packing plant, it became the dominant player in the profitable berry sector operating through its Mexican subsidiary and large network of local contract growers. The company's penetration in Baja further advanced the encroachment on San Quintín's land and water resources that, since the early 1980s, transformed the region into a major agroexport enclave along the

Mexico-U.S. border. In this juncture, Henry Clark served as an ethnic entrepreneur connecting this company with San Quintín's local growers. As such, he embodies a new generation of growers with an entrepreneurial spirit who have capitalized on the business opportunities that NAFTA and the globalization of the fresh-produce industry brought to Mexico.

The transnationalization of agricultural production in Baja has also consolidated the figure of contract growers. For growers like Joaquín Cuenca who inherited their farms from their parents, a business association with Driscoll's offered an opportunity to escape bankruptcy and enter the lucrative berry business. As a contract grower, however, Joaquín is limited as to what kinds of berries he can grow and how he can grow them, depending on Driscoll's for access to capital, supplies, and export markets, a system of tutelage farming. In this system, certification standards further accentuate smallholders' dependency, a phenomenon Susana Narotzky (2016, 308) calls "a neoliberal governance tool of control." From this perspective, contract farming serves large corporations by providing access to land, water, and labor resources, fomenting competition among local growers and externalizing the economic costs and legal risks and responsibilities of managing labor to local companies and growers. But transnational business arrangements go beyond the system of contract farming. In response to this model, some local growers in San Quintín like the Palma brothers seek to preserve their autonomy. While Joaquín Cuenca was satisfied to operate as a contract farmer, growers like Andrés Palma refused to be reduced to "disguised proletarians" by embracing the neoliberal idea of grower-entrepreneurship to penetrate the global market on their own terms. But even as an "independent" family business, Las Palmas had to "accommodate" to the demands and cultural sensitivities of buyers and consumers in the United States. The language of autonomy couched in terms of individual agency and choice, I argue, masks important power relations that link these firms with international brokers and buyers. In this sense, as Narotzky (2016, 310–11) points out, discourses on innovation and creativity reflect recent developments of late capitalism where an ideology of autonomy obscures dependency on powerful political and economic actors.

Whether undertaken by U.S. or Mexican transnational companies, contract farmers, or independent growers, berry production in Baja for international markets relies on a labor management system that treats workers as seasonal labor with limited if any labor benefits. As other studies have shown, this system is common in Mexico, providing access to a well-trained yet flexible and poorly remunerated workforce on which the profitability of producing high-quality berries depends (Echánove and Steffen 2005, 171). This labor regime that treats field workers as temporary has created what C. de Grammont and Lara Flores (2010, 241) call a "permanently temporary" labor force that provides maximum flexibility to agribusiness employers. This scheme rests on the symbolic construction of indigenous laborers as "migrant workers" that is often used to exclude them from access to health insurance and other basic labor benefits as mandated by the law, a long tradition justified in terms of indigenous workers' "cultural preferences." The current practices by which the agroexport industry in Baja relies on local labor contractors to recruit, discipline, and manage the labor force are discussed next.

3

Labor Recruitment

From Local to Transnational Labor Contractors

It is 4:30 on a chilly morning in mid-June 2010 when, along with Abbdel Camargo—then a graduate student in Mexico doing fieldwork in San Quintín—I go to Colonia Santa Fe to document farmworkers as they leave home for work. Before sunrise, the streets are mostly empty and quiet, the silence interrupted only by roosters crowing and a few dogs barking. The Trans-Peninsular Highway—actually a narrow two-lane road and the only paved motorway—usually busy with trucks carrying produce and buses taking farmworkers to work is still quiet, with only a few vehicles passing by. At the house of Esther Chávez, her partner, Raúl, told us she is having a bath before breakfast. A few minutes later Esther comes to the kitchen and explains that without a water heater she takes a bath with cold water every morning before going to work, which by now she has become used to. In the kitchen, she and Raúl fix breakfast and lunch to take to work at Monsanto, where both of them are employed this summer. On a gas stove three burners are on, cooking ground pork with sliced potatoes, *chilaquiles,* and tortillas. When everything is ready, Esther fixes eight burritos, wraps them in aluminum foil, and divides and packs them in two Tupperware containers for herself and Raúl, making four portions for breakfast and lunch. She then fixes coffee and pours it in two small plastic Coke bottles, which she says keeps it warm, and puts them inside their backpacks along with their food. While she finishes, Raúl gets dressed in blue overalls and protective plastic glasses provided by Monsanto. Esther is wearing jeans, a T-shirt, and black rubber boots, also provided by her employer. Before leaving home, she irons the white coat she wears every day while pollinating plants in a greenhouse. "Our *patrones* are very particular, and they check to see that our

FIGURE 8. Esther in her kitchen in Colonia Santa Fe, getting ready to go to work at Monsanto. Photo by Abbdel Camargo Martínez.

coats and boots are clean before we start working," she explains. If their clothing is not clean, they are not allowed to work.

As the sun rises the streets get busier and louder. A young man with a backpack rides a bike on his way to work, while on a street corner three men wait for the bus that will take them to work. A few minutes before 5:30 A.M. we accompany Esther and Raúl to an unmarked point along the highway where every morning a "rented bus" picks them up and takes them to Monsanto's ranch, located a few miles south of Colonia Santa Fe. As we arrive at the bus stop, six neighbors who also work for this company are already waiting for the bus. The highway is now busier with buses transporting farmworkers in both directions. Only a few of the buses bear signs with the name of the company that owns them; the rest are operated by labor contractors who specialize in recruiting and transporting workers from their colonias to the ranches where they work. At 5:40 A.M. the Monsanto rented bus arrives and we say goodby to Esther and Raúl as they get on. The vehicle belongs to the Fernando Amilpa Association, a company licensed to provide municipal transportation for passengers in the region but whose members often subcontract to transport farmworkers in the early morning and evening to make extra money on the side. As we walk back to the colonia, several groups of men and women farmworkers wait on the street for their contractors to pick them up. Buses run now in and out the colonia picking up workers in front of their homes and on street corners, slowly maneuvering around the many potholes in the unpaved streets. By 6:15 A.M., as most of the contractors' buses have left, some women come out of their homes and sprinkle a bit of water to sweep their lots clean of anything left on the ground after people leave for work.

This chapter focuses on the system of labor contractors and intermediaries that connects workers like Esther and Raúl with horticultural companies like Monsanto in San Quintín's agroexport industry. Since the early 2000s, when many large companies dismantled the labor camps that housed migrant workers, growers began recruiting farm laborers who had settled in local colonias through labor contractors. With time, a new system of labor contracting made up of several layers of contractors and subcontractors developed, allowing companies to shift the costs and legal responsibilities of recruiting and transporting workers to local labor contractors (Zlolniski 2016). This system allows companies to treat colonia residents as casual and flexible workers and provide them with few if any benefits. Based on individual case studies, this chapter depicts the four main types of labor contractors that developed over time in San Quintín's agroexport sector: independent contractors, part-time labor intermediaries, temporary agencies, and transnational companies that recruit local farm laborers to work in the United States. Rather than a remnant of the past, this assemblage of labor contractors speaks to a process of "labor intermediation," where the figure of labor contractor has reemerged as the main mechanism to articulate labor supply and demand. The system relies on the labor contractors' kinship and social ties as well as modern means of communication in order to secure a flexible and disciplined workforce. Labor subcontracting, I argue, embodies the neoliberal principles of labor market flexibility in modern capitalist agriculture, constituting a key pillar of the labor regime in the transnational Mexico-U.S. fresh-produce industry.

THE RESURGENCE OF LABOR CONTRACTORS IN MODERN CAPITALIST AGRICULTURE

Labor contractors have historically helped connect growers and workers in commercial capitalist agriculture. They help solve the problem of labor scarcity at times of high labor demand, especially during the harvest (Ortiz 2002). They also serve as a cushion against labor unions and collective labor resistance, diluting the legal nexus between employers and workers (Quaranta and Fabio 2011, 198). Moreover, labor contractors offer the advantage of recruiting workers for specific, usually temporary tasks, negotiating with employers workers' wage and piece rates, payment systems, and working conditions (Griffith 2014, xvii). Many contractors also provide transportation and housing for farmworkers, usually under exploitative conditions, and even serve as cultural and linguistic brokers between employers and workers who speak a different language and/or are migrant laborers (Griffith 2014; Sánchez Saldaña 2006; Krissman 2000).

The modernization of industrial agriculture, along with the growth of large transnational corporations with advanced systems of production and labor management, was expected to lead to the decline of individual labor contractors. Despite this expectation, scholarship on this topic has showed that since the late 1990s labor contractors have reemerged with renewed strength along with new forms of labor intermediation. The proliferation of labor intermediaries has been especially pronounced in Latin America, where neoliberal agrarian policies fostering export agriculture have contributed to the rise of contractors to enhance labor flexibility, reduce labor costs, and increase workers' productivity (Ortiz, Aparicio, and Tadeo 2013, 3; Ortiz, 2002). Some scholars argue that the need to train and discipline workers in the so-called good agricultural practices mandated by product certification requirements have also contributed to the reemergence of labor contractors. According to this view, modern capitalist agriculture places emphasis on product standardization and horticultural companies use contract labor to comply with them but avoid direct labor connections with workers laboring in their fields (Quaranta and Fabio 2011, 215).[1] In Mexico agricultural companies regularly use labor contractors for labor recruitment, especially in regions specializing in export agriculture that relies on indigenous migrant workers (Sánchez Saldaña 2006, 2015; Lara Flores and Sánchez Saldaña 2015; Saldaña Ramírez 2017; Zlolniski 2016). Contractors also serve as language and cultural intermediaries bridging the linguistic, ethnic, and class differences in a labor market sharply segmented along ethnic lines (Sánchez Saldaña 2006, 29–40).

Scholarship on contemporary industrial agriculture, however, reveals a large variety of labor intermediaries rather than a single type. While some contractors are full-fledged intermediaries who recruit, transport, supervise, and even carry out some administrative tasks, others perform only some of these roles, usually labor recruitment and transportation (Ortiz, Aparicio, and Tadeo 2013). In addition, new service companies have emerged in the recent past to recruit temporary workers for large agribusinesses (Quaranta and Fabio 2011, 210–14). In the end, as Sutti Ortiz (2002) argues, the diversity of labor contractors is the result of the new forms of labor control and scientific labor management strategies companies have devised to increase labor productivity (2002). Yet why and how different forms of labor contracting change over time and how labor contractors assess the advantages and disadvantages of operating as labor and social brokers between employers and farmworkers have not received much attention in the literature. In the rest of this chapter I unpack the different types of labor contractors that have emerged in San Quintín over time and the factors behind this diversity.

FROM LONG-DISTANCE TO LOCAL LABOR CONTRACTORS: THE CASE OF RAFAEL MONTES

Growers hire us when they need workers and say, "I need a busload of workers." We are the spokespersons for the companies, their subcontractors. We go to the colonias and tell people, "There is work at this company, they pay X pesos for doing this work." If people want to take the job, they jump in our bus and the company pays us for each worker we recruit.... Because, to be honest, growers are not interested in the workers, they are interested in growing beautiful and big tomatoes and that they don't go bad. That's their priority; how workers are hired isn't important to them.

—RAFAEL MONTES, FORMER LABOR CONTRACTOR, 2006

Rafael Montes's experience as a labor contractor provides a window into how Baja's agroexport industry has fostered the use of labor intermediaries and the opportunities and risks of the job. He represents the independent contractors, full-time labor intermediaries autonomous from the companies that contract their services. Independent labor contractors specialize in the recruitment and transportation of farmworkers and are affiliated with the associations of farm laborer transporters that, as I explain below, emerged in Baja in the early 2000s. They usually have long experience working and living in the region, own their buses for transporting workers, and after several years in the business often buy more vehicles run by subcontracted drivers. More important, they illustrate the change from long-distance enganchadores, who recruited migrant workers as indentured labor housed in labor camps, to the present system of local labor contractors who recruit settled workers. This change, I argue, has allowed horticultural companies to enhance labor flexibility and create a dual labor market in the industry.[2]

In the late 1980s Rafael began working for Agrícola San Simón contracting workers from rural communities in Oaxaca and bringing them to the San Quintín Valley. At the time, he recalls, there was no need for local labor contractors: "In the past many growers had their own labor camps, that was common.... Thus there was no need for subcontracted transport service and [local] labor contractors." However, when farm laborers began staying in San Quintín instead of going back to their home communities in Oaxaca, Agrícola started recruiting workers locally to save transportation and housing costs. At that point, Rafael decided to quit his job at Agrícola to become an independent contractor for this and other companies in the region. Not living in labor camps controlled by growers any longer, farmworkers had new freedom to choose their employers. Yet many workers, including newcomers with no social connections, relied on contractors to find work and connect them with employers in what had become an open and often competitive local labor market. Rafael commented on the benefits this change had accrued to workers: "Before all workers arrived in the region already contracted by a com-

FIGURE 9. Labor contractors' buses arrive early to pick up workers in the colonias. Photo by Abbdel Camargo Martínez.

pany; nobody came on their own.... Today is different, and workers don't come any longer contracted by a *patrón,* they are better off paying for their own ticket to come here because they can go to work for smaller companies that pay higher wages than the big ranches."

New government regulations regarding the transportation of farmworkers in Baja also contributed to the rise of labor contractors like Rafael. In the past, when the system of labor camps prevailed, workers' transportation was not regulated and growers used open trucks, pickups, and platform trailers to take them back and forth to the fields. There were frequent accidents as many of those vehicles were old and unsafe, and when riding in rough terrain and roads workers often fell from the trucks. After long years of inaction by the government, the CIOAC—an independent union popular among many farmworkers at the time—organized protests to denounce the dangerous transportation conditions and the abuses indigenous workers endured in the fields and labor camps. In response, the state government in Baja issued new ordinances in 1998 mandating the use of licensed drivers and buses to enhance the safety of farmworkers' transportation. To adapt to the new regulations, large companies began investing in their own fleets of buses to transport their workers. Midsized and smaller companies that could not afford their own vehicles searched for alternatives, often by encouraging some of their mayordomos to buy their own vehicles and become their labor contractors in exchange for financial help, higher wages, and bonuses based on the number of workers recruited. Rafael recalled how the government regulations opened new business opportunities for local contractors like him: "Smaller growers realized they could not afford to buy their own buses but still needed to provide transportation to their workers, and they went ahead and told their mayordomos, 'You know what? Buy your own bus and drive it yourself and then I will pay you for this service.' And that's how the transportation in 'rented buses,' as we call them, was born.... The arrangement was beneficial for the companies and contractors too."

The new transportation regulations led to the formation of numerous associations of bus owners to operate as service providers transporting field workers for agricultural companies. In 2005, Rafael Montes and fourteen partners founded Autotransportes del Valle, a company licensed to transport farmworkers in the San Quintín Valley. A year later, the association already had twenty-seven members with permits to operate forty buses, mirroring the rapid growth of local labor contractors. Rather than just transport farm laborers, the majority of the members of these associations were also in charge of recruiting them, combining two jobs that usually go hand in hand (Quaranta and Fabio 2011). In my conversations with him, Rafael was eager to emphasize the "advantages" independent labor contractors rendered to both companies and workers.

> The bus owner [contractor] takes good care of the vehicle because it's his patrimony, the instrument of his livelihood, and he wants it to be in good shape to attract his workers. [In contrast,] if I am a driver employed by a company, I get paid the same amount whether I bring ten or fifty workers; I earn 100 pesos a day just the same. That is why our rented buses have become so common because workers receive personalized attention. We make money if we provide good service to workers.

The proliferation of independent labor contractors allowed companies to reduce operating costs and increase labor flexibility. Agrícola San Simón, for instance, gradually reduced its bus fleet and instead used rented buses managed by contractors like Rafael. This system also allowed the company greater flexibility to recruit and lay off workers in a short-term and efficient fashion, creating a subcontracting chain. Thus as an independent contractor, Rafael was in charge of recruiting workers from their colonias, subcontracting drivers and mayordomos to supervise his work crews, and coordinating all his vehicles to run a smooth business. He was also responsible for negotiating all the pay details with the bus drivers and mayordomos in the subcontracting chain, freeing Agrícola and other companies for which he worked from the costs and responsibilities of forming their labor crews. The system of labor contractors that emerged in the early 2000s allowed companies like Agrícola to create a dual contracting scheme. Thus the company developed a segmented labor force composed, on the one hand, of its own workers and, on the other, of labor crews recruited by independent contractors. These labor crews occupy a secondary tier, often lacking access to even the minimum labor benefits, such as health insurance, that farmworkers directly employed by Agrícola and officially registered as temporary labor have. These companies often use a dual accounting system: some of their workers are registered as "temporary" in the Seguro Social; and those subcontracted by labor contractors only appear for internal accounting purposes.

As a result, there is no official record of the latter's employment and they do not accumulate seniority or pension benefits. Rafael, who in 2006 and for several years afterward recruited workers for Agrícola Colonet—the largest agribusiness in the northern San Quintín Valley, growing tomatoes and strawberries for a commercial partner in San Diego—was familiar with the dual labor system. The farmworkers he contracted were "alive" in the company's accounting office but did not show up in the state's official registers, saving the company from paying for mandatory health insurance. We discussed this situation.

RN: Let's say you have a company that employs 1,000 workers, and out of them about 400 or 500 are paid in cash daily with a fictitious payroll; fictitious, because it's never presented to the Seguro Social but used only for internal accounting purposes. The company gets the money to either pay the workers or the contractors to pay his workers.... This means that the labor relationship [between the company and the subcontracted workers] begins at 7:00 A.M. and ends at 4:00 P.M.

CZ: So these are [truly] casual workers.

RN: No, they aren't even temporal workers because there is no record they ever worked. Temporal workers are those who work between one day and six months, that is, 180 days or less, but these [subcontracted] workers don't show up in the [official] statistics as working even a single day; they do not exist.

CZ: They don't exist in the official payrolls.

RN: No they don't; that male or female field worker was never employed. She or he didn't show up in the [Seguro Social] even a single day.

But while the system of local labor contractors allowed Rafael to prosper, it also contained the seeds for his later decline. For a few years he prospered in the business, even purchasing three additional buses, all operated by subcontracted drivers and mayordomos. At that point, his job consisted of finding growers and companies that needed labor contractors to recruit workers, coordinating the drivers and mayordomos under his command, and negotiating and managing the payment of his work crews. With time, however, as more labor contractors began to proliferate in the region, competition grew, including contractors working in the informal sector without licenses who offered growers lower prices to recruit and transport farmworkers.[3] By 2010, the number of local contractors, cooperatives, and private companies specializing in transporting farmworkers in the region significantly increased, and what used to be an attractive business niche became increasingly saturated. In light of the diminishing returns, Rafael decided to sell three of his buses and retain only one driven by a family member, while he went back to school to study labor law and open a labor office on his own. He blamed the municipal government in Ensenada for giving "too many licenses" to people to transport farmworkers, inundating the market and driving prices down. Indeed, every year I returned to the region, I noticed the growing number of buses parked in the evenings in the local colonias, a visual signal of residents working as labor contractors or subcontracted drivers. Despite the market saturation, the development of a local labor market in San Quintín opened the doors for contractors like Rafael to capitalize on a new business niche and prosper.

PART-TIME CONTRACTORS: RECRUITING AND DISCIPLINING FARMWORKERS

In addition to independent labor contractors, part-time labor intermediaries are common in San Quintín, representing a second type of labor contractors in the fresh-produce industry. Part-time contractors occupy a lower status in the subcontracting pyramid and recruit field workers during the harvest season. They usually work for large companies as mayordomos to recruit, transport, and supervise work crews, receiving a salary as mayordomos and a bonus according to the number of workers they enlist. In the slow winter season, they often revert to their jobs as either mayordomos or field workers, reflecting a pattern of "internal labor subcontracting" that is common in export agriculture in Latin America (Quaranta and Fabio 2011, 215 n.). As such part-time contractors are an intrinsic part of the labor regime of export agriculture that combines flexibility to hire and discard workers with the need to train and discipline them in the requirements of modern horticultural production.

Arcadio Román, a Mixtec contractor born in 1963 in San Gerónimo Progreso, a rural town in the municipality of Huajuapan de León, Oaxaca, reveals the challenges part-time contractors face recruiting and disciplining workers in Baja's agroexport sector. Arcadio arrived in San Quintín in 1979 with his parents after having lived for six years in Tijuana. At thirteen years old, he began working as a farm laborer with his father in Oceanside in northern San Diego County, but a few years later, when legal restrictions on child labor in California's agriculture were in place, he went back to San Quintín to work at Rancho Los Pinos, which at the time recruited thousands of indigenous workers from Oaxaca. In 1999 he married Carmen, who he had met in the *surco* (field) while working for this company. They had five children, all born in San Quintín.

Arcadio's transformation from farmworker to part-time labor contractor shows the key role large agribusiness plays in fostering this type of labor intermediary. In 2000, Agrícola San Simón contracted him as a tractor driver to work with his brother Nemesio, who at the time was a supervisor overseeing the transportation of workers and produce for the company. In 2003, Nemesio bought a bus to become a labor contractor for Agrícola and asked Arcadio to quit his job and be his business partner recruiting fieldworkers and serving as their foreman. At the time Nemesio received 12 pesos for each worker he recruited for Agrícola, which he split in half with Arcadio. A year later, Arcadio decided to borrow money to buy his own bus and become a contractor himself. With a down payment of 5,000 pesos he bought an old bus from an American missionary organization for 40,000 pesos in monthly installments, which he repaired to put it to work. Then he joined the Frente Independiente de Transportistas de Trabajadores del Campo Rural, a cooperative founded by indigenous workers to transport farmworkers in the valley. As a labor contractor, he received 15 pesos for each worker he recruited for Agrícola. As Arcadio explained to me, about twenty-five other contractors belonging to the same cooperative worked for this company under a verbal agreement based on a piece rate: "The company says, 'You get workers for me and I'll pay you 15 pesos per worker. If you want to work as mayordomo of your crew as well that's fine; if not, you bring another person as mayordomo.'"

As a part-time subcontractor, Arcadio offers his employers a great deal of versatility by performing different functions and adapting to changes in the production cycle. He performs three overlapping roles: labor recruiter, transporter, and mayordomo. First, he is responsible for recruiting workers, for which he normally combs six different colonias in the south of the valley. Going street by street, sometimes house by house, he looks for workers in an effort to build personal relationships with them, as competition with other contractors can be intense. Second, he is the bus driver of his work crew. His daily routine in this job begins at 5:00 A.M. with a mechanical check of his bus, inspecting the tires and checking the oil and water to make sure everything is in order. By 5:30, he starts his route picking up workers in several colonias along the way to Agrícola San Simón, where he arrives at around 6:30. At 7:00, work in the field begins, at which point Arcadio switches roles from driver to mayordomo, the third facet of his job. As mayordomo, his daily tasks vary depending on the needs of the company; sometimes he brings his workers to open fields, others to any of the shadehouses to carry out tasks such as planting, cleaning, pruning, and harvesting. For this job, he earns 125 pesos a day, slightly above his workers' wages. When the busy season ends in the fall, Arcadio stops working as a contractor and becomes a field worker. The decision as to when to stop working as a contractor is the result of his calculations about income and expenses. As a labor recruiter, running and maintaining his bus costs him about 1,200 pesos a week, including gas. In addition, he has other expenses such as replacing the tires, renewing his license and insurance, and maintaining his bus to pass the mechanical inspections required. As he told me, recruiting and transporting forty or more people per day was good business, but when his employer asked him to bring fifteen or fewer workers, it was no longer profitable, at which point he parked his bus at home and worked in the fields until spring.

Like independent contractors, part-time labor recruiters help large horticultural companies maintain a segmented labor force. Arcadio is aware of the differences between the job stability and labor benefits of farmworkers recruited and transported by the company in its own buses and those part-time contractors like him recruit. Commenting on the contrast between the two groups, he said, "There

FIGURE 10. Arcadio Román's bus that transports workers to the fields.

is a difference; workers who come in the company's buses have work all year long, but the people who come in our buses don't. Usually around November or December, the company stops using our service when work slows down; at that point it starts laying us off one by one as work slows down. Sometimes we are idle one or two months, it varies, until the company calls us back when needed."

In addition to recruiting and transporting field workers, Arcadio is in charge of training and disciplining them in the standards for food security and quality. As Quaranta and Fabio (2011, 15) have shown, in Latin America horticultural companies that need to meet product certification requirements often use contract labor to comply with legal regulations, and rely on labor contractors to avoid direct association with workers. In Mexico this has created a work culture in which contractors are expected to "motivate" their laborers to work hard to meet the production quotas and quality standards set by their employer. A common folk expression used in San Quintín to persuade farm laborers to work hard is "echarle ganas," which means to work energetically without faltering to make the most of being paid at a piece rate. The creed "echarle ganas" is part of this work culture, persuading workers to internalize the demanding quantity and quality standards that predominate in this sector. As mayordomo at Agrícola San Simón, Arcadio is responsible for disciplining his workers; as he explained to me, during the planting of tomato plants, his job consists of "making sure people plant them well, that they don't use broken plants, and that plants are properly placed in their holes exactly where they have to be placed." Later, during the harvest, he supervises the workers to make sure they conform to the instructions on the size, color, and shape of tomatoes they pick and enforces the sanitation rules in the field. In addition, as he put it, "I [check] they don't leave tomatoes that should be harvested, don't pick tomatoes that are not ripe yet, that they don't throw tomatoes in the field, and that they carry the buckets properly."

Disciplining field workers is thus one of the key functions part-time labor contractors are expected to perform. Contractors and mayordomos often blame workers when problems arise; expressions such as "careless workers" or "*vagos*." (slackers) are commonly used to refer to "problematic workers" who do not pay enough attention to their work, "ruining the fruits," and causing economic damage to the patrones. Subjected to intense surveillance, mayordomos are under constant pressure to monitor and discipline their work crews. In charge of a crew of forty field workers, Arcadio uses different methods, ranging from persuasion to coercion to punishment. In describing how he deals with "rebellious workers," he highlighted the importance of using "gentle persuasion" without disaffecting them: "When workers take a rebellious stand, one has to know how to talk to them without mistreating, without insulting them. You have to explain the reasons the work tasks need to be done in certain ways. But you have to know how to talk to them calmly and with what I would call 'talent' so that they don't get offended.... You have to have some power of persuasion."

When persuasion does not work, Arcadio moves to more coercive methods, including temporary "rest periods" and layoffs. This is a paternalistic labor management strategy that places disciplining of subcontracted workers in the hands of the labor contractors. Arcadio explained what he does when workers show signs of defiance: "In cases when workers don't respond and exasperate me, I lay them off for a while to see if they change. I lay them off for one or two days, I then [wait] to see how they react, but many times, they don't change."

At the same time, he has to walk a fine line between disciplining his workers and keeping them content so that they do not quit and go to work for other contractors. Explaining how he navigates this narrow path, Arcadio emphasized the challenges labor contractors like him face in San Quintín.

> In addition to mayordomos like me who are in direct contact with the workers, there is also an inspector or supervisor in the company who, if someone is planting and not doing the job right, approaches us so we talk to the workers and tell them to do the work right.... I cannot fire them because it wouldn't make sense to fire people when we as contractors and *raiteros* [drivers who transport workers to their jobs for a fee] struggle to recruit workers; we cannot lay them off. My job is to teach them to do their work well so that I don't have problems with my supervisor.

Notwithstanding these trials and the instability of their jobs, serving as a mayordomo–labor contractor is considered a step up from working as a field worker in the occupational hierarchy of the agricultural sector. Despite his multiple responsibilities and the environment of intense surveillance in which he operates, Arcadio feels he is better off than when he was just a field worker. He especially appreciates the reduced physical drudgery. He also values having more job stability and a higher income than field workers, which keeps him employed year-round. Reflecting a common feeling I found among former field workers who moved up the ladder to become labor contractors–mayordomos, Arcadio underlined his relief at leaving the lowest position workers occupy in this sector: "The main advantage is that you don't work in the surco any longer because now you are a mayordomo and *chofer* (bus driver). The other advantage is that having your own bus, you earn more money, a bit more, about one and half or twice the wage of a field worker."

Part-time contractors generally live in the same colonias as their workers, helping to lubricate the connection between growers and farmworkers in the local labor market. Cell phones have made the system of labor subcontracting system even more agile, allowing companies to recruit workers for specific tasks at the moment and length of time needed. While occupying a lower status than full-time independent contractors, subcontracted labor intermediaries like Arcadio have experienced a modest but important degree of occupational mobility, holding a job that carries a higher social status than field workers' and is less strenuous and physically demanding. The result is a highly flexible labor arrangement in which part-time contractors are used as labor recruiters, mayordomos, or simply farm laborers according to the changing needs of their employers.

INSTITUTIONALIZING LABOR FLEXIBILITY THROUGH TEMPORARY AGENCIES: THE CASE OF MONSANTO

The system of local labor contractors is not the only form by which agricultural companies have access to a flexible labor force. By 2010 when this system was firmly in place, new forms of labor contracting emerged in San Quintín that further enhanced labor flexibility by distancing employers from labor and legal responsibilities with their workers. One such new form is the use of temporary work agencies to recruit and manage farmworkers on behalf of agricultural companies. The use of temporary contract workers through third-party agencies is a recent trend in the Latin American agroexport industry, a scheme that seeks to insulate large agribusinesses from legal responsibilities for their employees (Quaranta and Fabio 2011). The emergence of service companies specialing in contracting "outsourced" agricultural workers, I argue, constitutes another step in the process of labor intermediation in the modern export agriculture industry, one that mirrors a similar trend in manufacturing and service sectors.

Global Outsource Group, one of the world's largest temporary agencies specializing in outsourcing personnel for other companies, reveals how this form of labor intermediation is at work in Baja's agroexport sector. In 2006, Monsanto acquired Rancho El Milagro in San Quintín, a well-known company that hybridizes seeds for domestic and international markets that at the time was owned by Seminis, one of the largest multinational firms in this industry. A year later, Monsanto laid off most of its workers, including in-house administrators as well as supervisors, irrigators, machine operators, and fieldworkers, replacing them with temporary contract workers hired by Global. Monsanto used this change to lay off most of its older workers, offering them severance pay based on seniority. It also offered the rest of its workers the opportunity to be "rehired" by Global as "seasonal workers" with temporary work contracts. To keep their jobs, and despite losing seniority, many of Monsanto's field workers accepted the offer and signed contracts with Global. The change, however, came at a steep price. While in the past both Seminis and Monsanto employees received full benefits and accumulated seniority according to their years of employment, after being hired by Global they were considered temporary employees with limited benefits and health insurance only while employed. Under the new arrangement, Monsanto's temporary workers could not accumulate seniority as their contracts were renewed every year, and they lost the *aguinaldo,* an extra payment issued in December that farmworkers use as a cushion for the slow winter season. As outsourced labor, they were no longer entitled to *utilidades,* a share of the profits they received in the past at the end of the year; instead, they received these payments from Global Outsource, and they were significantly less.

The shift from in-house employees to temporary contract workers was facilitated by the acquiescence of the labor union representing farmworkers at Rancho El Milagro, reflecting the role of state-controlled unions in enhancing labor flexibility in the region. The Regional Confederation of Mexican Workers (Confederación Regional Obrera Mexicana; CROM) is one of the two largest labor unions for farmworkers in San Quintín. Founded in 1918, it was the first national union in Mexico and is regarded as a typical *sindicato patronal* (company union) that signs collective bargaining agreements with growers, often without the knowledge of workers. The CROM did not challenge Monsanto's decision to lay off its employees. Instead, it adopted an accommodation strategy and became the de facto intermediary in recruiting workers for Global. According to Arnulfo Quintanilla, CROM's president, with whom I talked about this case, the union wanted "to protect" laid-off Seminis workers and help them to be rehired by Global. In order to avoid losing them as union members, Arnulfo explained to me, the CROM created a new "membership category" that reclassified them as "temporary contract workers," keeping the right to "represent" them.[4] In the process, the union rather than Global, which was new in the region and did not have social contacts with farmworkers, took on the role of recruiting workers, a task that required close collaboration with this company and Monsanto.

Josefina Rodríguez, the union steward representing workers at the ranch, was at the heart of this labor contracting arrangement. Born in Puerto Escondido, Oaxaca, in 1964, Josefina had arrived in San Quintín in 2000 and for several years lived in a labor camp owned by Los Pinos, after which she was able to move to a land lot in a colonia in the town of Lázaro Cárdenas. She then worked in several of the largest horticultural companies in the region, until she was hired by Monsanto to hybridize flowers and melon seeds at Rancho El Milagro. Employing about fourteen hundred workers in the summer and three hundred in the winter, Monsanto contracted with Global to hire them as temporary contract workers, at which point the union began recruiting farmworkers using its social connections with laborers in the region. As a union representative, Josefina visited some of the largest colonias, posting flyers, talking to friends and acquaintances, and spreading the word with workers she knew from companies where she had worked in the past. As she explained to me, she compiled and carried a notebook containing a handwritten list of former Monsanto workers, their contact information, and when they last worked, deciding whom to call when she was asked to recruit additional labor. This pyramidal system of labor contracting entailed close coordination and communication between Monsanto, Global, and the CROM. As Josefina put it, "My job is to bring workers to Monsanto. When the field or greenhouse manager signs a form requesting so many workers, then the manager of Human Resources at Monsanto signs it [too].... Then the petition is passed to the people at Global, the other manager, and when it's signed, they pass it to me, and then I am in charge of recruiting the workers. This is my job, ... the company doesn't recruit workers, we [CROM] are the ones who do labor recruitment."

Josefina's job entailed recruiting workers for Monsanto every summer after they were laid off from other companies, a system in which workers continuously rotate among employers in the region. The CROM had contracts with other large horticultural companies in San Quintín, including BerryMex; every year after this company laid off its workforce when the strawberry harvest was over, Josefina contacted them "to find work at Monsanto" at the peak of the season for this company, June and July, as temporary employees. Having worked at Monsanto before, Josefina was aware of the consequences the new system entailed for outsourced workers, including loss of employment stability and labor benefits: "The difference is that before there were permanent workers employed year-round who received paid vacations. Now it is different. To keep them from getting seniority, Global lays them off for two weeks just before they are about to reach one year of working for the company. They lay you off so they can label you as a temporary worker; then they hire you again."

In addition to labor recruiting, Josefina's job at Monsanto consisted of disciplining workers and taming labor conflict when it arose. "I am responsible for disciplining my workers," she told me. She has to make sure they follow the rules and protocols established by the company and screen job applicants to discard "bad and irresponsible workers." As steward of a white union (one that signs "protection contracts" with employers), she considered "filtering problematic workers" part of her job. "It's a company union because the company pays us, it pays me; we are with the company," she commented, explaining the rationale for her approach. Not surprisingly, Josefina's role as labor intermediary elevated her status among her peers, who felt pressured to stay on good terms with her to be hired every season, a relationship that reflects the "instrumental friendship" that characterizes social relations between labor contractors and workers in agriculture and other employment sectors that rely on labor intermediaries (Griffith 2016). Every time I visited Josefina and her family after she had returned home from work, our conversation was interrupted by frequent calls to her cell phone from workers inquiring when the company was going to start hiring again and asking her to keep them on her call list.

On the other hand, Josefina also considered it her responsibility to inform workers about their rights and prevent sexual harassment and other abuses by unscrupulous mayordomos, reflecting an important facet of the work of labor intermediaries. She felt particularly proud of "teaching workers about their rights," something she considered a significant improvement compared to the old days when she was housed in a labor camp where workers never heard about labor rights. At Monsanto, she was in charge of ensuring that all new workers received the standard work equipment such as gloves, protective glasses, overalls, and shoes, which the company introduced to reduce work accidents. When labor problems arose at the ranch, she intervened "to mediate" between the company and the workers, "not antagonizing but dialoguing," reflecting the role labor intermediaries play as social and cultural brokers to maintain social order in the workplace. At one point, for example, as part of a new set of rules Monsanto introduced to "enhance job safety," it prohibited workers from carrying their cell phones at work. The union interceded with the company's top manager, explaining that most of the workershad children and families who may need to reach them in an emergency during the eight hours they spent at work. A compromise was reached, and field workers were allowed to bring their phones to work but to be used only in emergencies.

In 2016, a few years after arriving in Baja, Monsanto closed Rancho El Milagro, allegedly due to lack of water to keep production going, although according to rumors the company had acquired Seminis to stop the latter's competition selling seeds in Mexico. In 2017, Andrew and Williamson, another transnational American company that had arrived in San Quintín in 2007 to grow tomatoes and strawberries for U.S. markets, acquired Rancho El Milagro, marking yet another episode in the long and unstable labor history of this ranch. Although Monsanto left the region, it established the precedent of using temporary agencies, creating yet another layer of labor intermediation in Baja's agroexport sector.

FROM LOCAL TO TRANSNATIONAL LABOR CONTRACTING: THE H-2A PROGRAM IN SAN QUINTÍN

It was an early afternoon in July 2017 when I visited the local office of Sierra-Cascade Nursery in San Quintín. Having arrived in 2007, Sierra-Cascade was one of the first

U.S. agribusinesses that opened an office in the region to recruit temporary workers for its facilities in Susanville and Tule Lake in northern California, where this company grows strawberry plants. Workers were hired through the H-2A program, which, managed by the Department of State (which issues the visas), the Department of Labor (which certifies that there is a "labor shortage"), and U.S. Citizenship and Immigration Services (USCIS) (which authorizes the entry of workers into the country), allows U.S. employers to recruit foreign workers, typically from Mexico, to fill temporary agricultural jobs lasting from a few weeks to several months at a time. At the time, I met with Jorge García, the on-site manager and labor contractor the company had sent to launch this program in Baja, to learn about this new form of labor contracting in the region. Born in Sonora in 1946, García migrated in his teens to work as a farm laborer in the United States. Many years later, in 1986, he was hired by Sierra-Cascade Nursery, which later sent him to launch the H-2A program in Baja because of his fluency in Spanish and familiarity with Mexican farmworkers culture. The company located the office in the town of Vicente Guerrero, near some of the most populous indigenous colonias, and staffed it with two secretaries in charge of reviewing farmworkers' applications. In our first meeting, García was rather cautious because, he told me, "activist groups and journalists" had unfairly criticized the program. Contrary to this negative image, he said, Sierra-Cascade was led by "a Christian family" and offered a legal avenue for poor people in Mexico to work in the United States. Couching the labor recruitment program in religious terms, García added that the company's owner considered this program "a missionary project" because he was concerned about the high number of "illegal" workers employed in California. Recruiting seasonal workers in San Quintín was a way "to reduce the number of workers who died trying to cross the border" and offered a better alternative to H-2A labor contractors, who charged Mexican workers and U.S. employees high fees while also curtailing farmworkers' wages.[5]

By 2017, Sierra-Cascade Nursery was firmly established in San Quintín and had moved to a larger and more comfortable office in a new strip mall in the same town. Jorge García had retired two years earlier and was replaced by Alicia Reyes, a young Mexican woman who grew up in San Quintín in a family of immigrant farmworkers from Sonora. When I arrived at the new office, four male workers were seated waiting to be interviewed as candidates for the H-2A program. On the walls of the office there were flyers listing the prerequisites for prospective applicants, including having a Mexican passport, a *credencial de elector* (one of the most common IDs in Mexico), and a *carta de trabajo,* or employer's letter certifying they had experience as farmworkers in the region. On another wall there were pictures of workers who had gone to California under this program between 2007 and 2017, several of them smiling in the company's facilities in California. Other flyers encouraged workers to "follow the company on Facebook" and receive updates about contracting dates, interviews, and other pertinent information.

FIGURE 11. First H-2A labor recruiting office of Sierra-Cascade Nursery in San Quintín in 2007.

The consolidation of the H-2A program in Baja represents the latest development in the history of labor contracting in the region, one that marks a shift from domestic to transnational forms of labor recruitment. As such, the program constitutes another layer in the dense web of labor contracting that has evolved over time in which agribusinesses and contractors on both sides of the Mexico-U.S. border compete for experienced farmworkers. In the United States, the H-2A received renewed support from growers when border control policies slowed the arrival of undocumented Mexican farmworkers, leading to a sharp rise of workers coming under this program since 2006. Over time intensified migration control policies have made undocumented migration even more expensive, riskier, and less frequent than in the recent past, while the heightened activity of Immigration and Customs Enforcement (ICE) has increased the vulnerability of undocumented workers in the United States. In this context, U.S. growers have pushed hard to recruit H-2A workers, a move to provide them with additional and, as I argue below, more docile labor.[6] Unlike undocumented migration, temporary migration programs represent what Griffith (2014) calls government-managed migration, in which the state acts as a broker between employers and workers.

The case of Sierra-Cascade Nursery also illustrates the inner workings of the H-2A program, the type of labor contracting it generates, and its impact on farmworkers in Baja. While in 2007 the company hired 340 workers, by 2017 it had contracts with about 1,200 workers: 1,000 for the "short season" (six weeks beginning in September) and 200 for the "long season" (eight months starting in March).

About 60 percent of the recruited workers are men, a smaller proportion than other companies that recruit H-2A farm laborers in San Quintín. In California, H-2A workers are paid at a piece rate, and the company provides them with housing and food at a "subsidy rate." To ensure workers return to San Quintín after their work visas expire, Sierra-Cascade privileges those with "home and family stability" in the region. To "incentivize" them to return, Alicia Reyes explained to me, the company reimburses workers for the cost of the H-2A visa only after they finish their contracts and return to San Quintín, a standard practice among the other firms recruiting seasonal laborers in the region.

As a form of transnational labor contracting, the H-2A program introduced new means of labor selection and control. At the local office in San Quintín, Alicia and her coworker are responsible for screening the candidates who apply for the program, requesting proof of residence in the region, letters from employers in Baja attesting to their experience in strawberry work, and personal documents, all of which are required for applying for an H-2A work visa. After passing this first filter, however, the selected candidates must undergo a second screening in which they are "interviewed" by a company manager in California via Skype. Seated in San Quintín in front of a camera and wearing headphones, workers have to organize and count bunches of pencils following instructions provided live by a company supervisor on screen. Lasting about fifteen minutes, the test is used to assess worker's manual dexterity, agility, and speed, including keeping a mental count of the bunches of pencils. According to Alicia, of each ten workers who apply to the program, the local office selects an average of seven candidates, and this number is reduced by half after the virtual test from the company's headquarters in California. Digital technologies have thus become the latest component of the tool kit used by U.S. agribusinesses to select the most skilled farmworkers from Mexico as seasonal laborers in the United States.

In turn, for farm laborers in San Quintín, the H-2A program has opened new opportunities to work in the United States as legal rather than undocumented workers. With the militarization of the border, they find this program a viable option to travel safely as temporal workers to the United States. It is also an opportunity to save money to invest in their homes and their children's education or prepare for the low employment winter season in San Quintín. Anayeli Fernández—a Zapotec farmworker who was born in Nochixtlán, Oaxaca, in 1988 and has lived in Colonia Arbolitos with her husband and three children since 2003—is one of the hundreds of experienced farmworkers who have been recruited by Sierra-Cascade Nursery. Soon after this company began recruiting H-2A workers, she wanted to go to work in the United States. "I saw my brothers going every year and coming back home with money and presents for their children, while we here couldn't afford it," she told me, reflecting the social deprivation and local inequalities that often arise between households that receive migrant workers' remittances and those that do not (Cohen 2011, 106). Anayeli's break finally came in 2014, when Sierra-Cascade contracted with her to work in California for three months. She recalled being "very nervous" about taking the virtual test because she had never been subjected to this type of examination before and thought she had "flunked it." In California she worked trimming strawberry plants at a piece rate of $14 per 1,000 plants, earning $670 a week plus a "quality bonus," a significantly higher wage than farmworkers in the berry sector earn in Baja (about $90 a week). The higher earnings allowed her to save money to bring to her family in San Quintín. In her first year, the hardest as a new worker at this company, she returned with 20,000 pesos (about $1,500 at the time); in her second season and with more experience, she saved 40,000 pesos ($2,400); and in her third year in 2016, she brought back 60,000 pesos ($3,000).

Participating in the H-2A program also gave Anayeli a comparative transnational perspective. After several years in the program, Anayeli told me she prefers working in the United States because of the higher wages and better treatment workers receive. In 2017, before going back as an H-2A worker to California, Anayeli was employed at BerryMex, earning 220 pesos a day ($11.50). After three months, she quit the job because she considered it "not worth the money" and because of the drudgery involved; instead she opted to work for a smaller company where she could earn more money until she went to California in the summer. Anayeli also noticed a difference in the work environment in the United States, where she had to work harder but under better working conditions. "There they treat workers better, but they're also more demanding," she told me. In addition, she observed that Mexican workers in the United States are "more docile" than in San Quintín: "In the United States, we are more submissive, we don't say anything, you don't complain because if you do [the company] won't call you again to come; you shut up.... Here [in Baja] we protest more."

Anayeli's words reveal the discipline and labor-control components built into the H-2A program. As temporary workers they have limited ability to complain about and mobilize around their working conditions, which makes them a more malleable workforce than farmworkers contracted in the United States. Farmworkers like her are willing to trade the ability to protest working conditions in the United States for higher wages and a chance to bring savings back for their families in Baja. Despite this incentive, it is important to consider the larger context in which farmworkers' decisions are made. As Silverman and Hari (2016) argue regarding a similar program for seasonal workers in Canada's agricultural sector (the Seasonal Agricultural Worker Program, or SAWP), Mexican field workers' positive assessment of their experience is partially the result of the lack of opportunities in their own country, where neoliberal agrarian policies have rendered labor migration one of the few options to sustain their families via economic remittances. Without "real employment options," they argue, it is difficult to speak about real choices (2016, 97), and migration to the United States or Canada is one of the few avenues to get ahead at home. In Baja, farmworkers consider the H-2A program a good opportunity because of their experience of decades of labor exploitation in the region, especially at the hands of Mexican companies and growers who have historically treated them with contempt.

By 2017, several companies had opened local offices to recruit farmworkers in San Quintín, including Fresh Harvest and Elkhorn Packing, two of the top ten employers of H-2A workers in the United States (Karst 2018). The number of H-2A workers increased from 283,580 in 2015 to 412,820 in 2017, a trend that reflects the increasing reliance of U.S. horticultural companies on Mexican contracted labor, the second-largest sector using this program after the tobacco industry (Martin 2014, 51). In San Quintín the H-2A program gave workers some leverage to resist labor exploitation by local agribusinesses. For people like Anayeli, temporary labor migration to the United States represents a form of indirect labor resistance to the low wages, limited benefits, and long work hours that characterize farm labor in Baja. In the process, workers have also learned to use social media as a tool for resistance. Thus they often form WhatsApp groups to warn about "fake [H-2A] labor recruiters," people who come to the region and ask workers to pay in advance for processing their H-2A work applications. They also use social media to share information about their own employers, local contractors, and working conditions in San Quintín. *Denuncia Ciudadana,* for example, is a Webpage farmworkers created after a massive labor strike in 2015 to share information about labor abuses by local companies and contractors. This form of "digital citizenship" demonstrates the strength of the social and political organization that farmworkers have developed, which they deploy in an otherwise complex web of local and transnational labor contracting systems in the region. The last time I visited Anayeli and her husband, in the summer of 2017, they proudly showed me some WhatsApp groups their kin, friends, and coworkers have formed on Facebook to follow up opportunities regarding companies recruiting H-2A workers, gently teaching me (rather incompetent in social media) how to join and use them to stay informed and in touch.

CONCLUSION

In this chapter, I have provided a diachronic discussion of the emergence and transformation of different forms of labor contracting in San Quintín since the early 2000s. The different types of labor contractors, I have argued, allows the production and export of fresh produce at highly competitive prices while meeting the demanding food safety and quality standards that predominate in this sector. Rather than a remnant of the past, this assemblage of labor contractors emerged in the recent past and speaks of a process of labor intermediation by which agribusiness responded to workers' new freedom when they escaped the indentured labor regime that prevailed in labor camps until the 1990s. The change from migrant laborers housed in labor camps to settled workers living in the region opened a business opportunity for local contractors with vertical and horizontal social ties in the region to link growers and workers in the labor market. The multilayered system of labor contracting, which includes independent contractors, part-time labor intermediaries, and temporary contract agencies, also enabled companies to treat farmworkers as casual and flexible labor, constituting a vital pillar of the restructured labor regime of the fresh-produce industry in Baja. The result is a vertical subcontracting chain in which labor contractors and their workers are subordinated to large transnational companies in an asymmetrical power structure. The system allows agribusinesses to externalize the costs and legal responsibilities of labor recruitment, transportation, and discipline to labor contractors and workers themselves, creating a space of structural vulnerability in which contractors and their work crews absorb the costs and risks. The result is a sad irony. While global regulations on food safety and quality have been strengthened to benefit consumers, the reemergence of unregulated forms of labor contracting has heightened the precariousness of the very workers who produce these fresh and healthy crops.

A second argument I have presented is that labor contractors are not just labor recruiters but also serve to discipline workers in the norms of "good agricultural practices" at the heart of the fresh-produce industry. Labor contractors like Arcadio act as social and cultural brokers to convey, train, and enforce those norms among indigenous workers. As labor disciplinarians, they bridge the large class and cultural gap that separates them from the growers and managers of transnational agribusiness. Yet local contractors occupy a status vulnerable to the whims of their employers, which contributes to the uncertainty of their jobs. Despite their instability, for indigenous Mixtec, Zapotec, and Triquis, working as mayordomos and labor contractors is one of the few opportunities they have to move up in an industry that relegates them to the lowest position of field worker despite their skills and work experience. Because of this, labor contractors, particularly part-time contractors-mayordomos, occupy a liminal position in the community class structure, above their workers but in a vulnerable and insecure status. The ambiguity of their occupational status and class identity reflects the structural vulnerability the system of labor contracting has created that allows employers to use local contractors as either labor recruiters, supervisors, or field workers according to their needs.

Contract labor through temporary agencies such as Global constitute yet another layer of labor intermediation in Baja's agroexport sector. These agencies allow horticultural companies to institutionalize labor arrangements that combine labor flexibility with a strict code of labor discipline to enhance product safety and workers' productivity. Although Monsanto introduced changes that improved San Quintín the sanitary and safety conditions of workers, their wages and labor benefits were significantly undermined when Global converted them into temporary contract workers with fewer labor benefits. The complicit role of the CROM speaks of the central role of state-controlled unions to ensure a "climate of social peace," facilitating the flexibility of the labor force in commercial agriculture. As a result, most workers in San Quintín never develop a stable relationship with any of their employers but remain a permanent temporary labor force with limited rights and benefits. This, I contend, mirrors a structural trend in the political economy of the global fresh-produce industry. As the Spanish anthropologist Ubaldo Martínez-Veiga (2014, 109) has shown, Moroccan farmworkers employed in the tomato industry in Almeria in eastern Spain do not develop a stable labor relationship with any particular employer but permanently "rotate between bosses," creating the impression that they are truly casual workers rather than recurrent and necessary labor.

The recruitment of Mexican farmworkers in Baja to work in the United States as seasonal H-2A workers constitutes the latest form of labor contracting that has emerged in San Quintín's agroexport sector (Zlolniski 2016). The H-2A program, I have argued, adds a new layer in the complex web of labor intermediation in the region, denoting the consolidation of the San Quintín Valley as a transnational agroexport enclave. Farmworkers' labor experience and skills, along with the determination to improve their living conditions, make them ideal targets for U.S. growers to recruit them as a flexible and reliable labor source. Under this program, U.S. companies capitalize on farmworkers' skills and experience during their most productive years, externalizing the economic and social costs of raising, training, and maintaining them to their families and local communities in Baja. The use of digital technologies by U.S. agribusiness recruiting H-2A workers in Mexico allows them to refine the selection of the most productive and reliable workers, amounting to the extraterritorialization of labor control by these companies in Mexico. In turn, for workers like Anayeli, the program has made it possible to reconstitute themselves as a transnational labor force with valued skills and work experience that employers and contractors in Mexico and the United States compete for.[7] As a result, today Baja not only exports fresh produce but also the very laborers who produce them, turning this region into a new gateway for seasonal migrant workers to the United States.

4

"They Want First-Class Workers with Third World Wages"

The Workplace Regime of Transnational Agriculture

> Before we earned a bit more money working in the field. Now working in the shadehouses, the workload is higher and we are paid very little. . . . [I]t was easier before. Now they give us eight furrows to complete a work task planting, . . . and each furrow has two lines rather than one; . . . there're more plants, and it almost takes twice the work to complete a work task. It's so hard! Things are getting pretty hard for us farm laborers.
>
> —RODOLFO MORENO, A ZAPOTEC FARMWORKER, 2006

Rodolfo is a Zapotec farm laborer employed by Seleccionadora de Legumbres, a midsized company producing tomatoes and cucumbers for export to the United States. I originally met him through his wife, Adelina, while following the development of a community project led by women farmworkers in Colonia Arbolitos. After community meetings, Rodolfo would invite me to sit with him outside to enjoy the refreshing ocean breeze after his long day working in humid ninety-degree greenhouses and shadehouses. Slender, with a wide smile and bright white teeth, thick mustache, and intelligent eyes and wearing worn-out huaraches, he would sit on a bucket and we would chat until the sun went down or it got too cold. "Get away from there," he would yell, scaring away the chickens he and Adelina raised from the garden they kept to help feed their family.

Born in 1967 in Asunción Ocotlán, a small village in Oaxaca, Rodolfo has a story similar to that of other farmworkers who have lived in the region for years. His parents were peasants who combined dry-land farming with migrant labor in commercial agriculture in Sinaloa and Baja California. In 1986, after working three months on the tomato harvest in Sinaloa, Rodolfo arrived for the first time in San Quintín "to explore new lands" and job opportunities he had heard about. At first he lived in the labor camp of a large company, planting and harvesting tomatoes, chiles, cucumbers, and potatoes. A few years later, he met Adelina, a Zapotec who was employed by the same company. "We met in the field, we worked in the same crew, and I immediately recognized she spoke my same dialect," he explained, referring to his indigenous Zapotec language. Shortly afterward they moved together, first to a labor camp and then to a rented room to start a family. With two small children and after a great deal of sacrifice and time, they used some savings to buy a lot in Colonia Arbolitos, where many Zapotec farmworkers have settled. Despite their precarious situation, having their own lot and not having to pay rent felt like a major improvement compared to their early years in the crowded and unsanitary labor camps and rented rooms of San Quintín.

Despite their progress, Rodolfo's working conditions were getting tougher. Like many other farmworkers, he experienced the transition from working in open fields to shadehouses and greenhouses. In my conversations with him, Rodolfo often complained about the additional burden they endured because of this shift. "The work is more tiring, we finish later, and it's a bitch of a job," he summarized, reflecting the feelings of many other workers. He complained about his low wage—105 pesos a day ($8 at the time)—which was not enough to buy food for his family. For Rodolfo, the feeling of being subjected to increasing pressures and demands in the workplace translated into a mixture of resignation and defiance. "The day will come when the people won't take it any longer, when all this will come to an end," he told me during a conversation in 2009.

In this chapter, I examine the workplace regime in Baja's export agriculture industry and its effects on farm laborers like Rodolfo and Adelina. In the late 1990s, horticultural companies began to introduce new production technologies and labor management methods to increase productivity and adjust to food safety and quality requirements for fresh produce exported to the United States. But how have these changes affected labor conditions for farmworkers employed in this sector? How do workers themselves assess the impact of these changes? An ethnographic approach allows us to examine closely some of these changes and their effect on farm laborers in the fields. I use the concept of workplace regime as an analytical tool to elucidate the labor arrangements those changes have brought about. My central argument is that as a result of these transformations, farmwork has become more intensive and regimented than ever before, a workplace in which workers are under constant pressure and scrutiny to meet the "quality" requirements for export fruits and vegetables. I refer to this workplace regime as regimented flexibility, a system based on a reorganization of space-time arrangements aimed at extracting more surplus value from farmworkers, increase labor productivity, and achieve greater capital accumulation. In so doing I follow the British anthropologist Ben Rogaly's (2008, 497) call to map out the set of workplace regimes associated with modern capitalist agriculture with "region-specific and spatially aware research with a strong ethnographic component."[1]

"IT GETS VERY HOT HERE": WORKING IN GREENHOUSES

An important technological innovation in San Quintín's horticultural sector is the rise of production in sheltered environments, greenhouses and shadehouses. Known as controlled environment agriculture or indoor agriculture, horticultural production in sheltered facilities combines engineering, plant science, and computer-managed systems to optimize plant growing and productivity. Horticultural companies value production in protected environments because it requires less land and labor and lower herbicide and pesticide costs, and it yields more homogeneous and standardized crops. In Mexico, the expanded cultivation of water-intensive export crops in greenhouse facilities is considered the most important factor behind the intensification of horticultural production (González 2014). Between 1999 and 2005, for example, the increased production of greenhouse export crops such as tomatoes, green peppers, and cucumbers increased from 721 to 3,200 hectares in the main export regions of Sinaloa, Jalisco, Baja California, Baja California Sur, and Sonora (González 2014, 298–99). Greenhouses also raised productivity by 300 to 600 percent per hectare compared to open-air cultivation (González 2014, 299). Despite the increase in production in sheltered agriculture, studies of the working conditions of farm laborers employed in these settings are still scarce. One such study focuses on Mexican seasonal migrant workers employed in Canada's agriculture sector, portraying indoor agriculture as a "fast-paced and high-pressure work environment" and showing that workers' schedules are highly variable and unstable, depending on the numerous crop cycles in the greenhouses as well as fluctuating market demands (Paciulan and Preibisch 2013, 179–80).

In San Quintín, indoor agriculture began in the late 1990s after the collapse of the former capitalist model of extensive production in open fields that precipitated a water shortage crisis (Zlolniski 2011). Companies responded by investing in indoor agriculture, which sharply increased productivity. Thus, for example, open-field tomato production in 2011 yielded 60 tons per hectare compared to 92 tons in greenhouses. But the transition to cultivation in protected environments was an expensive endeavor. In the early 2000s, one greenhouse hectare required an initial investment of about 13,245.000 pesos (about $1,249,528), and one shadehouse required 4,644.000 pesos (about $438,113).[2] Due to the high cost, companies relied on financial investment by their commercial partners in the United States and, secondarily, on aid provided by Mexican government programs such as Alianza para el Campo to help growers invest in new technologies such as greenhouses and desalination plants. At the same time, the shift to production in sheltered environments had a major impact on farm laborers' working conditions.

FIGURE 12. Shadehouses and greenhouses have expanded in San Quintín since the early 2000s.

During fieldwork, I often heard farmworkers complain about the hardships of working long hours inside hot and humid shadehouses. They also experienced a significant increase in their workload and intense pressure from supervisors and managers to do a high-quality job. Anayeli Fernández, who was previously employed by Agrícola San Simón, illustrates this experience. Soon after arriving in San Quintín in 2003, she began working for this company in diverse tasks such as weeding, pruning, and harvesting, earning about 1,500 pesos a week (about $140). In 2005, after the company began producing in shadehouses, her work became more challenging. As she put it, "Shadehouses get very hot, which slows you down and you're less productive. [Also] they [company supervisors] are stricter regarding how you treat the plants; it wasn't like that in the open field, so there you could be a bit more productive. . . . In the shadehouses the plants are more fragile and you've got to be very careful; if you break them, you don't get paid for the whole work task."

Compared to work in open fields, surveillance in shadehouses is more intense, as companies seek to optimize the results of their costly investments. Explaining how her employer's supervisors were stricter than those in the open fields, Anayeli stated, "Because they don't want you to make any mistakes at work; they don't want any defects. If their wish would come true, everything would be carried on in an impeccable fashion, but as a worker you've to work fast. Sometimes your work isn't perfect because you want to make a bit more money and it's difficult to meet all the high requirements they have in the shadehouses. In the open field it wasn't like this."

Anayeli's comments point out two important dimensions of work performed in indoor agriculture. The first is the heat. With an average temperature of 90° to 95° Fahrenheit in the late spring and summer, high humidity, and the lack of a natural breeze, farm laborers' work can be more taxing and physically demanding than performing the same tasks in open fields. The second is the constant surveillance. Because greenhouses and shadehouses require high capital investments, companies often increase labor control to monitor workers' performance, deploying several layers of supervisors, including the contractors and mayordomos, field supervisors, and, occasionally, field agronomists. I often heard workers complain about the ubiquitous surveillance that slows them down and penalizes them for errors. More than in open fields, workers in greenhouses and shadehouses are expected to carry out their daily tasks with precision and to follow a prescribed script for each of those tasks to perform high-quality work.

Another challenge of working in shadehouses is the use of new tools. Because farmworkers have to do their work with more precision and care, they are often provided with and trained in the use of special tools like scissors and cutters. Anayeli noted a change related to the introduction of new tools that made her job more difficult when she was weeding tomato plants in greenhouses: "When weeding the plants in the open fields we used our hands; now in the shadehouses they give us pruning scissors that slow you down and make your job a bit more difficult. Also when working in shadehouses you have to step out of the furrow to bring your box when it's full to the containers [tinas], which is more tiring than in the open field ... [because] we have to walk longer distances."

When she has the option, Anayeli prefers working in open fields because she can "work faster," complete more tasks, and work in a more "natural" environment, with less heat and humidity than greenhouses. Although the tools she uses in the shadehouse have increased the precision of her work, Anayeli feels this has come at the expense of her time and income because it slows her down, decreasing her earnings, which are based on a piece rate. In her view, the shift to working in greenhouses and shadehouses has been detrimental because "you complete less [piece] tasks" and earn less than working in open fields, an observation found in Rogaly's (2008) analysis of work in sheltered environments.

Anayeli's critique of working in sheltered environments was common among many of the workers I met in San Quintín. Faustina Herrera, an old-timer from Oaxaca who arrived in the region in 1985, also experienced the shift from working in open fields to greenhouses. Like Anayeli, Faustina referred to laboring in greenhouses as requiring "more delicate," work as she had to be more careful and work under intense scrutiny. Her comments about working for a local company that grows strawberries and blackberries in tunnel houses for U.S. markets, reflects the microdimension of farm labor in these environments.

> I planted strawberries plants in the tiny holes as marked in the furrows covered by plastic and had to be very careful not to step on the tender plants when walking in the [narrow] furrows.... Also when the soil is hard, it's very difficult to plant the tiny plants; if you push too hard you run the risk of breaking them, so we use our fingers to press, and sometimes they bleed. When we have to clean the plants it's the same story; you must be very careful and cannot move forward as I used to in the open field, where you can walk faster without damaging the plants. Meanwhile [the supervisors] keep telling you to be careful: "Don't step on anything, be careful with the plants, take care of the tender strawberries!"

Faustina prefers working in open fields to closed environments and tunnel houses because, she said, "you feel freer, and it doesn't get as hot." In addition, after she started working in shadehouses, her blood pressure went up and she developed some health issues. Describing the difference between both settings, she told me, "Greenhouses are fine in the winter when it gets cold or if it rains so you're protected, but in a time like now when it's hot [summer] it's tough and my blood pressure goes high. Sometimes I get dizzy and agitated."

By 2010, the shift from open field cultivation to production in sheltered structures was well under way in San Quintín. As this change was taking place, farmworkers complained about being "caged" in closed shadehouses with suffocating temperatures and humidity and little ventilation. Luis Flores, a farmworker employed by Monsanto to grow seeds as well as a variety of fruits and flowers, complained about the heat: "You can't work at ease inside because of the heat; there is no breeze coming in. In the open field it's hot, but sooner or later there's always a breeze and you cool down a bit. In the shadehouse you are enclosed and you feel like you're burning." In addition, he noticed an augmented workload since he began working in the shadehouses: "Before [in open fields] they gave us six furrows per task and we worked in the field with the breeze. Now they give us seven furrows and you are closed up inside. You cannot work *a gusto* [at ease]; it's very hot inside; no, no, it's very difficult to bear it!"

The health hazards associated with working in greenhouses and shadehouses were a common theme among the farmworkers I spoke with. While there are no official statistics on workplace accidents in San Quintín's horticultural sector, I found considerable information in the field about health issues. Field workers complained about feeling dizzy, having episodes of high blood pressure, and fainting, as well as accidents, revealing a new set of occupational hazards in indoor agriculture. A case in point is Elisa Ortiz, a farmworker in her mid-thirties who was born in Mexicali and as a child picked cotton along with her parents and siblings until she moved to San Quintín in the late 1980s. A few years later, she began working at Los Pinos, which employs about 2,500 workers, and then got married and took a few years off to raise her children. In 2004, when she went back to work for the same company, she was assigned to a greenhouse. Like other workers, Elisa had a hard time adjusting to the new workplace. First was the problem of working in high temperatures and the effects on her health: "My blood pressure goes down in the greenhouses, I get dizzy, feel like vomiting, and can't breathe. I can't work there; I get sick and feel bad." She also had to learn to use new tools and, in the process, suffered an accident she could not forget.

> When I worked in greenhouses, they gave us scissors to do our job and I cut myself here in this hand, and I only got paid 80 pesos [$7.20] that day. I hurt myself and almost cut off one of my fingers. On top of that I got reprimanded by the mayordomo, who yelled at me, "Pendeja" [asshole], very upset.... There wasn't anything I could use to cure myself so they put my hand in a bucket of chlorine that was there, and I was bleeding badly so all the chlorine got red. I then bandaged my finger myself as best I could.... I couldn't work for the whole week because my finger got all swelled up.

After the accident, Elisa did not return to work for Los Pinos and avoided working in greenhouses. Like other workers I met, she prefers working for small companies and growers who still produce in open fields, where she does not feel the intense pressure and she is treated better by supervisors.

Not all the consequences of working in sheltered environments, however, were seen as detrimental. Because of food safety requirements, large horticultural companies have implemented new methods to reduce work accidents and increase safety in the workplace. They have also developed protocols to reduce farmworkers' exposure to pesticides, a major problem that was rampant for decades in northwestern Mexico's commercial agriculture (Wright 2005). To comply with food hygiene and phytosanitary requirements to prevent food contamination, companies also made portable bathrooms more readily accessible in the fields and greenhouses and shadehouses. Moreover, workers have cleaner lunch and working areas, as well as access to clean drinking water in the workplace, all of which they greatly value, especially the old-timers, who remember when none of these facilities was available until the late 1990s.

Workers' narratives, I contend, speak to the intensification of labor, the difficult microclimate conditions, and the rules and regulations that govern their performance. These conditions can magnify the common health risks farmworkers regularly confront such as work injuries, respiratory diseases, arthritis, and stress, which, as numerous studies have shown, make agriculture one of the most hazardous industries in the United States and Mexico (e.g., Arcury and Quandt 1998; Holmes 2013; Horton 2016). These health hazards reveal the effects of horticultural production in sheltered structures on the bodies of farmworkers.

As Jorg Gertel and Sarah Ruth Sippel (2014, 252) argue regarding the case of immigrant farmworkers employed in the fresh-produce industry in the Mediterranean, "Biopolitics are governing the social organization even of intimate spaces" in the workplace, a trait that also characterizes this industry in the U.S.-Mexico borderlands. It is not surprising, then, that farmworkers' narratives in San Quintín often held a longing for a past when they worked in open fields, "a more natural environment."

RATCHETING UP THE WORKLOAD: FROM DAY WAGES TO PIECE RATES

Until the late 1990s, most companies and growers paid their workers *jornales,* or daily wages, a fixed amount for working a day shift of eight hours. In the early 2000s, daily wages began to be replaced by a piece rate, a system in which the unit of product replaced the unit of time as the payment method (Hernández-Romero 2012, 74). Growers shifted to a piece rate to increase productivity and reduce labor costs as well as to compete for scarce labor during the harvest when many farm laborers moved out of labor camps and settled in colonias. Rather than an anomaly, piece rate has become a key tool in the fresh-produce industry to increase productivity. Companies use piece rate as a management strategy to keep the costs of specific work tasks constant while stimulating individual competition to enhance productivity (Ortiz 2002, 404; Ortiz et al. 2013). In turn, laborers prefer piece rate because it allows them to increase their earnings and gives them more freedom to decide when to come and go. Some scholars argue that piece rate "promote[s] individual competition among workers" and work teams (Paciulan and Preibisch 2013, 181). From this perspective, piece-rate remuneration not only seeks to enhance productivity, but also to break horizontal links of social solidarity among workers based on kinship, ethnicity, indigenous identification, and friendship.

In San Quintín, the introduction of a piece-rate system led to a quantitative intensification of labor, as workers had to work harder than before to earn the equivalent of a day's wage and meet the production quotas set by their employers. But as I observed in the field, rather than a single piece-rate system, companies use a great variety of piece-rate types throughout the production cycle to keep labor costs down. Thus some tasks are paid by individual piece rate, others are team based, and still others are paid by the day. Planting and harvesting, for example, are often paid at piece rate, while other "culture tasks," such as pruning and preparing the soil for the next cycle, are frequently paid by daily wage. This means that a worker employed by the same company is paid by several or all these systems throughout the year, depending on the task, crop, season, and whether work is performed in open fields or greenhouses. The latitude if not arbitrariness with which companies constantly change types of payment to reduce labor costs and increase flexibility is illustrated by the case of Ramón Suárez, a farmworker who lives in Colonia Santa Fe with his wife, Aurelia, and their six children. Born in 1972 in Tetujín, a Mixtec village in Oaxaca, Ramón worked since 2006 for Rancho Vigor, a company growing strawberries and tomatoes for a U.S. distributing company. From January to February 2013, Ramón worked pruning strawberry plants, an activity for which he was paid a daily wage of 110 Mexican pesos (about $8). During the harvest, from February to June, he was switched to a piece rate, earning about $19 a day, and in July he was sent to pick cherry tomatoes in a different field for a piece rate that barely earned him between $6 and $8 a day, which was less than the daily wage. When the harvest was over, his job consisted of removing the plastic that covers the strawberry beds, an activity he performed by hand with a knife for about ten days, and was still paid piece rate. In September, he prepared the soil for the next production cycle and was switched back to a daily wage of $8. Finally, from October to December, when work slows down, Ramón worked three to four days a week at a daily wage, supplementing his meager income with a temporary construction job. In my conversations with him, his frustration and resignation about how the company treated him and other workers often came to the surface. Conveying the sense of power inequality in which growers have the upper hand and workers little room to maneuver, he commented, "Wages always fell short. I think that growers take advantage of us because they know that all the people who live here cannot go to work somewhere else and that we can only work in the field, especially if we are not schooled. The patrones know that eventually we will end up working in the field, even if we don't want to. That's why they don't raise our wages."

Meanwhile his wife, Aurelia, who worked for Rancho Nuevo, a company that produces tomatoes and onions, experienced the consequences of piece-rate wages when, two years after quitting her job to raise her newborn child, she went back to work. Her employer had switched from a daily wage to a piece rate based on the number of furrows (100 meters long) workers complete per work task. The increased workload meant that she could hardly earn the equivalent of a day's wage: "To earn the equivalent of a day's pay, you have to complete four furrows. I went yesterday, and there were others harvesting onions and planting strawberries, but I only managed to complete three furrows.... Sometimes I don't even make a day's wage. Like now, we're planting onions and only get paid 25 pesos ($1.90) per furrow."

Ramón and Aurelia's predicament reflects the consequences of the structural transformations of San Quintín's export agricultural sector. Production in greenhouses and shadehouses employs fewer workers, increasing competition for jobs among farm laborers and pushing them to accept higher workloads at a piece rate. The slow winter season further destabilizes the precarious budget of farmworkers like them. Every year in September, when his earnings start to decrease, Ramón gets in debt buying on credit in the small food stores in his colonia. Unlike regular food markets, these are family-run stores that sell on credit to local residents, allowing farmworkers to buy food during the low season until they are back in full employment in the spring and can pay their debts in weekly installments after cashing their checks. The winter months are particularly difficult for Ramón and Aurelia as they struggle to put food in the table. Ramón talked about his anxiety:

> When I'm out of work, sometimes I don't even have enough money to buy a gas tank for the kitchen so I go around gathering wood to cook so we can have something to eat.... Sometimes when I'm in bed at nights, I start thinking about all the debts I have, that we don't have enough to eat. *Híjole,* there're moments when I'd like to walk in the hills to cross to the United States as I did before to work and send money to my family. Then I see on TV that things are getting very tough to cross and that holds me up.

Companies also use piecework to change the workload assigned to each task to enhance productivity. Elisa Robles, a Zapotec worker who lives in Colonia Arbolitos and was employed by Seleccionadora de Legumbres, explained to me that when her work crew managed to finish their task ahead of schedule to complete another half-task to earn extra income, the company's manager often increased the number of furrows per task, making it harder: "Sometimes they take advantage of us and give us many furrows per task, and then if they see we move forward fast they give us even more furrows! Only when we cannot complete a task at all they give us fewer furrows per task."

Moreover, piecework entails more pressure and surveillance by mayordomos and supervisors, further contributing to the intensification of labor and workers' stress. Workers employed in large companies often complain about mayordomos who yell and press them to work faster and do not allow them to take any breaks. Hermelinda Ramírez, a single mother employed by Agrícola San Simón who lives in Colonia Arbolitos, described being constantly pushed to her limits by mayordomos in this and other large companies where she worked: "In these companies the mayordomos are behind pushing and yelling at you to work fast: "'¡Apúrate!' [Hurry up!] The patrones give orders to the mayordomos not to let us sit and rest, to check the time we spend going to the restroom.... [They] keep saying 'Hurry up!' and '¡Échale ganas!' [Apply yourself!], because you aren't fast enough, or 'Look out, you're getting behind the rest of the crew.'"

Despite the high-pressure work environment, many farmworkers prefer piece rate to a daily wage because it allows them to earn more. In 2015, the daily wage was about 110 pesos, or $7.15, which was clearly insufficient to provide for their basic needs. In turn, growers estimate that the shift to piece rate has helped them reduce the number of jornales paid for many of the work tasks of the production cycle, especially the harvest. The flexibility to constantly change and readjust the form of labor remuneration in the workplace is, I argue, a key factor that has fostered the intensification of labor in Baja's agroexport industry and that distinguishes it from labor arrangements in California's agriculture sector.[3]

FROM HARVEST TO PACKING

A third change in the organization of production in San Quintín's fresh-produce industry is the consolidation of sorting and packing tasks as part of the regular workload. This is especially the case for workers harvesting berries, a crop that by 2015 had displaced tomatoes as the main produce in the region. While in the past these tasks were carried out in separate facilities, beginning in the early 2000s, they became part of workers' piece-rate harvest contracts. The integration of sorting and packing during the harvest is considered an important feature of modern industrial agriculture. Describing the work process with strawberries, table grapes, and lettuce in California's Central Valley, Manuel Hernández-Romero (2012, 75) points out that the harvest of these crops "is immediately integrated with packing, and the products leave the fields with the same presentation with which they will reach the consumers." This practice demonstrates the tendency in this industry "to increase profit margins at retail through value-adding" (Hernández-Romero 2012, 79), a process in which farmworkers are expected to enhance the attractiveness of the packaged produce for consumers.

The introduction of packing as part of the labor process among farmworkers in San Quintín gained momentum when transnational companies began growing berries in the region, importing many of their labor management methods from the United States. Farmworkers were required to sort and package the delicate fruits according to specific instructions on size, color, and degree of ripeness, integrating this task as part of the harvest in what amounts to an unpaid component of the work process given that they are paid piece rate based on the volume of harvested fruits. The labor intensification that resulted from this change did not go unnoticed. Amalia Tello, a former Mixtec field worker who later became a radio host at a public bilingual station in San Quintín, told me that she recalled the time when strawberry workers were paid by bulk just "filling big boxes" divided in two sections each. By the early 2000s, however, companies started to pack them in small baskets and implemented new quality norms regarding specific traits of the fruits with rigorous checkups in the fields, a system that became the new normal in the region.

One day while observing strawberry workers employed at a midsized company growing raspberries for Driscoll's, I had the opportunity to witness the implications of this change. It was midmorning on a summer day when a group of about eighteen field workers, mostly women, were in the last days of the picking season. As they explained, they were paid 14 Mexican pesos (about $1.00) for each box of fruit, each containing six "baskets" of twelve ounces, amounting to 2.3 pesos

FIGURE 13. A female worker inspects raspberries for BerryMex.

(17 cents) per basket. Experienced workers filled an average of 25 to 30 boxes at the peak of the harvest season when the plants are full of fruit, but when the harvest was ending they only filled about 10 boxes a day. Filling 8 boxes a day, they explained to me, was the equivalent of a day's wage; going above that threshold was considered good and an incentive to work hard. To be paid, however, the fruit each worker harvests has to pass a quality check that has several steps. Every time a worker filled two boxes, he or she had to bring them to a checking station where a *checadora,* or inspector, counted and checked them to make sure they met the instructions on type, size, color, and degree of ripeness specified for the day. Afterward, a truck took the boxes to the Driscoll's cooling and packing plant to minimize the time between when they are picked and when they arrive at this facility. That morning, shortly before I was about to leave this field, a pickup truck arrived from the Driscoll's cooling plant bringing back about a dozen raspberry boxes. When I asked the driver why he was bringing them back, he replied that these fruits had not passed a second quality check. Whenever berries arrive at this facility, he explained, they are inspected for quality, and if there are boxes that fail the test, they are sent back to the field where they were harvested. A tracking number on the boxes identifies the field and work crew that harvested and packaged the boxes. Once back in the field, the workers who picked, sorted, and packed the berries had to replace them with good fruits and repack the boxes to pass the inspection in order to be paid.

This incident reveals three important features about the labor arrangements in the strawberry industry. First, by integrating packing into the harvest, workers contribute to the added value of the produce in the consumer market but are not remunerated for this component of the labor process. In this system, companies extract value from field workers' labor, which increases the retail profit margins (Hernández-Romero 2012). Second, the dead time workers spend during the quality inspection process is not computed in the piece-rate system, which is based solely on the total number of boxes harvested after passing the quality check. This system is based on negative reinforcement, meaning that workers are penalized when the fruits do not meet the company's quality specifications. This quality check, conducted by Driscoll's, facilitates the social distance between the company and the subcontracted fieldworkers. Third, modern digital traceability technologies allow companies to track and monitor the performance of their workers and tie the piece rate to it. Watching this event in the field made me realize the irony that while horticultural companies use the most sophisticated technologies to keep precise internal records about who picks their berries, where the berries are picked, and when, they do not keep official records of workers or register them in the Seguro Social, a strategy to reduce taxes and avoid paying them health and other benefits.

ENFORCING FOOD SAFETY AND QUALITY

The set of norms for food safety and quality implemented by horticultural companies exporting fruits and vegetables to the United States mostly consist of the standardization of size, shape, texture, and color of fresh produce established by shippers and large supermarkets. Food safety and quality norms in the fresh-produce industry have been the subject of recent scholarship. Examining the experience of Maya farmers growing broccoli in Guatemala for consumer markets in the United States, for example, Edward Fisher and Peter Benson (2006) argue that quality standards are market driven and mainly aimed at shaping consumers' preferences for aesthetic traits and the appearance of freshness. Rogaly (2008, 507) refers to this trend as "commodity fetishism," whereby working conditions in modern industrial agriculture are rendered invisible to the consumers of fresh produce. The standardization of fresh-produce production, he argues, has increased the speed, care, and effort required from farm laborers.

As in other regions in Mexico that specialize in export agriculture (C. de Grammont and Lara Flores 2010; Stanford 2002), San Quintín experienced a renewed emphasis on fresh-produce quality in the late 1990s, which transformed the organization of production in the workplace. While in the past growers emphasized quantity or volume of production, in response to new certification requirements and market trends they began to emphasize "quality," by which they meant not the flavor or other natural properties of fresh produce but the external aesthetic appearance and homogeneity. In the process a new work culture developed, one in which quality became the new and dominant mantra. To meet these market requirements, horticultural companies specializing in export agriculture began implementing a set of Good Agricultural Practices (GAP), which are codified norms about "best practices" for fresh-produce regarding all aspects related to growing, handling, packing, labeling, storing, and transporting perishable produce (C. de Grammont and Lara Flores 2010, 236). GAP also include rules for sanitation, toxic pesticide residues, and workers' personal hygiene and appearance. This set of norms are usually passed top-down, from the growers and field agronomists to company foremen, labor contractors, field mayordomos, and, finally, field workers. In Morelos, for example, workers are required to attend training sessions about food safety and quality known as *escuelas* implemented by their mayordomos and supervisors in the field (Sánchez Saldaña 2016). These training sessions seek to socialize workers in the new efficiency and quality requirements and reduce the use of coercion as a tool of labor control (Lara Flores and Sánchez Saldaña 2015, 81). Some scholars also argue that GAP workshops serve as informal social institutions to convert technical knowledge into workers' language and daily practice (Hernández Romero 2012, 79).

In San Quintín, the renewed emphasis on quality created a new workplace milieu with heightened surveillance and labor control. Don Antonio, a retired farmworker in his mid-sixties who witnessed the shift from quantity to quality in the region, told me that "a change in growers' attitudes" had a direct effect on farmworkers' workload: "Now they [farmworkers] work until the point of exhaustion, and by the time they leave they look like rag dolls, very tired."

Growers also use GAP as a vehicle to instill corporate values about efficiency, "excellence," and the importance of responding to clients' demands. In my conversations with Esther Chávez, who for many years, until 2017, worked planting seeds and growing different varieties of flowers, tomatoes, and cucumbers for Seminis and then Monsanto, I learned how GAP workshops served to promote the values of obedience and respect in the workplace. After Monsanto took over Rancho El Milagro, it implemented a new managerial approach that included GAP workshops to enhance food safety and quality and to convey the company's emphasis on improving productivity. The workshops were carried out by the crew leaders of the company in the mornings every third day when laborers arrived at work. To enhance safety, in addition to providing new equipment to workers such as gloves, safety glasses, overalls, and boots, the company developed new rules regarding the personal hygiene of workers, most of them women, and the appearance of their work clothes. Women could not wear makeup or bracelets, rings, trinkets, or any other jewelry, and they had to wear their hair bound and their nails short. During my regular visits to Esther and her family, she often talked about the effects of GAP rules on her work, pointing to both the benefits and the new burdens.

They [company's managers] have folders with the list of all the *pláticas* [talks] scheduled for us, like what to do to avoid damaging the plants.... I am glad because they give us protective gear to wear at work, which is called protective personal equipment, given to each worker and not transferable. [We get] gloves, safety glasses, overalls, and boots, and if you don't bring your equipment, they don't let you in. We have to bathe at home and arrive clean; sometimes workers look dirty and get reprimanded. Once I remember a woman who arrived with a stained sweater and without combing her hair, as if she had slept in her clothes, and they told her, "You're going to work only until noon, and then you have to leave." Here the talks they give us insist on personal hygiene and being clean. They are very strict.

Esther's comments convey the mixed feelings I often found among many farmworkers in San Quintín. One the one hand, she was happy to have a work uniform to wear at work instead of her own clothes, which in the past got dirty and worn out. Wearing special boots made her feel safer than when she wore her own tennis shoes on the slippery floor of the shadehouses, diminishing the risk of falling down. She particularly appreciated talks about how to handle pesticides and having access to drinking water at work as well as clean portable restrooms. On the other hand, she experienced the consequences of strict norms about personal appearance. At Monsanto, workers were responsible for washing, ironing, and keeping their work uniforms clean and in good shape, activities they had to carry out in their homes on their own time and with their own resources (soap, water, etc.) with the cost externalized to them. Esther described her new responsibilities: "We have to wash the overalls every day because we work with different varieties of tomatoes, and if we don't wash them well, they say we can contaminate the plants and cross-fertilize them. We have to wash them every day at home to be ready the next day. Then the mayordomos check us when we arrive, and if our overalls aren't clean, she calls it to our attention, saying, 'Why didn't you wash your overalls?'"

GAP sessions at Monsanto also included a new protocol for interaction between workers and their mayordomos. These rules were aimed at increasing workers' "efficiency" and instilling the company's values. Describing the change she noticed when this company acquired Seminis, Esther stated:

The supervisors aren't called supervisors anymore, but now we call them our "clients"; I have to refer to them as my clients. My duty is to satisfy my client with my work; all this is contained in the quality policy the company teaches us when we are hired. The policy has several goals. The first goal is to deliver our products on time; if we satisfy our client, then they in turn satisfy their boss. The second goal is to increase our efficiency or productivity; we need to increase the quality of our work every day we work. Every day when we arrive in the morning they give us a *plática*, and they ask us, "Hey Esther, what is the first objective of the company's philosophy?" Sometimes they catch us in a blank, and we don't know what to answer.... Every third day they keep repeating, repeating, and repeating these principles, and we have to memorize them.

This managerial approach brings the neoliberal language of "customer satisfaction" from the supermarket to farm laborers in the field, seeking to naturalize the expectations on productivity and food quality. The language change from "supervisors" to "clients" can be read as an ideological device to conceal the intensification of labor that the new managerial system entailed. This was especially remarkable considering that officially these were temporary workers hired and managed by Global as a labor outsourcing company. The inner contradiction of this labor management system was well captured by an agronomist employed at SAGARPA who, commenting on the changes he had observed in San Quintín since the early 2000s, told me that transnational companies like Monsanto in the region "want first-class workers with Third World wages." This observation lays bare the gulf between employers' expectations as embodied in the GAP norms and the living conditions of farmworkers. While large companies emphasize strict hygiene for their workers, most houses where farm laborers live in San Quintín are made of cardboard, have latrines rather than bathrooms, and many colonias have no sewage system. I was always amazed how, in such conditions, workers like Esther and Raúl managed to stay healthy, maintain good personal hygiene, and keep their homes clean.[4]

THE FIGHT TO CONTROL THE WORKDAY

The last and most recent change in the work rules implemented by many agricultural companies in San Quintín is control of workers' time. Large companies began applying new rules on punctuality, lunch breaks, the length of the workday, and the use of time in the workplace to better synchronize laborers' activities and increase their overall productivity. To confront high labor turnover, many employers also instituted new policies to lay off workers for several days when they missed work, economic incentives to retain them, and more homogeneous and standardized work shifts. That meant that workers paid by piece rate who in the past had some leeway to go home after completing their work tasks were now required to wait until the end of the workday to leave.

The struggle over the workday is a theme with a long tradition in Marxist studies on work. The classic work by the historian E. P. Thompson (1967, 76) showed that irregularity of the working day and week prevailed until the early nineteenth century. The clock was then introduced as a tool to impose work discipline, including by agricultural employers who complained about time wasted by wage-earning field laborers (77). While at first workers resisted the new time discipline, in the next stage, Thompson tells us, they began "to fight, not against time, but about it" (85). As Harvey (2010, 135) reminds us, the quarrel over the length of the workday is thus linked to the social construction of time and temporality in the capitalistic mode of production and is an important feature of class struggle. Labor disputes about time involve when laborers should get to work, what and how long lunch and other breaks should last, and how to set the maximum hours workers can be employed in a day's work (Harvey 2010, 142).

Originally labor discipline was enacted to curb absenteeism among indigenous populations in colonial settings because authorities had difficulty getting indigenous peoples to work a "normal" working day in a cultural context in which the local conception of temporality did not fit the idea of clock time brought by capitalist production (Harvey 2010, 147). More recently, David Syring (2009) has examined the experience of indigenous rural peasants in Ecuador who were turned into farmworkers in modern industrial agriculture. Syring argues that rural workers with a peasant background resent and resist capitalist notions about the proper ways to organize time and labor and relationships between work and everyday life. This is because the workplace regime in commercial agriculture subjects them to a more exacting labor discipline, which he calls "transnational encounters with global capitalist temporality" (Syring 2009, 119). Moreover, workers resent the regularity, repetitiveness, and tediousness of work in industrial agriculture that is the result of the standardization of production and GAP rules (Syring 2009, 133).[5]

In San Quintín, the implementation of new rules to control the length of the workday and workers' time in the workplace became another tool for labor disciplining and an arena of struggle for workers who seek to resist them. The new rules were often met with resistance as laborers felt they had lost the flexibility to control and organize their own time. For example, Luis Flores, who worked for Monsanto, noticed the imposition of more rigid time requirements when this company arrived in town: "Before you could leave after finishing your work task.... Now you have to stay until 3:30 P.M. or the time the company says. Sometimes they give us additional tasks.... Moreover, if you don't want to continue working, they tell us not to come the next day because there won't be any work for us.... It's different than before because . . . you have to wait until everybody finishes, and then and only then they let us leave."

New rules about workers' time schedules most negatively affected women, revealing the gender dimension of labor discipline in industrial agriculture. Women with children felt especially constrained by the lengthening of the workday as it restricted their ability to combine work with caring for their children and other nonpaid work in their households. Laura Flores, Luis's wife, resented the new rules Monsanto had implemented to penalize workers who missed work: "What I don't like is the requirement we have to work every day. As a woman I'd like to work every day but I have children and sometimes they get sick and that's why I can't."

Some women I knew opted for quitting their jobs with large companies that had rigid work-time policies. Instead, they decided to work for *rancheros*, small companies and growers that had more relaxed rules and flexibility about schedules. Elisa Ortiz, for example, a single mother who in the past worked for Los Pinos, quit and began working for rancheros near her colonia in the southern San Quintín Valley because of the greater flexibility to leave the field early to go home to attend to her children after they get out of school at 2:00 P.M. rather than wait until 3:00 P.M. as is compulsory in large companies. Elisa explained why she prefers working for small companies.

> I like working for rancheros. They pay me daily, and there isn't an obligation to work every day. I can miss one, two, and even three days and they don't tell me anything. In the big companies, there's the commitment to work every day and you cannot miss work. . . . Anyhow, I normally work every day. Even if we have to work on Sundays I go to work, so I often work seven days a week. It's tough, believe me; I feel tired but still get up at 2:00 A.M. to get ready and go to work every day.

While working for small-scale growers is often less stable and rarely provides any benefits, the higher earnings, greater flexibility to organize their time, and less punitive discipline often attract farmworkers, especially women, to these employers.

Interestingly, the implementation of discipline to control the workday often increased rather than reduced labor turnover. As I mentioned earlier, growers in San Quintín frequently complained about a labor turnover problem in the region. In my conversations with them, they were often mystified that workers did not show up or missed work a few days in a row, which they often interpreted as lack of discipline, commitment, or ambition. This interpretation, however, did not take into account that settled workers who live in local colonias have other responsibilities and time commitments as they seek to balance paid work with family and household tasks. Celeste Hernández, a Zapotec single mother in her early forties who lives in Colonia Arbolitos, told me she sometimes could not show up for work at Seleccionadora de Legumbres, where she had been employed on and off for many years. When I told her about growers' common perception of farm laborers being *desobligados* (irresponsible), she replied:

> When I miss work it is generally because of family health issues, as, for example, when my children get sick and I have to take care of them or take them to the doctor. Otherwise, I always go to work. . . . Other times I miss work because I go to my children's school to sign their report cards or do household chores. For example, some days I start early in the morning washing clothes and I stay home until I finish, and the next day you wake up very tired, take the day off, and go to work the next day.

For women workers with children, the pressure to combine and coordinate work, family, and community responsibilities makes managing their time a real challenge. As Greta Friedemann-Sánchez (2012) argues in her study of female workers employed in floriculture in Colombia, their rationale for leaving their jobs despite the income they earn is shaped by household responsibilities such as caregiving, cooking, and child rearing in a cultural context where men are excluded from these tasks. In San Quintín, employers' expectation that women would work six or seven days a week without missing a day just by offering a modest economic bonus misses the fact that in addition to wage work, they have family and social lives of their own with multiple responsibilities competing for their time. When I talked with women workers about this issue, they often acknowledged that one of the main advantages of living independently in their own homes was the freedom to decide when and for whom to work, including quitting work to tend newborn children if someone else in the household was working and bringing in an income. With an exacting time discipline implemented by large horticultural companies, farmworkers' decision to miss work can be seen then as a micro form of resistance to work-time rules that undermine their autonomy, ability to tend to their families, and individual freedom.[6]

CONCLUSION: THE BRAVE NEW WORLD OF EXPORT AGRICULTURE

In today's advanced capitalist agriculture, farmworkers labor in a brave new world. Horticultural production in closed facilities, the use of piece rate to reduce labor costs and stimulate productivity, the folding of harvesting and packing into a single work task, the tight control of time in the workplace, and the implementation of "good agricultural practices" constitute the five pillars of the ecosystem of export agriculture in Baja. The stories presented in this chapter speak to workers' feeling of being caged in closed greenhouses and shadehouses with suffocating temperatures and humidity and of being subjected to strict rules that seek to standardize their jobs and discipline them into the work rhythm of modern industrial agriculture. This regime, I contend, has led to a deep transformation of the space-time arrangements in the workplace to increase the intensification of the labor process and enhance productivity, transforming peasants into wage workers for commercial agriculture. The reconfiguration of space and time arrangements has created a system of regimented flexibility characterized by the flexible rotation of workers through different tasks and assignments with constantly changing remuneration schemes, along with a set of rigid norms and regulations to control their performance and use of time. As a result, for many workers, farm labor has become a highly scripted, regimented, and monitored occupation.

Examining the workplace regime in San Quintín's export agriculture, I have argued, allows us to see how transnational companies incorporate the neoliberal principles of labor flexibility, efficiency, and individual responsibility in their management methods. Codified in the technical language of "product safety and quality," GAP norms embody the values of individual competition, workers' loyalty, "excellence," and productivity as a hegemonic discourse. This approach seeks to naturalize the idea that farmworkers should assume and identify with the demands and delicate tastes of the "clients" who consume Mexican fresh-produce in the United States. These principles reach all the way down to the micro-conditions in which workers perform their daily tasks, regulating even workers' bodies and their personal appearance. Biopolitics are thus deeply entrenched in the organization of labor in this industry, as medical anthropologists studying the health hazards Mexican farmworkers confront in Mexico and the United States have demonstrated (Holmes 2013; Horton 2016). As I have shown, while some changes and norms have improved sanitary conditions for farm laborers in the workplace, others have caused new health hazards and risks, especially for workers laboring in closed environments under intensive surveillance and pressure.

The workplace regime described in this chapter reveals the inner contradiction of a production system that places a premium on the preciousness of the plants and the need to tend to them with care and gentleness, on the one hand, and the treatment of the workers who grow them as an expendable commodity, on the other. But as I have also noted, some of these changes have opened new spaces for workers' discontent and opposition. The array of individual and collective resistance strategies by which farmworkers cope with the new workplace regime is the subject of the next chapter.

5

Resisting the *Carrilla* in the Workplace

Forms of Labor Protests

The labor problems haven't been resolved, and you'll see it when everything blows up. Workers are now like in a pressure cooker and the time will arrive when all explodes in a big boom.... There have already been episodes of despair, and the fact that the media doesn't cover but hides them won't matter. The time will come when it won't be possible to cover up all this any longer.... I'm committed to keep fighting until San Quintín explodes!
—JUSTINO HERRERA, LONGTIME MIXTEC LABOR AND
COMMUNITY LEADER, 2011

Ethnographic studies on labor resistance in modern industrial agriculture remain scarce. We know more about the technological and managerial changes that have transformed the global fresh-produce industry than about how workers have been affected by and responded to those changes. In her classic book *Strawberry Fields* (1996), Miriam Wells argued that despite the "impotence [of] the literature," which led her to expect unskilled workers' resistance to labor management would be "negligible," she found that strawberry workers in California's Central Valley were actively involved in forms of struggle that shaped the terms and rewards of their labor (2–3). Wells urged scholars to pay close attention to the individual and collective forms of workers' resistance in advanced capitalist agriculture rather than focus solely on its structural changes. She uncovered a variety of ways in which Mexican migrant workers opposed labor management methods, arguing that beneath these expressions of resistance there was a struggle for equality and justice in the workplace (11).

In the recent past, an emergent body of scholarship has contributed to advance the empirical and theoretical knowledge on forms of labor resistance in the production of fresh fruits and vegetables for international markets. These studies point out two different types of labor protests. One type is small-scale, everyday forms of resistance by which workers seek to cope with and push back against the intensification of labor imposed by structural changes in the industry. In Great

Britain, for example, Rogaly (2008, 504–6) has documented the rise of workers' resentment of the piece-rate system that has undermined their ability to earn incomes beyond the minimum wage. Likewise, in Mexico, Lara Flores and Sánchez Saldaña (2015, 84) identify "spaces that denote workers' resistance" to the competitive labor environment of tomato production in Sinaloa. They argue that farm laborers' complaints are the product of perceived inequalities in work assignments by their employers and mayordomos. Workers' protests are not aimed at the companies but rather at other workers because of the competitive nature of the labor market, thus serving "to reinforce [managerial] labor control" (Lara Flores and Sánchez Saldaña 2015, 90). The second type of labor resistance is what Alonso-Fradejas (2015, 504–5) calls "structured forms." In an ethnographic study of sugarcane and oil palm indigenous Q'eqchi' workers in Guatemala's lowlands, he shows that in addition to traditional defensive strategies such as walk-offs to protest low wages, they engage in "offensive strategies" to increase wages and "de-flexibilize labor arrangements." While incipient, this body of literature indicates that along with the transformation of methods of production and management, old and new forms of labor resistance have also surfaced in the fresh-produce industry.

In dialogue with this literature, this chapter examines the resistance strategies and labor protests farmworkers in San Quintín have developed. My goal is to map out and analyze the different types of resistance I found in the field that farmworkers use to confront abuses by their employers. While in many cases workers sought to negotiate, contest, or repudiate the increased workload and redefine their piece rates, on other occasions they rejected the rigid rules that have lengthened their workday and the heightened pressure to work faster to meet quality standards. First, I discuss work stoppages as a strategy farmworkers use to negotiate a reduction in their workload. Then I analyze a less common but strategically important form of labor contestation in which workers sue their employers, which I show represents a more structured form of resistance, as well as the case of workers who leave agriculture to work in other sectors. Next, I explain the role of government-controlled unions that favor growers' interests and the response by indigenous leaders like Justino Herrera to channel and voice workers' labor and civil rights demands. In the last section, I depict the labor strike of 2015, discussing its goals, organizational strategies, and the outcomes it produced over the next years. These varied individual and collective forms of labor resistance, I contend, speak to farmworkers' political agency as they respond to the intensification of labor shaped by the restructuring of industrial capitalist agriculture and the struggle for economic and social justice in the region.

WORK STOPPAGES

One of the most common ways in which farmworkers in San Quintín have traditionally coped with the intensification of labor is by engaging in *plantones,* short and company-specific work stoppages. This is in response to what workers in the region commonly call *carrilla,* a folk term that refers to the pressure to work fast, often under intense surveillance by mayordomos and supervisors to meet the work quotas established by the piece-rate system. As an idiom, "carrilla" conveys the feeling of being pushed to the limit and is thus associated with the physical drudgery of having to work fast, often without any rest periods or breaks. In this context, fieldworkers often engage in plantones and localized labor strikes to negotiate for higher wages, a reduction in the workload, or both. Usually workers engage in sporadic mobilizations to demand higher wages, fewer furrows per work task, or permission to go home after concluding their tasks. Celeste Hernández, for example, explained that when she returned to work for Agrícola San Simón in 2006, the company assigned each worker six furrows per work task, well above the three furrows she was assigned the previous year. As a result, workers could not finish the task and ended up earning less than a day's wage. Taking advantage of the harvest season, workers pressed the company to negotiate a reduction in the workload. To that end, they used their labor contractor–mayordomo's support to negotiate on their behalf. As she recalled:

> No one in my crew could finish and earn the 105 pesos [about $9.20 at the time]; most people completed two or three furrows. Six furrows is too much work! Then we went to talk to our mayordomo, who in turn talked to the managers in the company to ask about reducing the number of furrows because it was too much work and most workers could only complete half [three furrows], earning 52 pesos [$4.50] for a whole day of work. Then they reduced the number of furrows to three per task, and, even so, we barely complete our tasks by 3:00 P.M. because each one has many plants.

The arbitrary nature of the piece-rate system and employers' ability to change it according to their needs appears to be a major motivator of worker protests. Because work crews are often composed of individuals from extended families or connected by kinship, ethnic, or neighborhood ties, work stoppages are facilitated by a sense of organic solidarity, which contributes to the internal solidarity of the group and avoids disagreements. Sudden changes in the piece rate often motivate work crews to react. Elisa Robles, who worked on and off for Seleccionadora de Legumbres for more than a decade, explained to me that the arbitrary increase in the workload in piecework and flat wages pushed her work crew to mobilize and confront their employer.

> Every year the company kept increasing the number of furrows per task, but our wages remained the same. Then one year we asked the owner, "Why do our wages never go up?" . . . We asked him to give us a raise because it had been many years that

we were earning 78 pesos a day [$6.80]; we told him that if we didn't get a raise we'd stop working. We talked to people in all work crews, and they conveyed the same demand to their mayordomos until they all agreed and went to talk to the grower.

Knowledge about labor rights is also an important factor that motivates workers to get involved in labor protests. Unlike migrant workers in labor camps, settled workers usually have more information, are more conscious about their labor rights, and are in a stronger position to demand higher wages and better working conditions (Lara Flores and Sánchez Saldaña 2015). Over time, they learn from different sources about basic labor rights, such as the obligation of their employers to register them in the Seguro Social while they are employed and the right to report their employers for labor violations and mayordomos who mistreat them. Even single mothers like Celeste Hernández, for whom losing her job involves a high economic cost, expressed her knowledge about some of her labor rights and eagerness to participate in plantones if she felt there were no other alternatives. Conversing with her about her position, she proudly told me that in contrast to when she first arrived in San Quintín—when she did not know anything about farmworkers' rights—after years of living and working in the region she was more informed and felt more motivated to act. Much of what she learned came from listening to Radio XEQUIN La Voz de la Valle (The Voice of the Valley), a small local radio station that has been broadcasting since the late 1980s. Part of a large transnational network of associated radio stations in rural areas in Mexico and the United States, Radio XEQUIN offers a variety of programs, in Spanish as well as Mixtec, Triqui, Zapotec, and other indigenous languages spoken in the region, that address issues relevant to the people in the area, including information about labor rights. Celeste emphasized how this knowledge had made her more secure about getting involved in labor protests, despite her fear of losing her job: "There're many of us here who are single mothers who need to work, who want to work. If we get fired it is a big blow, and because of fear sometimes we let them [employers] take advantage of us. But now it's different because there's much more information, for example, on the radio; thank God the radio provides a lot of information [about labor rights]. And now we sharpened our nails, so to speak, to fight back [laughs]; we can extend the fight longer. Before we couldn't; we were frightened."

Despite standing on firmer ground than migratory workers, however, settled farm laborers are still highly vulnerable when engaging in work stoppages and collective forms of labor protest. The reduction of production in open fields and new technologies have decreased the need for workers, undermining their power to negotiate. In a region characterized by enormous power disparities between large agribusiness and poorly paid farm laborers, even participating in short-term work stoppages and brief labor strikes can entail a significant risk of losing their jobs and being blacklisted. Such responses by companies represent a form of retaliatory disciplining. One afternoon when I was visiting a group of Zapotec women at Elisa Robles's home who were chatting and eating after work, I asked them to talk about their experiences when involved in protests to demand higher wages. With no hesitation, Elena and Celeste answered that the threat of being fired was the most common response.

Celeste: There's some ranches where workers protest, but others won't let you and tell you, "If you want to work that's fine, if not just go." And since we need to work, what can we do?

Elisa: Or they [employers] threaten us and tell us, "Don't stir up other workers!"

Celeste: Exactly! For example, if you speak up at work then the company's mayordomo tells you the next day, "You know what? There isn't work for you here anymore," or the company's bus just doesn't come to pick you up anymore. That's why people are afraid, especially now that there isn't much work; they really take advantage of us, a lot.

Elisa: Employers and mayordomos react immediately when we protest or try to negotiate for higher wages.

These comments were similar to those I heard from other workers who participated in labor protests and, as a result, confronted open retaliation by their employers. Companies and growers routinely deploy retaliatory disciplining to suppress collective expression of labor resistance, a central form of management control in the horticultural industry.

LITIGATION AS FORMAL RESISTANCE

Work stoppages and short-term labor strikes are not the only ways in which farmworkers resist the intensification of labor. After years of living and working in the region and gaining knowledge about political and legal resources, some workers are willing to take a step further and engage in more formal types of labor contestation. While in the field, I learned about workers who sued their employers for labor violations. Sometimes they would bring their grievances to the Subsecretaría del Trabajo, a state government office overseeing labor disputes in the region. On other occasions they complained to a local state office of human rights, hoping government officials would mediate on their behalf. Less frequently, they hired a lawyer to litigate when they were fired for participating in labor protests or were not paid by their employers.

One such case involved a group of workers employed by Seleccionadora de Legumbres who in 2009 hired a *licenciado* (lawyer) to sue the company for improperly firing them after they mobilized for higher wages. Nicolás Robles, Elisa's husband, was at the center of this dispute and became engulfed in a legal battle that many Zapotec neighbors in Colonia Arbolitos still remembered many years later. According to Nicolás, it all started when a few workers protested after the company unilaterally increased the number of furrows to complete a piece rate. In response, several crews decided to confront the patrón to reduce the workload. As he recalled, this approach produced good results, at first.

> The ranch was paying very low wages and kept increasing the number of furrows to complete a task. One day the workers of five crews [cuadrillas] asked to talk to the company's general mayordomo to reduce our workload so we could earn at least the equivalent of a day's wage, because it wasn't fair that we arrived home at 3:00 in the afternoon having earned only 30 or 40 pesos [$2.20 or $2.90].... The next day the company's administrator arrived around 10:00 A.M., and we told him that just as the company was increasing the number of furrows, it should also raise our wages because the furrows were going up and our wages were staying flat. He responded that he'd talk to the patrón and see what he could do. The next day the patrón came and we arrived at an agreement with him; he agreed to raise our wages.

This initial victory, however, was later complicated when one of Seleccionadora's main labor managers got the names of the leaders who initiated the protest and blacklisted them. Shortly after, Nicolás said, the company began firing the leaders of the mobilization, including him and the mayordomo of his crew. Upset by the turn of events, two days later Nicolás and his coworkers decided to go to the company's office to talk to the manager and ask him to rehire them. The meeting did not go well. The manager dismissed them contemptuously. "Don't bother me; there isn't more work for you. Do what you want and go protest wherever you want," Nicolás recalled him saying. Angered by his response and dismissive attitude, the fired work crew decided to file a complaint with the local office of the Procurador de Derechos Humanos (Human Rights Ombudsman), which handles many labor discrimination cases against indigenous workers in the region. The human rights attorney promised to intervene and mediate on the workers' behalf, and, as a result, the company sent a lawyer to negotiate with them. The meeting, however, fell well below the workers' expectations. Nicolás thought it was a *burla* (mockery). Retelling what happened at that meeting and the bad feelings it elicited among the workers, he said:

> Given that the manager had already fired us, we asked the licenciado to get us our retirement funds. I had been working for this company twelve years and another worker had fifteen years of seniority, so we have the right to collect our pension. The lawyer responded, "It's fine, I'll get you your pension." "How much will we receive?," we asked him, and he said we would each get 700 pesos [$52.20]. "What?," I asked him, "not even 1,000 pesos for all these years we've been working here? Keep your 700 pesos and we'll see what to do next."

Unlike "everyday forms" of labor resistance, litigation sometimes delivered better results. After that failed meeting the case slowly unfolded, producing an outcome that surpassed Nicolás's expectations. Unable to negotiate with the company's lawyer, the workers decided to hire their own lawyer to fight for their pension. On advice from their former mayordomo, they hired a labor lawyer from Ensenada, the largest city close to the San Quintín Valley, because, Nicolás told me, the few labor lawyers in the region had a bad reputation as *vendidos* (sellouts) who often accepted bribes from the growers. The lawyer in Ensenada met with them and prepared the lawsuit, but they had to wait eighteen months before the case was adjudicated. Unable to find a job as a farmworker, Nicolás began working part-time in the mornings as a helper in a small carpentry store run by his brother in-law. In October 2009, a judge finally ruled on the case: Seleccionadora was ordered to pay a pension to the group of workers who had brought the suit. Of the twenty-five workers who made up his crew, however, only nine had joined the lawsuit and continued the legal battle through to the end; the rest found jobs in other companies. For Nicolás, who fought this legal battle to the end, this was a major victory despite "the high fees" they had to pay to the attorney. With pride in his voice he explained the outcome of this labor dispute: "We won the case; at the end the company paid us! For us the settlement was significant. Each of us [nine workers] got 100,000 pesos [$7,462], our lawyer took 40,000 [$2,985] from each of us, so we ended up with 60,000 pesos [$4,477] each. . . . [Afterward] the company blacklisted us and sent our names to other companies, but it didn't last long."

As a vehicle of labor resistance, litigation reveals the advantages and limitations of more formal types of labor contestation. Because of its costs, risks, and long duration, litigation is not a common path field workers can afford to follow. Though a rare victory, however, the case of Nicolás and his coworkers indicates the opportunities settlement opens up for some farmworkers. Despite growers' traditional practice of treating farm laborers as temporary workers regardless of how long they employed them, they were able to win a pension because they could demonstrate they had worked for Seleccionadora longer than a decade. But Nicolás could not have won this battle without the help of his family. As it became clear when he told me this story, having their own home and the financial support of his wife while he was out of work was critical to withstanding the long time it took this lawsuit to be resolved. This shows that, with time, settled workers develop economic and social means of resilience that can enable them to deploy more formal, challenging, and effective forms of labor resistance.

SILENT RESISTANCE: LEAVING FARMWORK

While some workers seek to contest the exertion, arbitrariness, and mistreatment endured in farmwork, others follow a silent strategy: leaving farm labor and finding employment in better-paid and more dignified jobs. Population growth in San Quintín has enabled the rise of employment opportunities outside agriculture, leading to a more diversified local market economy. Service jobs, in particular, are occupied by one-third of the employed population and have experienced significant growth since the 1990s, after the massive settlement of thousands of farmworkers and families in the region. The service sector, however, comprises mostly low-paid jobs in retail, restaurants, small food establishments, and personal services, many of which operate in the informal economy (Velasco, Zlolniski, and Coubes 2014, 104). While such jobs offer low and often fluctuating wages, many farm laborers I met, especially women, preferred them over farm labor because they are less physically demanding, involve less carrilla and pressure, and allow them to escape the abuse and humiliation of their mayordomos, most of whom are men.

The case of Justina Sánchez, a resident of Colonia Santa Fe who I first met in 2006, shows the goals, challenges, and perseverance it takes for farm laborers in San Quintín to escape economic dependency on wage work in commercial agriculture. When I met her, Justina worked as a farm laborer during the day and ran a small food store from a room in her home in the evenings. During my numerous visits to her store, she spoke about her life history and the reasons that compelled her to open a food store. Born in 1966 in a small rural village in the district of Silacayoapan in Oaxaca, Justina was the third of ten siblings. She left school in her early teens to help her father, a farmworker who periodically migrated to work in Veracruz, Sinaloa, Chiapas, and occasionally the United States. At eighteen years old, she married and left her hometown to go with her husband to work in the tomato industry in Sinaloa. Two years later, in 1986, they arrived in San Quintín and rented a room in a *cuartería*, a dormitory with common bathrooms built to house seasonal workers, where she stayed for five years and where their two children were born. Shortly after, her husband went to the United States to work and send money to her, but after a few years he abandoned her. At that point, she sent her children to her parents in her hometown while she worked as a migrant farm laborer in San Quintín and Sinaloa and occasionally in California as an undocumented worker, returning every year to visit her children in Oaxaca. In 1996, she married her second husband, at which point she returned to San Quintín with her children and lived in a small house in Colonia Santa Fe. Her second marriage, however, did not turn out well, because, as Justina explained to me, her husband was a heavy drinker, had other women, and hardly contributed any money to the family expenses. Because of that, she had to work longer hours in the field. During the strawberry season, between March and May, she worked twelve hours a day making about 900 pesos a day ($78.90 at the time); in the summer when work declined, she worked six to eight hours earning about 400 pesos a day ($35.00); and the rest of the year, especially in winter, she only had work three to four days a week, making 90 pesos a day ($7.80).

After many years as a farmworker, Justina decided to open a small food store at home. As she explained to me, she just wanted to leave agriculture and escape the "humiliations endured for years in the field." She started in 1999 with 5,000 pesos ($438) she had saved on her own, and a few years later, with the support of the Fondo Regional para el Desarrollo de los Grupos Étnicos—a government program that helps low-income indigenous workers to start their own businesses—she received a grant of 12,000 pesos ($1,052) to buy merchandise for her business. She angrily recalled what led her to open her store: "I wanted to have my own business so that no one would boss me, because I was humiliated for nineteen years working in the fields. . . . That's why I told myself, 'I want to have my own business so nobody will scold me anymore.'"

While it provided some economic respite, the income from her store was not sufficient to maintain her family and she had no option but to continue working as a farm laborer. To combine both occupations, she readjusted her schedule working in the field from 7:00 A.M. to 2:00 P.M. and tended her store between 3:00 P.M. and 9:00 P.M. During summer vacation, her teenaged daughter ran the store in the mornings while Justina was at work. In 2006, she finally left her husband, which brought her major relief but also left her with the sole responsibility of providing for her two teenaged children who were still in school. Later that year she began having health problems, with pain in her ankles and legs, which she attributed to the long years of working as a strawberry picker bending her knees all day. Unable to work, she sought help from her employer, Felipe Ruiz-Esparza, an old-time grower who owns Rancho Seco, a midsized company that grows tomatoes as well as strawberries for Driscoll's. Justina asked for his help to pay her medical bills, but he declined, instead telling Justina that "strawberry workers make good money" and that she should cover the cost of the treatments on her own. By 2007, her pain was so acute that Justina had to undergo surgery on both legs and gave up working in the fields. With a mixture of sadness and anger, Justina explained to me in her store why she promised herself to work full-time in her business.

> Because of the problems with my legs, my meniscuses broke, and I lost all strength in my legs and I'd often fall down at work, so they didn't want to employ me anymore. . . . [Besides,] I didn't have a husband to help me and my children were studying in school. My employer told me, "You know what? You can't work anymore; you fall down twice or three times in the field. There isn't anything we can do for you." Like telling me, "You are useless." . . . They [company] were more concerned about losing the damaged berries than about my health. I felt bad and if I wanted to fight for my rights as a worker I'd lose because I did not have any use value for my patrón any longer. . . . I couldn't work and decided to devote myself to my small food store.

Justina's forced "retirement" from farm labor changed her life, illuminating the role that self-employment plays as a space for labor resistance. No longer able to work in the fields, she focused on running her food store and trying to grow it.

FIGURE 14. Justina Sánchez's tiendita in Colonia Santa Fe.

Every summer I visited her, I noticed the slow but steady progress of her business. It was furnished with cookies, fruits, vegetables, milk, water, canned goods, and other everyday items residents in the colonia buy. She sells to neighbors, most of them farmworkers, who buy on credit and pay her back, usually at the end of the week when they receive their paychecks. Based on trust, this informal credit system gives farmworkers access to basic goods when they lack cash while creating a stable and loyal clientele for her store. Comparing the work of running her food store with her previous employment in the field, Justina pointed out several advantages. These included the comfort of working from home, the flexibility to combine it with her household chores, the ability to control her own time, and the opportunity to grow her business. As she put it, "I am much better here because I can eat at home every day and keep my house clean; I have everything I need here. It doesn't matter how much money I make. I never run the numbers to see how much I earned, and I reinvest most of the earnings in the business. Don't you see that my store has many more items than before?"

While having a source of income other than wage work was important, for Justina leaving work in agriculture was a conscious decision and an open expression of repudiation of the exploitation and humiliation she endured over decades of work as a jornalera, even if her business did not generate much money. In a labor market where indigenous women are relegated to the most labor-intensive and poorly paid jobs in agriculture, small family businesses offer an attractive alternative.[1] Working in their own businesses provides them with a refuge that shields them from the abuses and discrimination and serves as a "pension plan" when, because of their age and/or health, they are "retired" by their employers without pensions.[2] Self-employment in informal occupations constitutes what Sergio Schneider and Paulo Niederle (2010, 381–82) call "resistance and diversification strategies" by which farmworkers confront the pressure of the labor regime in the agrofood industry and seek to preserve their autonomy. The last time I saw Justina, in July 2017, she told me that her two children had married and moved out of her home. She proudly commented that her store had grown bigger than last time I saw it and had many more items for sale.

WHITE UNIONS AND THE POLITICS OF ACCOMMODATION

The diversity of individual and collective forms of resistance by which farmworkers confront the effects of the labor regime in agriculture is largely the result of the absence of credible labor unions to defend and represent them. In the mid-1980s, when export agriculture was rapidly growing, the first unions were formed to negotiate wages and labor benefits with growers and the associations representing agribusiness in the region. These are what in Mexico are known as *sindicatos patronales* or *sindicatos charros,* namely, white unions that sign collective bargaining agreements, or "protection contracts," with employers without the knowledge of or consultation with the workers they represent.[3] Protection contracts generally represent the interests of the employers and the government, seeking to ensure a political climate of "social stability" and prevent the formation of independent unions that can cause labor and social unrest (Zlolniski 2017, 2018). In San Quintín, the largest union for farm laborers is the Confederación de Trabajadores Mexicanos (CTM; Confederation of Mexican Workers), originally founded in Mexico in 1936 as one of the pillars of the political structure of the PRI. The second is the Confederación Regional Obrera Mexicana (CROM; Regional Confederation of Mexican Workers), and the third and comparatively smaller union is the Confederación Revolucionaria de Obreros Campesinos (CROC; Revolutionary Confederation of Farmworkers). Historically, these labor unions have controlled the majority of labor contracts and blocked any attempts by independent unions to set foot in the region. The CTM and CROM sign protection contracts every two years with the two main growers' associations in the region, the Unión Agrícola and the Consejo Agrícola.

Not surprisingly, when I arrived in San Quintín, the CTM and CROM had a public image as corrupt unions that signed contracts with growers in backroom deals and collected bribes from companies to keep workers quiet. In 1984, the CTM had signed the first collective contract in a move promoted by growers and the government to prevent the formation of an independent union to represent farm laborers. Following a typical procedure by the political party in power, the PRI, local growers pressed the government to prevent any workers' protests that could jeopardize agricultural production. As a result, the Unión Agrícola decided to sign the first collective contract with the CTM led by its delegate in Baja, Jesús Espinoza. The first time I went to visit with Jesús Espinoza in June 2005, more than twenty years after he signed the first collective contract, he was still the president of the union. Waiting in my car before entering the CTM's office, located in the town of Lázaro Cárdenas, I saw a large black sedan pull up and park in front of the office. It was driven by Espinoza. The image of his ostentatious official automobile in the midst of the dusty, muddy roads and the humble, rundown cars of the few workers who could afford a vehicle surprised me.

When a week later, after making an appointment with his secretary, I returned to talk to him, Espinoza disdainfully directed me to sit in a chair in the lobby and asked me to proceed with my questions. He appeared suspicious and uncomfortable talking with outsiders, an attitude similar to that of some old-time growers who openly professed a dislike for "outsiders." Uncomfortable myself, I proceeded with some of the questions I had prepared, starting with the history of the union in the region. With a mix of arrogance and pride, Espinoza stated that the CTM was the "first union for farmworkers in Baja," arriving at a time when neither the Secretaría del Trabajo (Secretariat of Labor) nor the Junta de Conciliación y Arbitraje (Council of Conciliation and Arbitration) was present in the valley.[4] At the time, he added, the farmworkers' major problems were working long hours and on weekends, not having health insurance, and the dangerous conditions in which they were transported to the fields. Rather than being confrontational, Espinoza reiterated, the union espoused a conciliatory approach to avoid labor protests and preserve the "social peace" in the region. Casting it as a "socially responsible" policy, he emphasized that the union used "dialogue with growers" to address labor conflicts, emphasizing the role of negotiation to avoid companies leaving the region and with the paramount goal of "protecting workers' jobs." The CTM's approach, he continued, distinguished it from the "irresponsible" behavior of independent leaders and organizations. During work stoppages and episodes of labor unrest, Espinoza explained, the union intervened to mediate and find a solution: "We approach the companies to talk to them and make a compromise to avoid a work stoppage and strike, collective protests and all kind of mobilizations that could jeopardize the social peace in San Quintín. . . . We must preserve our job sources and take care of the companies that provide these jobs, not eliminate them."

The CTM's accommodative approach to the needs of growers also implied that it identified the state government in Baja as the source of many labor problems farmworkers confront. Traditionally aligned with the ruling PRI party at the national level, in Baja the union found itself in opposition to the state government when the right-wing National Action Party came to power in 1989. Regarding, for instance, the intense opposition from growers to register their workers in the Seguro Social, Espinoza blamed the state government for the poor health infrastructure and services rendered by the IMSS.[5] This, he argued, explained the little interest that both companies and workers showed in enrolling in the system. Espinoza also blamed workers themselves for many of their health problems. Reflecting a common view shared by many of the growers, he commented that indigenous "migrant workers' culture" prevented them from understanding and following the safety norms and protocols companies had established in the workplace. "The problem originates in their place of origin and travels here," he observed, referring to the issue of child labor in agriculture.

The leader of the CTM also portrayed the efforts of independent organizations and indigenous leaders as illegitimate and counterproductive to "workers' interests." He claimed those leaders were "agitators" who by inciting workers' protests put in jeopardy their jobs and livelihood. Independent attempts to organize workers around labor demands, he argued, were the product of "irresponsible" actors with a "personal political agenda" who did not care about whether farm laborers kept their jobs. Explaining his position, he stated, "Here growers in the 1980s and 1990s suffered deplorable labor strikes organized by subversive organizations that thought that stopping companies' production would solve [workers'] problems, but it was only a radical politics of disorder."

Espinoza's view reflects the dominant discourse by white unions in San Quintín, which seek to preserve the status quo and maintain the monopoly on representation of farmworkers in collective contracts with growers. This political discourse identifies the government and indigenous workers' culture as the root of many labor and social problems farmworkers confront, a position that closely resembles that espoused by growers. Historically these unions have opposed the organization of collective forms of resistance by workers, casting a negative image of independent leaders and organizations who showed support for labor protests in the region.

INDEPENDENT UNIONS AND VIOLENT REPRESSION

Despite the collusion between white unions and the government, there were efforts by independent unions to organize farmworkers in San Quintín. This was the case of the Central Independiente de Obreros Agrícolas y Campesinos (CIOAC), a national independent union founded in 1975 in the state of Sinaloa—Mexico's largest export agriculture region—to organize migrant farmworkers (Velasco 2005). The CIOAC first started operating in Baja in 1984 to protest the crowded and unsanitary conditions in which indigenous farmworkers were housed in labor camps. To block this attempt and pressured by local growers, the Mexican government denied the CIOAC permission to register as a labor union, instead conceding to the CTM the rights to be the first union to represent farmworkers in the region. Despite its lack of legal recognition, the CIOAC established a local chapter to protest the conditions of migrant workers in labor camps such as that operated by A.B.C. Farm in the mid-1980s. In the 1990s, when many workers moved to colonias, it shifted its focus to organize residents to demand the provision of basic services such as water, electricity and education in their new communities (Martínez Novo 2006). It also focused on labor demands, helping to organize strikes and work stoppages, blocking the highway to stop trucks exporting crops to the United States, and occupying local government offices to bring public visibility to workers' grievances (Velasco 2005).

Yet from the beginning the CIOAC confronted major challenges from the local power structure. When it was first founded, the federal and state governments had a weak presence in the region, leaving farmworkers at the mercy of employers who often used guardias blancas for repression, blacklisting, and violence against leaders who organized labor mobilizations. One such episode was the murder in 1987 of Maclovio Rojas, a twenty-four-year-old charismatic Mixtec leader of the CIOAC who was killed a few months after becoming head of the organization. Two years earlier Rojas had published an open letter in ZETA, a weekly publication with wide circulation in Baja California, denouncing the labor exploitation and abject poverty of farmworkers in San Quintín (Velasco, Zlolniski, and Coubes 2014, 243). His death dramatically illustrated the determination by powerful barons in the region to use violence to quash any attempts at labor mobilizations by independent unions.[6] Later in the 1990s, the CIOAC began focusing on community demands by farmworkers, merchants, and other workers in the colonias, including the Triquis of Colonia Maclovio Rojas, named to honor the memory of the killed leader.

In the early 2000s, however, after the right-wing PAN won control of the national government, the CIOAC began a period of rapid decline. Its leader, Julio César Alonso, blamed the PAN for confiscating the properties the CIOAC rented in Colonia Maclovio Rojas that financed the organization. It also accused the new government of jailing Beatriz Chávez, a pioneering charismatic female leader of farmworkers. When I met Julio César Alonso in 2005, the CIOAC headquarters that once flourished with activities was reduced to a single room with a desk, four chairs, and a desk lamp, with no phone line and a leaking roof. He accused the PAN for being a "corrupt and racist government" and for using the courts to prosecute civic and labor organizations. "This government seeks to disintegrate, disarticulate, and disappear social and labor organizations," he complained, denouncing the PAN's harsh approach and "lack of disposition to dialogue." He also denounced growers who, despite the large number of settled farmworkers, still recruited migrant laborers in the spring and summer growing season to saturate the labor supply and decrease wages. The death of Julio César Alonso in 2009 accelerated the decline of this organization, but his pioneering work helped pave the way for the emergence of a new independent labor union with the farmworkers strike in 2015.

INDIGENOUS LEADERS AND ETHNIC ORGANIZATIONS

The failure of white unions to respond to farmworkers' concerns and the problems confronted by independent organizations like the CIOAC created spaces for alternative forms of labor and political representation. Over time, several indigenous organizations emerged to give a voice to farmworkers, who had been excluded from the labor and political scene despite their rapid demographic growth since the 1980s. These are pan-ethnic organizations that combine labor, civil, and political demands to address farmworkers' needs not only as workers but as residents in the region as well. Some of the most notable organizations are the Frente Indigena de Organizaciones Binacionales (FIOB; Front of Indigenous Binational Organizations) and the Movimiento de Unificación de Jornaleros Independientes (MUJI; Movement for the Unification of Independent Day Laborers), which throughout the years changed their names but remained a fixture in the region's political landscape. Unlike labor unions, indigenous organizations are transnational in nature, encompassing leaders in numerous rural communities in Mexico and the United States with a sizable number of farmworkers. Chapters of these organizations are found especially in California, Oregon, and Washington, where many Baja farmworkers have kin and friends from their hometowns in Oaxaca.[7] In San Quintín, the leaders of these organizations have taken on the labor demands by farmworkers such as the refusal of growers to register them in the Seguro Social, abuses and mistreatment by patrones and mayordomos, and the lack of benefits. Known simply as "leaders," they are individuals with public recognition in their communities who act as ethnic and political brokers with growers and government authorities at times of labor unrest and social conflict. As ethnic brokers, they also serve as conveyor belts for top-down government programs that target indigenous communities in the region, giving them the power and visibility needed to act as mediators (Velasco 2002).[8]

Justino Herrera, with a thick mustache, dark complexion, and penetrating eyes, is one of the most recognized and respected Mixtec leaders with a long history of mobilizing for labor demands in San Quintín. A former migrant farmworker and member of the CIOAC, Justino had participated in farmworkers' mobilizations in Sinaloa and Oregon. His brother, Bonfilio Herrera, was a legendary labor leader in San Quintín who organized some of the most important workers' mobilizations in the mid-1990s to demand that the state government construct a hospital for indigenous residents in the region.[9] Following in his footsteps, Justino has been since 1998 among a group of indigenous labor leaders mobilizing for agricultural companies to register their workers in the IMSS after the Mexican Congress approved new legislation for health insurance for farm laborers. He developed a reputation for independence, openly denouncing the labor abuses of growers in the valley and the complicity of the state government. Later, in 2010, with the support of residents in the town of Vicente Guerrero, he was elected government officer to deal with community affairs and improve public services in the locality and surrounding colonias. His passion is to raise public awareness about the labor abuses farmworkers confront in San Quintín and push growers and the state government to address them. When I first visited with him in summer 2011 in his office at the San Vicente Guerrero town hall, Justino identified the sindicatos patronales as a major reason growers did not respect farmworkers' labor rights.

> Unfortunately, there isn't a labor contract as such or a real labor union to defend workers' rights because the CTM we have here is a "[sindicato] patronal." . . . In the CTM we have Jesús Espinoza, . . . but he is useless; he's only there to receive the money the companies pay him. He claims to be the legal representative of farmworkers when to be one he should meet with them as the labor law stipulates. . . . But this doesn't occur and he just signs the collective contracts without workers' knowledge.

To Justino, the lack of true union representation is the central reason for the persistent violation of farmworkers' rights that historically has predominated in the region. At the base of this problem, he explained, was the "shameless complicity" between growers, government officials, and white unions like the CTM and CROM. Denouncing the common violations of the labor law that regularly take place, he commented, "No farmworker receives paid vacation, even if he has been working twenty years for the same company. They don't receive a Christmas bonus or windfall profits as the law mandates. Access to health care is the most important thing for a farmworker because if he isn't healthy and is not treated, how on earth is he going to work? When a farmworker is unprotected, all the members of his family are unprotected too."

Justino also blamed state officials for ignoring these problems and constructing a "false narrative" of social peace in the valley. This, he added, was "a facade" to conceal the subterranean flow of discontent, frustration, and anger that many workers felt. Scolding the government and local media for looking the other way, he predicted that sooner or later, the underlying labor and social discontent would explode and cause a major public uproar, as expressed in the epigraph to this chapter. At the time, I thought he was overstating his case and that a major labor strike was unlikely anytime soon. More focused on their mobilizing to improve living conditions in their communities, I did not envision farmworkers rising up in a major revolt that could jeopardize their jobs. Moreover, while ethnic leaders like Justino had public recogni-

FIGURE 15. Justino Herrera, a longtime labor and community leader at his home in July 2017.

tion, the strong alignment between the growers' associations and unions like the CTM and CROM conferred hegemonic power on growers, who ruled with an iron fist. Time, however, proved me wrong: four years later the undercurrent of workers' discontent Justino had identified exploded into the largest and most powerful labor strike in the modern history of the region, revealing the limitations of the power structure horticultural companies had built over time.

THE LABOR STRIKE OF 2015

On March 17, 2015, several thousand farm laborers mobilized a massive strike in the San Quintín Valley. They marched to demand higher wages, registration in the national health system, and an end to the abuse and sexual harassment of female field workers by mayordomos and field supervisors. They also denounced the sindicatos charros that for decades dominated the in region and demanded the right to form an independent labor union. Lasting about twelve weeks, the strike took growers, government authorities, and the media by surprise with its wide scope, encompassing the whole valley, and workers' resolve to stay away from work until their demands were met. State and municipal government authorities responded harshly, using rubber bullets and tear gas to disband the protests and reopen the Trans-Peninsular Highway, which workers had blocked to prevent agricultural companies from shipping produce to the Tijuana–San Ysidro port of entry. More than a dozen leaders and participants in the protests were jailed, many were injured, and police even entered homes in two colonias where many Triqui families lived to repress the movement and detain some of its leaders.

Martín Fernández was among the many workers who showed up at the town hall in San Quintín to support the leaders negotiating with growers and government authorities to end the strike. Because the main road was blocked, he rode his bicycle from his home in Colonia Arbolitos on side roads for about eight miles. After arriving, he joined a large crowd standing in front of the town hall awaiting the results of the leaders' negotiations, surrounded by the police and the military who had come to "prevent any violence." At some point, he recalled, someone in the crowd began throwing stones to protest the intimidating police presence; in response, the police started to shoot rubber bullets into the crowd. Alarmed, people began running in different directions. Martín jumped on his bike and began pedaling as fast as he could to avoid being hit. Instead of using the road, he went under the dry stream bridge so the police would not see him, then took a trail through the fields to avoid the roads, which were heavily guarded. Until then he had never participated in a labor protest in San Quintín, yet this time he joined the strike because he wanted to support the leaders' demand for higher wages for farmworkers like him. He was not alone in this endeavor; residents of Colonia Arbolitos, he told me, had been organizing for several days to support the strike by collecting donations of money, food, water, and sodas and sending them to the people congregated at the town hall. Martín joined an eight-member committee formed in his colonia to coordinate the donations and gather support for the strike. Going home by home, they knocked on their neighbors' doors to persuade them not to go to work and "support the strike because it was for the benefit of all workers." Many residents gave donations in kind but stayed home rather than participate in street protests "because they were afraid of being hit by the police if they went to gather in front of the government office." As the strike continued for several weeks, however, some divisions began to emerge. While some residents continued to support the strike, others wanted to go back to work because they did not have anything to eat, and the local stores had run out of food, water, gas, and other basic items. Despite the hardships, Martín continued to be involved until the end. In his view, supporting the strike was worth the effort and risk: "It led to a raise in our wages from 120 pesos a day to 200, although some companies are paying 180 pesos," he said.

Unlike previous labor mobilizations, the strike was organized by a new organization called the Alianza de Organizaciones Nacional, Estatal y Municipal por la Justicia Social (Alliance of National, State, and Municipal Organizations for Social Justice). This was a new coalition composed of old-time labor leaders, including former members of the CIOAC, and new ones banded together to denounce farmworkers' exploitation and their systematic exclusion from basic labor rights. The strike started after several leaders of the Alianza sent a letter to the governor of Baja California, Francisco Vega de Lamadrid, to meet and discuss the grievances of farmworkers in San Quintín. Not receiving a response, they called for a wide regional strike, contacting members and sympathizers in colonias throughout the valley. From the beginning, the Alianza took an innovative approach to gathering support for its cause. When in the past labor protests erupted, both growers and government officials tried to contain the conflict by regionalizing it. This time the Alianza leaders sought to avoid being cornered into a regional political context in which it had little political power and instead developed a concerted strategy to gain national and international attention. To that end, they organized a march to the international Tijuana–San Ysidro border to gather support in the United States, coordinating with transnational indigenous organizations in California to promote their demands in international public forums and media. The strategy succeeded, and, unlike earlier and smaller labor protests, this time the strike galvanized attention and support from wide social sectors in Mexico and was prominently featured in the national and international press, especially in the United States (see, e.g., Marosi 2015; Domínguez 2015).

The novel transnational approach and robust support from indigenous ethnic organizations across the Mexico-U.S. border delivered some tangible results that earlier labor mobilizations had not accomplished. With the crops unharvested, the Trans-Peninsular Highway blocked, and workers organized in local colonia committees to support the mobilization, the largest companies and growers agreed to negotiate with the Alianza to avoid further financial hemorrhaging. Federal and state authorities intervened to serve as "intermediaries" at the negotiating table. The Alianza presented a pliego petitorio to be met to get workers back to work. After intense negotiations, an accord was signed in June 2015. The agreement contained fifteen resolutions complying with those demands, including a wage increase, overtime pay, the registration of farmworkers in the Mexican social security system as either temporary or full-time employees, and labor benefits such as a Christmas bonus. The accord also revoked the reviled collective contracts signed by the CTM and CROM and established a compromise by the government to invest in social programs for the local population. As a result of the arduous and lengthy negotiation that took place in Baja and Mexico City, wages increased from an average of 120 pesos to 280 pesos ($18) a day, the largest raise in decades although still insufficient to cover the subsistence costs of farmworkers. Large companies that in the past refused to register their workers in the IMSS finally began complying, putting pressure on other companies to follow suit. Equally significant, the leaders of the Alianza also demanded the right to organize and form independent unions to end the long-standing collusion between growers and state-controlled white unions, which they argued was at the heart of farmworkers' labor and political disfranchisement. As a result, only a few months after the agreement was signed, two new independent labor unions were formed. One, the Sindicato Nacional Independiente de Jornaleros Agrícolas y Similares (National Independent Sindicate of Agricultural and Related Workers), was founded by Justino Herrera and a group of collaborators in November 2015 after breaking away from the Alianza. The other, the Sindicato Independiente Nacional y Democrático de Jornaleros Agrícolas (SINDJA; National and Independent Sindicate of Agricultural Workers), was founded in January 2016 with the support of the Alianza. The birth of two independent unions was a significant victory and watershed moment in the troubled labor history of the region that since the 1980s had been dominated by the CTM and CROM.

The push for independent labor unions exposed the cultural and political transformation experienced by indigenous laborers in the region. The tapestry of indigenous organizations and the organizational support union leaders received from the colonias' local committees are key components of this transformation. The articulation of the labor movement with indigenous organizations with a history of mobilizing for labor and community demands was crucial to the success of the strike. This was particularly visible in the case of the Triquis, who, as mentioned before, had formed several organizations in the region. In January 1998, for example, Triqui workers founded the Frente Indígena de Lucha Triqui (FILT), an ethnic organization to negotiate with government authorities to deliver public services to the new colonia (Camargo 2014, 325). A few years later, in early 2000, Triqui residents decided to adapt three of their traditional political and religious institutions in Oaxaca to strengthen their internal cohesion and political representation in San Quintín.[10] The organizational experience of these and other ethnic organizations and their leaders provided significant support to the labor strike of 2015, one for which many paid a high price.

More significant was the strong interethnic grassroots support the strike received from the local committees of the colonias. The shift from the ethnically isolated labor camps that prevailed in the past to the more ethnically diverse and integrated colonias of the 1990s brought together farmworkers from different ethnic backgrounds and home communities, including mestizos, Mixtecs, Triquis, and Zapotecs. The diverse ethnic makeup of the population allowed a higher degree of interethnic cooperation and solidarity, highlighting the class-based demands they had as workers and community residents. In Colonia Santa Fe, for example, the committee included Mixtec leaders as well as mestizo women from Sinaloa and other regions who live in the colonia. Mobilizing the organizational structure residents had built over the years to improve living conditions, workers collected donations to support the leaders and supporters of the long strike. Esther Chávez, the main community leader and *promotora* (lay community worker) of several government aid programs for low-income residents such as Progresa and the DIF (National System for Integral Family Development), helped coordinate the efforts of many neighbors. Women prepared food, coffee, and beverages for the leaders when they traveled to Mexicali, Tijuana, and Ensenada and collected small donations of 10 or 20 pesos by going door-to-door. To hide her identity, Esther covered her head with a scarf because as the liaison between some government programs and residents in her community she "could be sanctioned by SEDESOL [Secretariat of Social Development] for supporting the strike." The long-lasting protests took a toll on local residents. "The stores ran out of goods, there was no gas, and we had to cook with wood outdoors for several days," Esther told me, recalling those days when workers struggled to buy food for their families. Ramón and Aurelia Suárez also supported the labor mobilization but lived in anguish while it lasted. "Estuvo muy feo [It was very ugly]," Ramón commented. "I had to kill several chickens so we could eat," Aurelia told me, explaining how her family survived after the local stores ran out of supplies. Like the residents of other colonias, Ramón and Aurelia supported the strike but did not get directly involved. "We supported the strike morally but didn't participate in the marches because we were afraid of police reprisals or that they would put us in jail," Aurelia explained, conveying the approach many other farmworkers took at the time.

Shortly after being formed, the new labor unions sought to break with the closed and top-down power structure of old white unions by establishing a more democratic, transparent, and inclusive constitutional framework. For example, in its foundational by-laws, SINDJA espoused an innovative approach to labor politics, stipulating that its leaders must be farmworkers to avoid the top-down political structure the PRI historically used to appoint state and regional delegates. The by-laws also established democratic election procedures and term limits to prevent them from staying in power indefinitely, as is the case of state-controlled white unions (Fregoso 2016). The infusion of new faces in the leadership of the Alianza contributed to bringing fresh air to labor organizing in the valley. Joining old-timers like Justino Herrera were new leaders like Fidel Sánchez Gabriel, a Mixtec farmworker with experience organizing tomato growers in Immokalee, Florida, who had been formerly affiliated with the CIOAC. Signing a new labor contract with an independent union, Fidel Sánchez argued, would open new opportunities for farmworkers to address not only labor grievances but also demands about housing and living conditions in local colonias. In a press interview shortly after the agreement was signed, he declared, "It opens up many opportunities because I know that the moment we sign a new collective labor contract with the [agricultural] companies, we will be able to integrate all the major demands, including labor benefits to which we are entitled by [Mexican] law. These include health benefits, housing, better wages, overtime, mandatory rest period, and many other benefits that can be integrated in the new agreement; it's a great opportunity for all farmworkers in the country" (Hoy 2016).

The labor mobilization created high expectations for the leaders and followers of the Alianza as well as for sympathizers of the farmworkers' cause in Mexico and the United States. The raising of wages and pressure on large companies to improve labor and working conditions brought the hope that it would create a political space for workers to negotiate the terms of their employment as represented by new and more democratic unions. The Alianza leaders also envisioned a labor movement that would surpass regional boundaries and include farmworkers employed in commercial agriculture in other regions in Mexico as well as in the United States. Capitalizing on its transnational connections after the strike was over, SINJDA developed formal collaboration with independent labor unions representing farmworkers in the United States. This is the case of the Familias Unidas por la Justicia (FUJ; Families United for Justice), an independent union formed in 2013 in the state of Washington after work stoppages and other labor protests organized by blueberry pickers against Sakuma Farms, which grows berries for Driscoll's. Many of the workers employed at this farm were Mixtecs and Triquis with relatives in San Quintín. In 2018, the leaders and committee members of both SINJDA and FUJ met in Washington to share their experiences of forming an independent union and mobilizing for higher wages and improved labor conditions.[11]

THE BACKLASH: THE POLITICS OF DIVISION AND RETALIATION

Although it delivered significant benefits, the strike of 2015 also generated a strong backlash from companies and their allied white unions. The aftermath of the labor strike and the formation of the new unions reveal the structural challenges that, as Sian Lazar (2017) argues, alternative forms of labor organizing face at a time when old labor unions and the established political structure begins to crumble. The difficulties the new unions confronted came from both external and internal sources. First, shortly after the strike ended, many growers retaliated by increasing the workload attached to work tasks and by using *listas negras* (blacklists) to punish workers who had openly supported it. Some companies asked their general mayordomos to check farm laborers returning to work and stop those who were regarded as "agitators." When Aurelia Suárez went back to her job, she learned that the requirements to complete a work task had been increased. "Although wages went up, the workload has increased," she told me with resignation, as if implying she was not surprised because growers had always had the upper hand. Likewise, when Elisa Robles returned to work she noticed that her employer asked workers to sign contracts for less than six months to avoid classifying them as "permanent workers" with full benefits and seniority. Although they can receive a sum for the time worked and a small retirement payment, she told me, they cannot accumulate seniority and are rehired as "new workers" when they go back to work. The old white unions also responded in order to maintain their turf and workers' contracts with the largest horticultural companies. The CTM and CROM began affiliating workers individually rather than as groups by companies as they had done in the past, to collect the largest number of signatures and win the legal right to represent them. Focusing on the largest employers and with their tacit support, delegates of the white unions collected workers' signatures when they received their paychecks at the end of the week, giving them a strategic advantage over the new unions, which were denied access to the ranches and companies.

Internal divisions and factionalism among the Alianza's leaders further contributed to weakening the new labor movement. Shortly after the strike ended, the Alianza, which amalgamated leaders from different indigenous organizations and colonias, began to fracture, revealing the enormous challenges that independent unions face in Mexico, where white unions have dominated since the 1930s. The first fracture occurred within a few months after the agreement with growers was signed, a period in which internal disagreements about political tactics and conflicting leadership styles led to the splitting of the Alianza into two separate unions. After the split, the two unions began to compete for members and public recognition, often seeking to delegitimize each other in the media and public opinion. Disagreement about political tactics and the course the labor movement should take also proved divisive. Justino Herrera, for example, resigned his post in the Sindicato Nacional Independiente de Jornaleros Agrícolas y Similares, disappointed about the course the union had taken under its *secretario general,* Enrique Alatorre, who he accused of undermining the democratic process they had agreed on to elect and renew the union's board on a regular basis. When I visited Justino at his house in the summer of 2017, he expressed his disappointment with several leaders of the Alianza for "putting their personal interests" ahead of the collective goal of fighting for the rights of farmworkers. "I am ashamed of talking about this because the workers' cause was betrayed," he told me, condemning the political fracturing that occurred in the next two years after the strike. Among the most contentious issues during and after the negotiations was the demand for higher wages. While at first the Alianza proposed a single wage increase for all workers, the final agreement signed with growers established three different wage levels—180, 165, and 150 pesos—depending on the size of the company and type of work, which Justino and other leaders rejected. The agreement also left intact the controversial *salario integrado* (blended salary) by which companies avoid paying windfall benefits and the *bono navideño* (Christmas bonus) to farmworkers by instead raising their weekly paychecks by a few pesos.

Moreover, despite higher wages and moderately better working conditions, the piece-rate system at the crux of the labor intensification in San Quintín's agroexport industry was left untouched. As Martín told me, thinking about the outcome of the strike, "While growers raised our wages, they also increased our workload," reflecting the feeling I heard from many other farmworkers who supported the labor mobilization. Moreover, while several of the largest companies were forced to register their workers in the Seguro Social, others, especially midsized companies and old-time growers, remained defiant and continued retaliating with increased production quotas attached to the piece-rate system. The external and internal pressures on the new unions significantly detracted from the high hopes with which they were born after the strike. By 2017, the two unions were only able to register a few hundred workers as members, struggling to gain traction with a precarious organizational structure and a small budget that made it difficult to grow.

Despite its limitations, the labor strike transformed the landscape of political power in San Quintín. For the first time, farm laborers forced the government and growers to sit at the table to negotiate face-to-face labor demands without the meddling of white unions. In the process, workers gained a renewed political awareness and were more willing to engage in open forms of labor contestation. The political strategy to focus the strike on large companies like Driscoll's with international brand recognition paid some dividends. The high visibility of this company captured the interest and support of sympathizers, facilitating the organization of a consumer boycott in the United States.[12] Caught in the public spotlight, Driscoll's was forced to increase wages and improve working conditions in San Quintín. In 2016, it joined Fair Trade USA to certify organic berries produced in Baja, using the price difference with conventional berries to fund community programs selected by a workers' committee, and later that year, it signed on to the Joint Committee on Responsible Labor Practices.[13] During lunch at a local restaurant in San Quintín with Henry Clark, he acknowledged that because of the strike the company was compelled "to do things better so our workers stand up for us next time there is a strike." In fact, unlike many old-time growers in the region who resented pressures to improve wages and labor benefits of farmworkers, Clark recognized the bad management practices of many companies and tried to improve conditions in BerryMex to set a good standard. While holding a more progressive view than many other growers, however, he nonetheless used workers' demands for services as an opportunity to deflect the blame of workers' poor living conditions to the government. He thus referred to the labor strike as a "social movement" of workers mobilizing for better community services that the government should provide, a political deflection traditional in the region that minimizes the role of agribusiness in workers' poor living conditions. "It's the lack of services in their communities, especially water, and many other deficiencies such as lack of garbage collection, unpaved streets, and the like," Henry stated. From this perspective, the government was to blame "for not doing its job," a political discourse traditional among many growers in the region.[14]

CONCLUSION: SOCIAL MOVEMENT UNIONISM AND ITS CHALLENGES

Despite its ubiquity and intensity, the labor regime of Baja's fresh-produce industry did not go uncontested. As I have shown, changes in the organization of production and new labor management methods opened new spaces for resistance and contestation by which workers sought to cope with the significant effects of labor intensification. These include a variety of everyday forms of resistance, from work stoppages and brief strikes to negotiate wages, piecework, and the length of the workday to more structured strategies such as litigation and lengthy strikes. In addition, self-employment and other forms of "pluriactivity" (Schneider and Niederle 2010) such as petty commerce, I have argued, not only serve as economic strategies to get ahead, but are also spaces farm laborers carve to cope with the exploitation of agricultural employment and to preserve a sense of individual dignity and respect. While seemingly unrelated, these varied forms of labor resistance are organically connected, fostering a synergistic interaction. Small-scale forms of labor organization and protest provide the building blocks, funds of knowledge, grievance language, resilience, and political experience that over time enable the organization of large and more structured labor strikes. Together, these individual and collective forms of labor resistance are a reflection of both farmworkers' political agency and the structural tensions and limits that the labor arrangements of export agriculture have engendered in Baja. In San Quintín, settlement provided workers with the economic, social, and political resources to progressively engage in more organized and forceful forms of labor protests that reveal their consolidation as a social class eager and ready to confront many of the labor abuses that for decades prevailed in the region.

Underlying most forms of labor resistance is a collective struggle to "de-flexibilize labor arrangements" that have become the norm in modern capitalist agriculture (Alonso-Fradejas 2015, 505). While shaped by historical and regional features, farmworkers' forms of resistance in San Quintín reflect the gamut of strategies that recent studies in the global fresh-produce industry have documented, whereby workers rebel against the piece-rate system and inequalities in work assignments that are at the heart of the workplace regime (Rogaly 2008; Lara Flores and Sánchez Saldaña 2015). Prompted by different circumstances and factors, these protests share what Wells (1996, 11) called "aspirations and notions of workplace justice," which motivate workers to mobilize not only for better wages and labor conditions but also to defend and preserve their individual sense of dignity and pride.

At the same time, the grievances and political discourse articulated by farmworkers' protests in Baja reveal that rather than mobilize for labor issues alone, they combine labor and community demands that are central to them as both workers and residents. The flexible inclusion of labor and community demands speaks to the notion of social movement unionism, in which labor protests go beyond bread and butter issues alone to include other claims related to their subordinated status along ethnic and class lines. Underpinning this holistic approach to labor protests are the extreme ethnic and social inequalities that have prevailed in the region since the rise of industrial agriculture in the 1980s. The Alianza's success in capturing the support of thousands of farmworkers in Baja reveals the outdated nature of traditional white unions. The Alianza reflects the emergence of a new labor movement that better reflects farmworkers' grievances and aspirations as workers and citizens. Like modern agribusiness corporations that operate on a global scale, the new labor movement capitalizes on the transnational social and political connections farmworkers and indigenous organizations have built across the Mexico-U.S. border to advance their claims and cultivate the support of consumers in the United States. The labor strike of 2015 marked a new threshold in the history of farmworkers' labor resistance, resituating the struggle from a regional to a transnational political arena.

An important argument presented in this chapter is that the settlement of thousands of farmworkers in the region has enabled the development of alternative and more resilient forms of labor resistance. Compared to migratory workers, farm laborers who live in San Quintín have a long history and cumulative experience of collective mobilizations to improve the living conditions in their colonias. In the process they have learned to demand to be treated as citizens rather than seasonal migrants, developing a strong sense of community and solidarity that was an essential ingredient for the success of the labor strike in 2015. Settlement also allows workers to diversify and muster more economic resources, to develop funds of resilience that enable them to engage in more structured resistance strategies and longer-lasting labor strikes. Farm laborers' resistance strategies are then shaped by their broader kinship, social, and community resources and demands, a situation similar to farmworkers employed in other regions in the global agroexport industry (Friedemann-Sánchez 2012; Schneider and Niederle 2010).

From a broader analytical perspective, the development of an independent labor movement in San Quintín speaks of the opportunities and challenges alternative forms of labor mobilization encounter. Rather than an isolated regional phenomenon, social movement unionism has gained traction in different employment sectors and countries in which disenfranchised workers are pushing for alternative, more decentralized and democratic forms of labor organizing (Durrenberger 2017). But the hurdles the new unions encountered reveal the structural challenges that, as Lazar (2017) argues, alternative forms of labor organizing face at a time when old labor unions and the established political structure begins to crumble. Unlike in the United States, where language, ethnic, and cultural differences among workers constitute an important barrier to effective union organizing (see, e.g., Stuesse 2016, 147–67), the main obstacle independent unions still confront in Mexico is the political alliance between the state and white unions that prevent them from gaining ground. Seeking to provide an alternative, independent unions formed by farmworkers operate in the larger political context dominated by powerful companies and state authorities that often maneuver to undermine the new movement's cause. This is the context of structural vulnerability these unions and their members still confront in the region.

6

Colonizing and Establishing Roots in Arid Lands

We build the house very slow, little by little, because we hardly make enough money to eat; it's hard, it's very hard!
—RAMÓN SUAREZ, MIXTEC FARMWORKER IN COLONIA SANTA FE, 2013

In 1991, when Ramón Suárez first arrived in San Quintín from Los Angeles after being deported to Tijuana, he was looking for a fresh start. As he told me, "I came to San Quintín because I heard many people saying there was work here and it was a quiet and good place to live." His first job was working for a company growing tomatoes in Camalú on the north side of the San Quintín Valley, where he shared a room with some of his coworkers. Two years later he met Aurelia, a field worker from San Juan Mixtepec in Oaxaca, who was employed by the same company. Soon afterward they moved together to the town of Vicente Guerrero in the central valley where they rented a room in a cuartería. Their life began to change three years later when they had an opportunity to buy a lot in Santa Fe, a colonia in the same locality. "They were offering land to people who didn't have a place to live so they could build their homes," recalled Aurelia. With a small down payment saved from their jobs, Ramón and Aurelia bought a 20 by 20 meter lot and moved to live there, agreeing to pay the rest in monthly payments. Their first house was a small room made of plastic. "We lasted in that *cuartito* [little room] two years until it fell apart, and then we built another one made of cardboard," Ramón explained. Life at the time was tough in Colonia Santa Fe, as there was no running water or electricity, and its unpaved streets got flooded whenever it rained, making it difficult to access the Trans-Peninsular Highway farmworkers use to go to work. A breakthrough occurred in 2002 when, with financial aid from PRONJAG, the government program designed to help low-income farmworkers, they received materials to build a *pie de casa* (basic construction starter kit) with which they built their first cement and wood room. As years passed, they added two more rooms, which Ramón patiently built with his own hands in the evenings and on weekends after work to accommodate their six children, four boys and two girls, all born in San Quintín.

Moving from labor camps or rented rooms in cuarterías to their own land parcels and homes was a watershed experience for thousands of farmworkers like Ramón and Aurelia in San Quintín. The settlement of former migrant farmworkers was the result of companies producing a larger variety of fresh fruits and vegetables for export markets and the demand for a more stable labor force that could be employed throughout the year. Poverty and the lack of job opportunities in their home communities in southern Mexico resulting from agrarian policies that withdrew support for peasant subsistence farming contributed to the desire of many farmworkers to settle in San Quintín hoping for a better future for their families. Farmworkers who moved to their own lots after having lived in labor camps or cuarterías enjoyed the benefits of this change. Living independently in their own homes, having more space for their children to grow, and being property owners brought a sense of pride and progress to many workers. It also allowed them to send their children to school without the disruptions of migrating from one place to another in search of work.

But moving into their own homes was not an easy endeavor, and farmworkers who followed this path confronted daunting challenges. The costs of building their rooms and houses, sending their children to school, and paying the bills as independent home owners brought enormous challenges to farm laborers who earned low wages (about $8 a day in 2005) and faced times of low employment in the winter. To make ends meet, they often had to take on additional jobs, work in the informal economy, and even migrate as temporary workers to send money to their families in San Quintín. After moving to Colonia Santa Fe, Ramón resumed traveling to the United States as an undocumented immigrant between 2001 and 2003, sending Aurelia about $1,000 a month when he was employed to finance the construction of their home. Meanwhile, Aurelia raised chickens in their backyard to feed her children when she did not have enough money to buy food and later applied for assistance from a government program called Oportunidades that provided financial relief to families living in poverty. As Ramón told me during one visit to his home in 2013, it took many years of saving and hard work to build his home—one room at a time.

In this chapter, I discuss the experience of farmworkers like Ramón and Aurelia who went from being seasonal migrant workers to settled farm laborers in San Quintín's horticultural industry. Moving beyond the analysis of their experience as laborers, I focus on their lives as settlers, the challenges they faced, and the ways in which they coped with them to set down roots in this region. Examining the strategies farmworkers deploy to settle, I argue, is central to explaining the subsistence and social reproduction of the labor force employed in the transnational fresh-produce industry in Baja. I provide a historical account of settlement as a social

FIGURE 16. Ramón Suárez and his family at their home.

and political endeavor from the time workers lived in labor camps to when they consolidated their roots in the region in the 1980s and 1990s. I examine the challenges they confronted in colonizing their lands as well as the benefits accrued from living on their own properties. I also analyze the economic and social strategies by which settled farmworkers confronted the costs and multiple challenges of life as low-wage agricultural workers. Finally, I document the new types of labor migration that emerged during and after settlement. At its core, I argue, settlement is a social and political process through which farmworkers have reterritorialized these arid lands, succeeding where many past attempts to populate this region failed. The chapter also exposes the close articulation between settlement and labor migration strategies in the lives of farm laborers employed in the transnational U.S.-Mexico fresh-produce industry.

BREAKING AWAY FROM LABOR CAMPS AND CUARTERÍAS

The history and settlement experience of farmworkers employed in the fresh-produce industry in the United States has been the subject of a body of anthropological scholarship (e.g., Palerm 2002, 2010, 2014; Du Bry 2007; Santos-Gómez 2014; Hernández-Romero 2012). As several studies reveal, the evolution of this industry toward the production of fresh produce year-round transformed its labor needs, requiring not only seasonal workers but also a more sedentary labor force. This major shift began in California in the late 1970s as the agricultural sector moved to the production of profitable specialty crops such as berries, table grapes, and citrus, which requires a more permanent labor force of full-time workers to irrigate, spray, and maintain them (Palerm 2002; Hernández-Romero 2012). As a result, farmworkers began moving from labor camps and other types of temporary housing to live in homes of their own, a "homesteading" process that transformed the demographic, ethnic, and class profile of many rural California towns (Palerm 1995, 8; 2010). Examining the settlement of farm laborers in the Coachella Valley in California that began in the 1990s, Travis Du Bry (2007, 133) argues that workers leave labor camps to move into their own single-family houses to pursue more stable and better-paid jobs, reunite with family members, and search for better education opportunities for their children. Breaking ties with labor camps that restricted farmworkers to working with the growers who owned the camps was one of the incentives that propelled them to move to their own homes. Farmworkers' desire to leave labor camps is not surprising. As other studies have shown, harsh housing conditions prevail in many company-owned camps, often consisting of plywood shacks with no insulation, exposing them to inclement weather in summer and winter (Holmes 2013, 47–48). The lack of separation between workplace and home keeps workers under constant surveillance and deprives them of privacy, reflecting the system of structural violence farmworkers commonly confront in the camps (Benson 2008, 608; Holmes 2013).

In Baja California, the demand for a more permanent workforce by the agroexport sector also propelled the settlement of farmworkers beginning in the mid-1980s. Previously, most farmworkers were housed in labor camps, often migrating back and forth to the region, arriving in the spring when employment began to pick up. The first labor camps were built in the mid-1980s to accommodate the growing number of field workers employed by large companies such as A.B.C. Farm, which, as discussed earlier, used enganchadores to recruit and transport indigenous Mixtec workers from Oaxaca. Some camps were rather large, like that of A.B.C. Farm, which in the summers housed about five thousand workers. The camps were rudimentary: barracks made of sheet metal, bedrooms with dirt floors, and shared restrooms. Workers had to cook with wood outdoors. Nonetheless, at the time labor camps were considered a sign of progress compared to when farmworkers lived in shacks they built with recycled plastic and cardboard in open spaces without bathrooms, water, electricity, or other basic services. Despite some improvement in housing conditions, farmworkers in labor camps confronted a new model of segregated living quarters with a highly regimented surveillance regime that was new to the region. Companies hired camperos to enforce the rules, sometimes with the help of armed guards who did not hesitate to use violence under a system of "patronal control" (Velasco, Zlolniski, and Coubes 2014, 236). Overcrowding was common—two or three families shared the same room—while child labor was also prevalent, preventing children from attending school and contributing to high infant mortality rates (Garduño, García, and Morán 1989; Clark 1985).

The poor housing and strict control that prevailed in labor camps left a deep and long-lasting mark on the individual and collective memories of farmworkers in San Quintín. Early pioneers who arrived in the 1980s vividly remember the crowded conditions. Such was the case of Agustín Mejía, a mestizo farmworker born in 1957 in Salina Cruz, Oaxaca, who arrived in San Quintín in 1991 at the labor camp La Campana along with a crew of forty-eight workers recruited from La Paz in Baja California after having previously worked in Sinaloa. The work crew was enticed to go to San Quintín by a recruiter who offered them good pay and comfortable conditions in the camp. Upon arriving, they were sorely disappointed: "We arrived at a labor camp called La Campana, but we didn't like it because they had promised us a lot of things that weren't true. They had promised us our rooms had gas tanks and bunk beds, but when we arrived . . . there were no stoves, no gas tanks, no beds, nothing. And they told us, 'To cook you have to gather your own wood in the hills.'"

Likewise, Hermelinda Ramírez, an indigenous woman of Nahuatl descent who was born in 1967 in Igualita in the municipality of Xalpatláuac, Guerrero, who arrived in San Quintín in 1989, recalled the harsh conditions at the San Simón labor camp, a property of A.B.C. Farm. When I asked her about her experience there, she replied, "It was very difficult because the barracks were made of sheet metal and there were two or three families per room. Everyone gathered their own firewood as they could to cook. For me it was very difficult because I arrived with nothing, only a frying pan and a pot I brought with me."

The harsh conditions in the camps with a spatially segregated and captive labor force provided the original impetus for many farmworkers to seek better alternatives. Some moved to cuarterías; unlike labor camps, these living quarters offered the advantage of being located in colonias closer to the main towns, breaking the spatial isolation of the camps and giving workers easier access to services and commerce. More important, independent cuarterías freed workers from the obligation to work for the company or grower who owned the camp. While an improvement compared to labor camps, cuartería living conditions were still bleak. Workers had to pay rent, bringing constant pressure to earn additional income to meet the monthly payments and avoid being evicted. Most cuarterías had deficient sanitation, frequently lacking running water, and the few restrooms and bathrooms that existed had to be shared by dozens of tenants; in addition, rooms were overcrowded, with families often having to share them with strangers

(Camargo Martínez 2015, 119). Hermelinda Ramírez, who after leaving San Simón moved to a cuartería where she lived with her husband and children for several years, shared her memories about life in such a setting. She singled out the pressure to pay rent, the crowded rooms, and the constant quarrels among tenants: "In the cuartería there isn't just one but many families, and there're always quarrels, especially because of our children.... In my case in the cuartería where I lived I had several problems because my child was always fighting with other children.... And then to take a bath you have to wait in line to gather water first with a bucket. It was *mucha batalla* [a big struggle]."

By moving to their own lots, workers began to tear down the regime of indentured labor that prevailed in the region at the time. As labor in agriculture became more intense with the expansion of production beyond the harvest season, the earlier model of labor camps for housing migrant workers became increasingly obsolete. While in the 1980s there were forty registered labor camps, by the mid-1990s there were only twenty-two camps with an estimated total population of 6,880 (Velasco, Zlolniski, and Coubès 2014, 84), and by 2010, fewer than half a dozen camps were still in operation. The push for residential autonomy showed farmworkers' resistance to this system and the desire to be free workers with the ability to choose when and for whom to work. By settling in colonias and building their own homes, they marked a new chapter in the labor history of this young region.

THE STRUGGLE FOR RESIDENTIAL INDEPENDENCE

In a seminal piece about the experience of settling in new lands, the rural anthropologist Thayer Scudder (1985) conceptualized it as a social and political process that evolves over time. According to him, settlement involves four stages. The first two critical stages consist of setting up the material infrastructure for the newcomers to work the lands and ensure the basic subsistence of their families (Scudder 1985, 161–64). In the next two stages, settlers develop a new sense of belonging, get involved in civic organizations, and attain self-sufficiency from government and private subsidies, a stage marked by the birth of a second generation of children raised in the new settlements (167–68). While originally developed to explain the experience of farmers who settle in new lands under government-sponsored projects, Scudder's analysis is helpful for interpreting farm laborers' settlement experience in San Quintín. When farmworkers began moving to new colonias, they embarked on a long and arduous process of colonization that would transform the physical and social landscape of the region. Unlike the government-sponsored colonization projects described by Scudder, however, settlement in San Quintín was a process largely driven by poor farmworkers who, for many years, received little or no help from the federal, state, or municipal government. For the new settlers, the transition from labor camps or rented rooms to living in colonias in their own homes was difficult, often taking many years of hard work, careful planning, and savings from meager wages.

The initial stage of this experience took place from the mid-1980s to the mid-1990s, during which workers either bought a lot or took it over by squatting. The first task after moving to their own lots consisted of taming the land before they could even build a room to live in. This task typically entailed clearing pastures, leveling the terrain, getting rid of venomous animals, and otherwise preparing the land to make it habitable. Esther Chávez first moved to Colonia Santa Fe in 1995 along with her husband and seven children. She was among the dozen or so families who received a lot from a "community leader" who was giving away parcels to families who wanted to settle there. Esther described the daunting living conditions at the time.

> Uggh! There wasn't anything here, no one, only *pitayas* [dragon fruit], cactus, *chamizo*, just hard plants and shrubs that were hard to remove! And the terrain was so dry and hard. Our lot was full of stones, very ugly.... We didn't have a bed, and all the family slept on the hard floor. By the morning when I woke up my back and ribs hurt. And there were lots of insects and bugs that would climb onto your head, hair, arms, and blankets, and there was a plague of fleas. Little by little we would clean and level the land, remove the stones, cleaning the land with a mixture of water, soap, and chlorine to get rid of the fleas. We didn't have electricity or water; we had to buy water from water trucks. At nights we would light candles and the colonia looked like a cemetery, everyone with their candles in small rooms covered with plastic recycled from the fields when growers throw them away after the harvest is over.

Esther's narrative depicts the zeal and commitment farmworkers deployed to achieve much-desired residential independence. After long days of hard work in the fields, they worked arduously preparing their parcels and building their homes. And unlike Scudder's model, this was a self-propelled movement in which workers depended on their own limited resources. Agustín Mejía, another early settler in Colonia Santa Fe, recalled his struggles.

> When I arrived there were only nine little houses here in Santa Fe; that was around 1993 or 1994.... And I built my first room made of *puros estacones* [logs], cardboard, and nylon; that was my first room. Little by little and with a lot of effort, we began to clean because it was full of animals; there were many tarantulas, lots of snakes that are very poisonous, big spiders. There were lots of cacti too, but little by little we cleared the land.

The lack of government support during the early years of settlement left people in a precarious state. Laura Flores recalled the hardships her family endured for several years after they moved to their lot in Colonia Santa Fe.

> We got here around 1997, and there were only nylon and plastic houses in the colonia. We lived in a house made of nylon and plastic for six years. We didn't even have

bathrooms, not even latrines, just a little hole, and when it rained the water would fill in and we had to make another hole to go to the bathroom. Then the rain came and the water came through and carried it off, and [it was] time to make another hole. It used to be all plastic houses here, cardboard, whatever people were able to use.

Conditions for farmworkers began to improve in the mid-1990s, when government agencies finally arrived in the region, marking a second stage in the modern history of settlement. To a large extent, the activation of government agencies was the result of pressure by farm laborers who organized in committees to demand basic services such as water and electricity for their communities. In addition to local committees, many settlers organized collectively under the umbrella of the CIOAC to demand that the government improve housing conditions (Velasco, Zlolniski, and Coubes 2014, 267–69). The arrival of the state government signaled the recognition of settled farmworkers as social and political actors that government authorities could no longer ignore. At this point, settled workers began receiving the first windfall of support from a few federal and state government programs aimed at helping low-income farmworkers and families.

One of the first programs was launched by PRONJAG, a significant development because until the late 1990s this program exclusively focused on migrant farmworkers housed in labor camps. However, confronted with the new reality of thousands of workers living in colonias and the declining number of labor camps, it began helping settled workers improve their housing conditions. The most popular initiative provided basic building materials, brick and concrete. In turn, workers were responsible for providing the labor to build the rooms and attending meetings organized by the agency. While housing conditions began to improve, the service infrastructure in the colonias was still precarious, including the lack of water and electricity. Agustín Mejía recalled:

> They gave us four hundred brick blocks, one ton of cement, one can of tar, two packets of sand paper, two insulation sheets, eight sheets of plywood, and twelve steel bars. And we *echamos ganas* [applied ourselves], and I made good progress building my first room.... After that we started living better because this was a small but more decent home; we finally could buy a small bed, a stove. Back then there wasn't electricity so we used candles; then I bought a car battery and adapted a small twelve-volt bulb so we could have some light at night at dinner.... We had to buy water in barrels of two hundred liters. There was a water truck that came to the colonia, ... and we had to be very careful not to waste any water, and we lived like that for several years, ... for about seven or more years.

To achieve residential independence, farmworkers relied on what in Mexico is called *la cultura del esfuerzo* (the culture of persistent effort), which refers to the work ethic poor people and those without political connections (*palancas*) must muster to get ahead in life. Indeed, for farmworkers in San Quintín, building their homes was still a slow and painstaking endeavor of incremental improvement that often took many years of sacrifice and hard work. In 2013, for example, Ramón and Aurelia Suárez were still building a fourth room to accommodate their family sixteen years after first moving to Colonia Santa Fe. Ramón reminisced:

> *Híjole,* it was very difficult! For example, this small room of 4 by 4 meters I built it in about three years, perhaps a bit longer. It took three years because first we [he and his adult sons] had to build the foundation, the next year we built the walls, the next season we put on the roof, and so we built it in stages along the years. . . . [We raised it] slowly, very slowly. The problem is that we hardly made enough money to eat, so to build this house was very hard, really hard.

Farmworkers were also required to pay for the registration of their properties. In seeking to regulate housing and the growth of new colonias in the region, the state government in Baja began requiring settlers to obtain property titles for their lots and pay the corresponding fees, a move to transform them into tax subjects. Despite their precarious economic status, farmworkers then had to pay property taxes, adding pressure to their family budgets. Esther Chávez, for example, paid 13,000 pesos ($1,300) in 2002 after the state agency in charge of regulating housing sent letters instructing all residents in the colonia to register their lots.[1] With farmworkers struggling to keep their families afloat with their low wages, confronting the costs of housing and registering their lots was a major challenge that tested their will and determination to stay put.

Workers' success in settlement, however, entailed more than individual efforts; it often involved forms of mutual help, solidarity, and collective organization. In many cases, neighbors living in the same colonia helped each other build their homes. For example, in Colonia Santa Fe, when PRONJAG began providing material resources for residents to build their first rooms, neighbors developed a system in which all beneficiaries provided free labor to build rooms for each family on a rotating basis, an adaptation of the traditional Tekio communal work system practiced by indigenous Mixtecs in Oaxaca (Stephen 2007, 57). In addition to housing, neighbors developed other forms of mutual help. During the winter months when employment declined and when many residents were trying to build their first homes, it was difficult to provide food for their families. Esther Chávez, who with her first husband was building the first concrete and wood room with materials provided by PRONJAG, explained how colonia residents organized to gather seafood when there was no work in the fields: "It was January when we moved to the pie de casa, but it was a very difficult time because that month it rained a lot and we couldn't work. A group of people in the colonia would get together to go in a small car of anyone who had one to the beach to collect clams and fish, and that's what we would eat because otherwise we didn't have anything to eat." Over time, neighbors developed other forms of mutual help. As in many other colonias, residents commonly participated in "tandas," informal rotating savings and credit associations (ROSCA) (Vélez-Ibáñez 2010). Groups of individuals, usually six to ten women, contributed fixed payments to a central fund for a fixed period of time, then received the entire pot once during the cycle and used it to make basic repairs to their homes, buy implements for their kitchens, help pay their children's educational costs, and other projects.

Although settlement was a long and arduous enterprise that involved a great deal of ingenuity and the mustering of individual and collective forms of mutual help and solidarity, over time the early settlers would begin to enjoy the fruits of their labor.[2]

MATERIAL AND SOCIAL BENEFITS OF RESIDENTIAL INDEPENDENCE

Among the dozens of old and new colonias that grew up in the late 1990s to accommodate the newcomers arriving in the region is Colonia Arbolitos. Located near the town of Lázaro Cárdenas and largely populated by Zapotec workers and families, it is a small community encompassing six blocks of houses, some made of cardboard and plastic, others of wood and concrete. Founded in 1990, the colonia lacks public lighting; it had no running water until 2008, and its dusty streets are dotted by potholes that make driving difficult when it rains. In 2005, when I first met Celeste Hernández, she lived in this colonia with four children, a 15-year-old daughter and three boys ages 15, 12, and 1, the latter "adopted" from a niece who got pregnant in her early teens. On a large parcel of about 20 by 20 meters, her house consisted of three separate rooms aligned and detached from each other, each built in a different year whenever she had enough money to expand the house. The first and oldest room was a kitchen and "dining room" of about 4 by 3 meters with a concrete floor and containing an old secondhand four-burner stove, a one-door refrigerator, a sink, a water barrel, and a round wooden table with five chairs. The second room belonged to her eldest daughter, Estela; it contained a twin bed, a small desk, a small TV, and a stereo DVD player. The third room, shared by Celeste and her youngest children, had a queen bed, a twin bed, and a two-seat sofa. The "bathroom" consisted of a detached small structure made of uncemented concrete blocks stacked on top of each other, with a hanging blue plastic curtain family members used for privacy to shower, using buckets as there was no running water in the house. On a corner of her property in the backyard was a latrine with a septic tank. Neither this nor any other colonia in the region has a sewer system. Celeste had embellished her parcel with a garden. There was a small orchard in the back of the lot where she had planted fruit trees and different types of plants, and in the front she had planted petunias, bushes, and a few colorful flowers. Despite the rough unsteadiness of her housing, Celeste, like many other workers I met in San Quintín, considers living in her own home a sign of progress and a source of pride. Having previously lived in a rented room in a cuartería, she was proud of finally having her own house. Every afternoon, after returning from work and preparing dinner, she tended her garden and plants, a task she enjoyed for the peace it brought her after a long day in the fields. Her children enjoyed running and playing outside on her ample parcel.

The scarce literature on farmworkers' settlement in Mexico indicates they have benefited because they have diversified their employment opportunities and sources of income for their families (Lara Flores and C. de Grammont 2011; Velasco, Zlolniski, and Coubes 2014). Settlement, however, is also a social and cultural process by which workers engage in place making and develop a new sense of belonging and community. For farm laborers I met in San Quintín, moving to their own parcels was a transformative experience that shaped their individual and collective memories. When discussing the motives and goals that helped them endure their sacrifices, workers pointed out both the material benefits and the less tangible but equally significant considerations that speak to the social and cultural dimension of settlement. First, there are the economic and material benefits derived from living independently in their own homes, even in uncertain conditions. Not paying rent and living on their own lots brought a sense of privacy and space farmworkers did not have when housed in labor camps and cuarterías. It also gave them a sense of stability and safety, something that is especially appreciated by workers who in the past had to constantly move from place to place. Adelina and Rodolfo Moreno, who after more than a decade of living in several labor camps and cuarterías moved to a lot in Colonia Arbolitos, conveyed a sense of relief, stability, and progress. As Adelina explained, "We don't have to pay rent anymore. We now have a lot where we live that is ours; it's progress. We don't have to tumble from one place to another, renting rooms in different cuarterías. It's an improvement."

In addition to better housing and more stability, many farmworkers were motivated by the desire to improve the educational opportunities of their children. After years, sometimes decades, of living as migratory workers, settling down allowed them to send their children to school year-round, an opportunity they highly value as many grew up in migrant families and could not complete elementary school. Faustina Herrera, for instance, emphasized the opportunity to send her children to school as a major incentive to settle in Colonia Santa Fe: "[It gave me] a chance to have my children grow up healthy, free from vices, because, well, I'm lucky to have my kids in school. Not all of them, you know, because the older ones didn't go to school, since they were working.... [But] I know we're getting ahead. First, because, as I tell myself, 'My children are in school.' I know they have their goals, and if God grants us life, they'll go as far as they want to."

By investing in the education of their children, farm laborers hope they can escape the rigors of working in the fields and find less physically demanding and better-paid jobs. I often heard parents inculcating in their children the importance of finishing school so they can find jobs outside agriculture and have lives that are more comfortable. Josefina Rodríguez, the Monsanto union representative who arrived in San Quintín in the early 2000s, established her home in Colonia Graciano Sánchez after a life as a migratory farmworker in the Oaxaca–Sinaloa–San Quintín circuit. Her decision to settle in San Quintín was motivated by her desire for her children to finish school and have better lives than she had: "My daughter started to go to school, and that's what made me want to stay put here. I bought a lot here so that she could study, that's what motivated me to stay. And when my second child [a boy] was born I stayed here because I wanted my children to study. . . . I did it for my children because I realized that if I continued moving back and forth, my children would not be able to go to school and graduate."

For farmworkers with children raised in San Quintín, settlement often entails a new sense of attachment and belonging to the region. While still maintaining an emotional connection with their communities of origin in Oaxaca, they regard San Quintín as their adopted land, one that has given them employment and economic opportunities not available back home. Faustina Herrera, for example, expressed a sense of attachment to San Quintín as her adopted home while developing a feeling of geographic and emotional distance from her hometown in Oaxaca: "I feel like this is home because I'm not thinking of going back, even though I like where I'm from. It's been a long time since I've been back, and I would like to go but for a visit, to take a trip, you know? But I couldn't go back to live there because my children are used to living here, they're all married here. What would I go back there for? . . . I like it here."

After struggling to establish roots in the region, settlement also enables farm laborers to nurture their social lives and build a sense of community they rarely experienced when housed in labor camps or cuarterías. In the colonias, they organize and enjoy family celebrations, especially those marking important stages in their children's life cycle such as quinceañeras, school graduations, and marriages. Developing strong ties with kin, friends, and neighbors brings a sense of joy, a less tangible but important social and emotional dimension of settlement that cannot be reduced to its material dimension. Women particularly appreciate the ability to develop personal relationships in their colonias. During field work, they often told me that getting together with female friends, even if only for a few moments during the week, is a source of pleasure that takes their minds away from work in the fields, their households, and their husbands. This set of social relations not only provides material and emotional support but also speaks to the larger process of community building at the heart of settlement that many residents treasure as one of the most enjoyable experiences of their lives in the region.

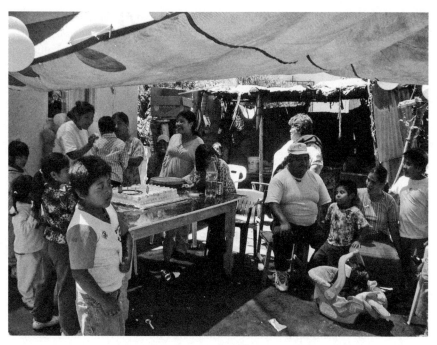

FIGURE 17. Kin and friends at a weekend birthday party in Colonia Santa Fe.

DEVELOPING A SENSE OF BELONGING AND PLACE

As place making, settlement is fundamentally a political endeavor (Oliver-Smith 2010). Thus place attachment, Oliver-Smith (2010, 165) contends, refers to the belonging of people to places, whereby place is in itself "socially constructed and contested in practice." For farmworkers in San Quintín, moving to their own lots and setting down roots in their new communities was a collective political endeavor as they had to mobilize for their rights as citizens in the region. Getting involved in local civic and regional organizations reflects what Du Bry (2007) conceptualizes as "community building," whereby participants become firmly integrated into the social fabric of their local rural communities.

The indigenous ethnic and cultural background of many farm laborers in the region, however, adds a new layer to the theoretical conceptualization of settlement as a political process. As mentioned before, indigenous workers in San Quintín have had a long history of ethnic and racial discrimination since first arriving in significant numbers in the 1970s. Growers, particularly local farmers, systematically engaged in labor and political processes that isolated and discriminated against indigenous workers from Oaxaca and southern Mexico. While in the field, I often encountered white and mestizo middle-class workers and residents who espoused a form of "cultural racism" (Martínez Veiga 2001), which portrays indigenous workers as culturally backward, blaming them for many of the social problems that afflict the region. Affluent and middle-class growers and professionals often referred to indigenous workers in pejorative terms: the "indiada" refers to indigenous people from different ethnic groups; "oaxacos" refers to people from Oaxaca; and the "mixtecada" singles out Mixtecs, the largest ethnic group in the region. In other cases, mestizos referred to them as "paisanos," a vernacular that in the region is commonly used to portray indigenous workers as an uneducated, low-class, and "migrant" population. Indigenous workers are often represented as a social and culturally distinct population that keep to themselves and are unable or unwilling to adapt to the more developed and modern society of northern Mexico. For instance, a physician at a public clinic who also runs a parallel private practice in San Quintín, as is common in Mexico, told me that the problem of contaminated water in Colonia Nueva Cali where he lived was the result of the latrines and septic tanks workers have at their homes. Many growers and middle-class professionals were eager to point out that indigenous farmworkers in San Quintín "lived much better" and more comfortable lives than in their home communities in Oaxaca. "The people in [Colonia] 13 de Mayo have TVs at home and even cars they don't have in Oaxaca," another doctor told me when explaining that San Quintín offered an opportunity for indigenous workers from Oaxaca to have jobs and improve their living conditions.

The business elite of old-time growers and middle-class professionals also espouses a form of nativism against indigenous workers along class and ethnic lines. An ingredient of this nativist ideology is the claim that indigenous people in San Quintín are privileged by government programs that shield their language, culture, and traditions at the expense of mestizos, who do not receive the same treatment. This form of "reactive nativism" blames the government for capitulating and pleasing ethnic leaders to keep them appeased. In addition to the government, middle-class mestizos often identify indigenous leaders as "a main problem." Ethnic leaders are blamed for "manipulating" their own people to engage in labor strikes and other forms of political protests, taking advantage of their ignorance. Indigenous farmworkers are presented as victims of corrupt and unscrupulous ethnic leaders who only want to advance themselves financially and politically. "The indigenous paisanos are manipulated by their leaders who subjugate them to their customs and rules and don't allow them to get loose," the doctor cited above told me, reflecting a common discourse by the middle class in the region. This nativist elite also seeks to minimize the demographic weight and cultural significance of the indigenous population in the region, arguing that government officials overstate their number and needs. Felipe Ruiz Esparza, a grower in Vicente Guerrero who employs Mixtec and mestizo workers, stated in an interview that the government exaggerated the number of indigenous people living in the region:

"The *indiada* is much less in numbers than what commonly people think," he argued. Middle-class growers, merchants, and professionals who form the core of a business and political elite see themselves as the key actors who can bring progress and modernity to the region, while the leaders of indigenous organizations are portrayed as keeping their own people frozen in the past.

Despite the cultural politics of exclusion and the long tradition of racial discrimination, farmworkers began to engage into different forms of political mobilization to improve the living conditions in their colonias. The mixed ethnic makeup in many of these communities prompted new forms of interethnic cooperation as residents from different language and cultural backgrounds and occupations began collaborating to press government officials to respond to their demands. Residents formed local colonia committees—usually made up of a president, a vice president, a secretary, and a treasurer—that served to organize, coordinate, and channel residents' main concerns. The experience of local micro mobilizations and cooperation forged a collective memory of struggle and accomplishment as well as a sense of belonging and place that are at the heart of the political agency indigenous and mestizo workers have deployed since the 1990s. Particularly in old colonias, the memories of collective struggles shape the fondness with which many farmworkers recount their experiences. In Colonia Santa Fe, for example, Aurelia Suárez told me that organizing to bring public services brought "progress" to the community, improving living conditions for its residents: "We feel like we've made progress because of the opportunities here. Other than that, we've also made progress because we have services like electricity, water, and all that we didn't have when we first arrived here. There was nothing; we didn't even have a barrel to put water in. We had no water for four years. Now I have electricity, I have water, and I have my little house."

Early settlers, who arrived at a time when there were few if any public services in rural settlements, are among the residents with a stronger sense of collective pride. This is the case of Agustín Mejía, who, like many other settlers who arrived in Colonia Santa Fe in the early 1990s, proudly talked about the individual and collective efforts it took to improve the housing and living conditions in his community: "We felt we were working for something worthwhile, and despite all the sacrifices and missing many basic things, we had our own lots and place. And we began to love this land, to love our small parcels, our own homes even though they were humble. We told ourselves that this was ours and nobody would take it away from us. And little by little we started to get ahead. . . . Little by little we began to see the results of our efforts, even if it took a long time."

Agustín's reflections reveal the close links between the collective political struggle to improve living conditions in the colonias and the development of a shared sense of belonging and place. After working long hours in the fields, farmworkers returned home to help each other build their homes, participate in community fund-raising, and join committees to negotiate with government authorities for public services such as water, electricity, and accessible roads. Esther Chávez, who before working for Monsanto had many other jobs as a field worker and in several local canneries, became one of the most visible and charismatic leaders in Colonia Santa Fe after moving there in the early 1990s. She soon joined the local steering committee to petition state authorities to build a child-care center as most women were field workers and had no place to leave their children while they worked. The committee also became involved in securing the construction of an elementary school and in raising funds by organizing raffles, dance parties, and other public events to build a community center. Ever since, the center has been used for community meetings, skill-training workshops, and celebrations and as a base of operations for government programs that assist low-income residents in the colonia. Having gone through years of collective struggles provided Esther with a strong sense of place, community, and accomplishment.

> I've lived here at ease and feel very happy about being in this colonia because I've lived together with neighbors from many different places, and whether you like it or not you develop affection for them and they do the same for you.... I like it here very much and think I won't move.... I've struggled a lot on behalf of this colonia; we have many years here fighting together, first to bring electricity and water, then schools, a kindergarten, and a community room for our activities, everything. We organized dance parties to raise funds to build a basketball court for the kids who live here.

By organizing in local committees to bring public services to their colonias, farmworkers forged a new political consciousness eager to mobilize not only for their rights as laborers but as residents and full-fledged citizens as well.[3] While ethnic cultural differences still persisted and sometimes were the basis for racial stereotypes, settlement transformed the cultural basis for collective mobilization. By facilitating a higher degree of interethnic collaboration and solidarity, settlement strengthened farmworkers' political agency and their ability to mobilize for labor and community demands, despite the class and ethnic discrimination they still faced in their work lives.

CONFRONTING THE COST OF SETTLEMENT: INFORMAL ECONOMY AND SELF-PROVISIONING

Despite the sense of progress and accomplishment farm laborers experienced when moving to colonias, the cost of living as independent workers is quite high. Examining the challenges farmworkers confront in settlement, I argue, is an important analytical task in explaining the maintenance and reproduction of those employed in export agriculture. In addition to building their homes and obtaining property titles for their parcels, farmworkers have to cover their children's school expenses, pay household bills for water, electricity, gas, and other basic services, and sustain family members who are not employed. Thus, unlike in labor camps, workers in colonias usually live in larger families and have more members to maintain, elderly relatives as well as children.[4] Low wages in agriculture compound this problem. In 2015, for example, average wages for field workers oscillated between 800 and 1,200 pesos ($55–$83) per week. With wages insufficient to cover even the most basic living expenses, many farm laborers also work in secondary jobs in the informal economy. Men usually work as manual laborers in construction, especially in the winter when agricultural employment slows down, while others work in carpentry and other trades. Women engage in informal home-based economic activities such as giving haircuts, sewing and tailoring, baking breads and cakes, selling sodas and other drinks, or working part-time as domestic workers. The earnings from these jobs are rather modest. Women with sewing experience, for example, can earn about 275 pesos ($19) a week working in the afternoons after laboring in the fields; those who cut hair at home earn around 500 pesos ($35) per week during the summer and about 75 pesos ($5) a week the rest of the year. Although their earnings are modest, they value these jobs not only as extra income for their families but also because of the opportunity to work from home in less labor-intensive jobs.

Farmworkers who are single mothers confront significant challenges supplementing their wages with income from other jobs. The significance of this problem cannot be overstated given that about 17 percent of families living in colonias are headed by women (Velasco, Zlolniski, and Coubes 2014, 170), reflecting the feminization of labor in the region's horticultural sector. Celeste Hernández illustrates the hard choices single mothers often face in San Quintín. Married to her husband, Bernardo, since 1987, she found herself in a critical situation when he abandoned her in 2006 while working in San Diego County after obtaining a green card through the IRCA legalization program of 1986. In response, Celeste began working longer hours in agriculture and looked for additional sources of income to support her four children. One such activity was cooking tamales to sell. Every weekend she prepared about four hundred tamales to sell in the colonia and at a local flea market in the nearby town of Lázaro Cárdenas. While she had the opportunity to work in the fields on weekends, particularly in summer, she preferred selling tamales because she could make more money and have a break from the onerous farmwork. She explained, "Sincerely, I make more money selling tamales than working in the field. I invest about 400 pesos [$36] in preparing them and get about 1,200 pesos [$110]; hence it's good business. But I also get very tired because I don't cook them in the stove but with firewood."

When not selling tamales on the weekends, Celeste was busy selling second-hand clothes, collaborating in the business with a sister and her sister-in-law who also live in Colonia Arbolitos. They bought shirts, sweaters, and pants in bulk from a vendor who arrived every month from California and sold them on the weekends at the flea market and a large labor camp run by Los Pinos, earning about 600 pesos ($55) a week. In addition, once a week Celeste worked as a house cleaner for a family who owns a ranch in San Quintín, earning 200 pesos ($18) for six hours of work, almost twice what she earns in a regular day as a farmworker. Overall, from Monday to Sunday, Celeste worked several jobs, combining them to optimize her earnings while still managing to keep her job as a farmworker. Her work strategy illustrates what the Mexican anthropologist Mercedes González de la Rocha (2001, 78) calls "occupational heterogeneity," an economic and social scheme used by the working poor in Mexico in which a single worker or several workers in the household work in different occupational niches to compensate for low wages and temporary unemployment.

After moving to their own homes, some workers rent out rooms to migrant workers to earn extra income. Renting out rooms provides a safe and predictable income, while for migratory workers renting rooms in homes is often a better option than living in a labor camp or cuartería because the rooms are generally in better condition and have their own latrines. Martín Fernández, for example, who lives with his wife, Nayeli Fernández, and their children in Colonia Arbolitos, built two separate rooms in the back of their property to rent to temporary workers. To this end, in 2009 he went to his hometown of Asunción in the municipality of Ocotlan, Oaxaca, to sell a parcel he had inherited from his father, and with the income he built two rooms that he rents every year for 250 pesos ($18) a month. Having their own parcel opened up an investment opportunity in rentals to supplement his work wages. A few years later he and his wife bought another lot in an adjacent, newer colonia, and by 2017, they had built two additional rooms to rent, allowing them to increase their income from non-farmwork. For him and many other workers, settlement in San Quintín entailed severing economic ties with their hometowns in southern Mexico to reinvest their resources and energies in their adopted land in Baja.

Living on their own land also gives farmworkers an opportunity to grow food for their own consumption and for sale, an important economic strategy to cope with their low wages in agriculture. Most workers I met use part of their parcels to grow vegetables and herbs and to raise animals such as chickens, turkeys, and rabbits for themselves, for sale, or to barter with kin, neighbors, and friends. This "backyard economy" falls within what economic anthropologists call "non–labor market activities," those that occur outside the monetary exchange market (Chibnik 2011) and that often go hand in hand with wage labor. Particularly common is the cultivation of vegetables, fruits, and medicinal plants and herbs in backyards. In this endeavor farmworkers combine traditional peasants' knowledge about particular crops and herbs learned in their home communities with agricul-

FIGURE 18. A sign outside a farmworker's house in Colonia Arbolitos announces haircuts and sale of sodas.

tural techniques and skills learned as farm laborers in San Quintín. Hermelinda Ramírez, for example, raises turkeys, chickens, rabbits, and pigeons in her backyard in Colonia Arbolitos for both her family and to sell. She appreciates this type of work and is eager to invest time to take care of her animals in the evenings after working in the fields. As she put it, "At any moment, if I run out of money, I can kill a turkey and prepare it with mole and rice." Likewise, Aurelia Suárez grows vegetables in Santa Fe cultivating *yerba mansa,* which she uses in the form of tea for medicinal purposes, and squash and prickly pear cactus for her family. "When there's no food, I eat that," she explained. To water the garden, her husband, Ramón, installed small drip-irrigation tubes recycled from the agricultural company where he works after they were discarded, using the skills he had learned at work.

By raising food for self-provisioning, farmworkers create a cushion for hard times of unemployment or underemployment, especially in the winter months. Drawing from a repertoire of skills and activities they learned growing up in Oaxaca allows them to meet the challenges of making a living in their new land in Baja. This reveals that in settlement farmworkers re-create their funds of knowledge about nonmarket economic activities and integrate them into their everyday survival strategies. As I watched indigenous farmworkers in San Quintín engaging in food production for self-provisioning, it struck me that this is as an important part of their new identity as residents, one that values autonomy and self-reliance. Having their own lots, they find in farming and raising animals a source of *gusto* and

FIGURE 19. Chickens and pumpkin flowers are common in workers' backyard gardens.

pride, particularly adults like Aurelia and Hermelinda who grew up as peasants in rural villages in Oaxaca and Guerrero before becoming wage workers in San Quintín.

THE GENDERED NATURE OF SETTLEMENT

Many farmworkers receive financial and material support from government programs in the region. Most state programs arrived in San Quintín in the 1990s, when the laissez-faire policies of the Mexican government ran into a dead end, resulting in high levels of labor exploitation, poverty, violence against labor and community leaders, and public health problems caused by workers' exposure to pesticides and unsanitary conditions in labor camps (Garduño, García, and Morán 1989). Since then, the government developed a new policy approach to combat poverty and prevent further social unrest, seeking to retain foreign investment in the lucrative fresh-produce sector. While for farmworkers these programs provide a modest but welcome addition to their meager income from wage work in agriculture as well as much needed funding for community projects in their colonias, they also entail considerable work for women, who are at the center of most of these government initiatives.

The centrality of women in government programs to combat poverty and strengthen local communities in San Quintín can be illustrated by the monthly meetings I often attended organized by social workers employed by these programs in numerous colonias where farmworkers live. One afternoon, I attended a meeting at a community center in Colonia Santa Fe organized by the Sistema Nacional para el Desarrollo Integral de la Familia (DIF), a federal program aimed at strengthening the welfare of Mexican families. The meeting was scheduled for 1:00 P.M., and by 1:15 around forty women had arrived, most of them Mixtec and Triqui farmworkers who live in this colonia and its vicinity. As they signed DIF's attendance roster, they were asked to add their names to a list distributed by PRONJAG. Meanwhile Esther Chávez used the opportunity to say a few words about yet another government program, Oportunidades, designed to combat poverty through cash transfers to mothers, reading the names of women who were registered as beneficiaries. A few minutes later the women attending the meeting walked outside to wait in line for a DIF van to unload food baskets. Once a month, DIF brings food baskets to the community center and distributes them for a subsidized price to registered residents. A social worker from DIF began calling out the names of the people waiting in line, handing each of them a food basket. At a cost of 20 pesos apiece ($1.80), each basket contained a handful of "basic food" items such as oil, beans, flour, sugar, rice, and lentils, as well as less traditional products like soya oil to promote the use of healthy cooking. Although women sometimes have to miss a workday to receive these baskets, it provides an important source of help they do not want to miss.

While DIF delivers subsidized food, other government programs provide cash transfers to alleviate poverty among low-income families channeling them through women. Oportunidades, the largest and most popular government program among farmworkers in San Quintín, shows the importance government welfare programs have for the family economy. Founded in Mexico as Progresa in 1997, it was rebranded Oportunidades in 2002 under the PAN government of Vicente Fox (2000–2006) and then Prospera under the administration of Enrique Peña Nieto (2012–18). This federal program was designed to combat poverty by breaking its intergenerational transmission through calibrated cash transfers earmarked for food and education for women and children. Under the umbrella of SEDESOL, the program espoused a new approach to reduce poverty by replacing the former model of government-mandated price controls for basic food items with individual cash transfers. These are "conditional cash transfers," based on the principle of "co-responsibility," that require mothers to participate in community tasks, attend monthly meetings held by the program coordinators, and collaborate in sanitary initiatives (Wilson 2015).

The program was devised as a more effective policy instrument to reach families in poverty while preventing political clientelism that affected social welfare programs in the past (Ansell and Mitchel 2011), reflecting a neoliberal ideology that emphasizes personal responsibility as a basis for receiving welfare support.[5] One of the most popular components of Oportunidades, known by farmworkers

FIGURE 20. A monthly IMSS-Oportunidades health checkup community meeting in Colonia Santa Fe.

in San Quintín as "family grants," provides cash for children to stay in school and for their mothers to cover food and other basic household expenses. The grant amounts vary according to several factors such as family size, income, and age of children in school, among others.

The impact of Oportunidades for settled farmworkers is significant, revealing the important role of welfare programs in subsidizing the low wages paid in the fresh-produce industry. In Colonia Santa Fe, for example, with an estimated population of about 1,900 inhabitants and 217 households, 135 families (62 percent) received help from this program. While modest, this economic aid is crucial for many farmworkers whose meager incomes cannot cover even their basic family maintenance needs. This monetary aid is especially important during the winter months, when workers are employed only a few days a week. Aurelia Suárez, for example, received 400 pesos ($31) every two months as well as 700 pesos ($55) for a son who is in secondary school and 240 pesos ($19) for another child who is in primary school. Commenting on the forms of support she receives, Aurelia emphasized their significance for clothing and keeping her children in school: "For me it's a great support and has helped a lot. Especially when we are out of work and when my children begin the school year, I know that at least that money is waiting for them, that when it arrives I'd be able to pay the basics for their school. Yesterday, for example, I collected my grant and bought clothes for my children now that school is going to start. I'll buy the rest, backpacks, notebooks, and the like, with my money."

Economic aid from programs like the former Oportunidades is crucial to keeping children in school. Adelina Moreno, a Zapotec resident of Colonia Arbolitos, told me that although small, the grants she receives on behalf of her children are crucial for keeping them in school and covering some of the basic education-related expenses she could otherwise not afford on her wages alone. She commented, "It's very helpful. For example, by the end of this month, I'll get paid, and the first thing I'll buy are shoes and school uniforms for my children because they need to replace them. [The money] doesn't stretch much further but it helps. When school starts we have more expenses and we need to borrow money because our wages aren't enough. Thus we buy the school supplies, not all of them at once, though, but little by little as we can so they can have what is needed to go to school."

Economic aid from government programs, however, is not free. In exchange, the beneficiaries are required to provide time and labor for government community projects. Because programs such as those sponsored by DIF and Oportunidades / Prospera designate women as either de jure or de facto beneficiaries, women are disproportionately burdened with additional responsibilities. Thus they are required to regularly attend monthly meetings and to "volunteer" in community activities such as sweeping streets, removing graffiti from walls, and cleaning public clinics and schools, as well as helping in ad hoc projects in their colonias. Most women "community leaders" chosen by government officials also have to contribute unpaid time and labor to conduct a census of local residents enrolled in government-funded programs, coordinate the community meetings, and keep track of people who are added or dropped from these programs. These requirements rest on the assumption that women do not have other demands on their time and on the ideology of "good motherhood" in which those tasks are considered natural (Wilson 2015). This "feminization of community labor," I argue, reflects the gender ideology of Mexico's welfare policy culture that constructs community work as a natural extension of women's domestic activities. These requirements add to the heavy workload women farmworkers like Esther carry, juggling wage labor, household work, and secondary jobs in the informal economy with community responsibilities. While cash transfer programs have empowered women workers in terms of financial decision making in their households, they have also added a new layer of responsibilities to the "double shift" associated with the feminization of employment in export agriculture (Kay 2008, 925; Lara Flores 1995). As a result, women have less time for other important income-generating activities and often have to miss work to attend the mandatory monthly meetings,

FIGURE 21. Community work by farmworkers is often performed by women.

a particularly harsh choice for women who are heads of their households (Wilson 2015, 211). As an economic, social, and political endeavor, settlement is thus a gendered process in which women carry a disproportionately but often unrecognized burden as family keepers and community organizers.

COMBINING SETTLEMENT AND MIGRATION

While building homes in San Quintín and settling with their families have reduced labor migration outside the region, it has not stopped this tradition as both men and women farmworkers often seek to find better job opportunities in other regions in Mexico and in the United States. In fact, labor migration to the United States has a long historical tradition in San Quintín that precedes settlement and has continued afterward, although in different forms and often involving new migratory routes. Thus, except for the early phase of settlement when many workers concentrated their energies on procuring a lot to build a first room, the settlement process often entailed workers migrating out of the region for different lengths of time to support the economic costs of achieving the goal of residential independence.

During the early years of settlement, many workers migrated north of the border to send remittances back to their families. This was the case of Rodolfo and Adelina Moreno in Colonia Arbolitos. As a farm laborer and despite Adelina's part-time informal job as a hairdresser and the monthly stipend she received from Oportunidades, Rodolfo felt his income was well below the bare minimum to sustain his family and was compelled to migrate to work in the United States, where, as a single man, he had worked in the past. In 2003, after building their first room, he decided to go back to the United States to help finance the costs of expanding their home and maintaining their children and keeping them in school. When I asked what drove him to leave San Quintín again after all the sacrifices to move to their own house, he pointed out the higher wages he earned in California and the ability to save to help his children: "My goal was to save some money to help my children because here it's very difficult to save anything. . . . Simply put, here [San Quintín] you earn much less, you work hard, and get very tired; over there you make more money."

Rodolfo's decision to migrate as a seasonal worker to the United States reflects a common pattern I observed among many farmworkers. After moving to their own lots, they confronted rising living expenses, especially for housing and maintaining their children, who in the past were either left behind in home communities or brought along on migrations. By migrating to the United States, workers were able to send money back to their families to help with housing, subsistence, and school expenses. Luis Flores, for example, who had first gone to work to the United States as a single male in 1982, resumed migration after marrying Laura and moving to Colonia Santa Fe. For several years, he spent five to six months at a time as a seasonal worker in the United States, sending money to build their house and maintain their seven children, while Laura worked in San Quintín cleaning houses, washing clothes for others, and running the household. Luis felt that without the ability to work in the United States, he would not have been able to support his family.

> For me to support everyone, I didn't make enough, and it's a little more money if you work over there. There I make $200 or $250 a week; that's good money, about 2,000 pesos. Here you can't make 2,000 pesos a week. As a driver I make 700 pesos a week, and I pay 1,500 pesos a week for food. It doesn't work. So when I was in the U.S., I would send $150 to $180 a week so they could eat, except the week when I had to pay rent there, I would send less.

Over time, however, undocumented labor migration became a more expensive, riskier, and less common option for farm laborers in the region. The militarization of the border, especially in the San Diego–Tijuana region, significantly increased the cost of crossing the border and the chances of being caught. The economic recession that started in 2008 also reduced job opportunities for farmworkers in

California. Some workers who still managed to get across often went back to San Quintín after not being able to find work and with considerable debts to the people who helped them finance their journey. Luis Flores was among those seasoned migrant workers who after years of going back and forth stopped altogether because of the rising costs and physical struggle of crossing the border.

> Before, when we would go through Tijuana, it wouldn't take long, just around four hours and we would be through. Later on, we started walking more, day and night for a week. And later, at the end, at the very end, we would just walk for one day and one night. That's how long we walked last year [2008]. The coyotes used to charge $100, later they started charging $300, and after that it was $700. And last year they charged me $1,400, walking twenty-four hours a day, day and night.

Without the option to continue migrating to the United States, workers like Rodolfo Moreno and Luis Flores had to make important adjustments to reduce family expenses. In several cases, I witnessed some farm laborers who could no longer afford the educational expenses of their children, including a few who had graduated from high school and wanted to go to college. But as the path of undocumented migration to the United States began to narrow by the late 2010s, new forms of migration began to emerge, including to the United States, revealing the dynamic and continuous rearticulation between settlement and migration in workers' lives.

WORKING AS SEASONAL H-2A FARM LABORERS IN CALIFORNIA

When crossing the border as undocumented migrants to work in the United States became a more costly, riskier, and more uncertain enterprise, farmworkers in San Quintín began looking for other options. Low wages that hardly increased over the years and the rising cost of living in Baja placed them under constant economic strain, pushing them to find alternative ways to deal with their predicament. An opportunity to begin or resume migrating to the United States emerged when transnational labor contractors started recruiting experienced farmworkers in San Quintín through the H-2A Temporary Agricultural Workers program. As mentioned earlier, the H-2A program received renewed support from growers when border control policies slowed down the arrival of undocumented farmworkers from Mexico. With the fortification of the border, the program opened new opportunities to farm laborers in San Quintín to work in the United States for a few months at a time, earn wages in dollars, and save money to invest in their homes, their children's education, or prepare for the low employment winter season after coming back home.

Celeste Hernández was among the hundreds of experienced farmworkers who were recruited by Sierra-Cascade Nursery to go to California shortly after this company opened a recruitment office in San Quintín. She first learned about this company through the local station Radio XEQUIN and decided to apply. A few weeks later, she was interviewed about her work experience, her family, and her properties in San Quintín. After paying the 1,300 peso ($125) fee for the visa application, she was selected to work in Susanville, California. In her first season, she worked from mid-September to the end of October cutting strawberry seedlings, earning $400 per week and saving $2,200, which, upon returning to San Quintín, she used to pay tuition and living expenses for her eldest daughter who was attending college in Ensenada. Her first time as a seasonal worker in the United States was the hardest, not only because it was the first time she left home after settling in San Quintín, but also because she had to leave behind her youngest child, Marco, who was four years old. In order to leave, she arranged with her relatives to take care of him and watch over her teenage children during her absence. Recalling her first experience working north of the border, she described the incentives, difficulties, and help she received from her relatives in San Quintín: "It's nice because you learn to do a different type of work, but at the same time it's sad because I'm far from my children, I'm not with my children. At night sometimes I cry while I think of them. I thank them [her sisters] because they're the ones who support me. If it weren't for them I wouldn't go there and my daughter wouldn't be in school because here [San Quintín] I don't earn enough money to give her the schooling she wants."

Despite the emotional cost of leaving her children behind, Celeste continued migrating to California as an H-2A seasonal worker to bring money back to her family in San Quintín. The following season, Sierra-Cascade Nursery called her again to work for two months because of her good performance and behavior the first year. Having learned the work routine in California, this time she was able to increase her earnings and save $2,500. After that, the company hired her every year to return to California, benefiting from her experience and reliability and the low risk she posed of staying in the United States after her work permit expired. In 2010, during her third season in the program, she saved $3,500, which she used to cover her daughter's university expenses, make repairs on her home, and create a financial cushion to support her family during the winter. Celeste, who was single after being abandoned by her husband several years earlier, appreciated the opportunity the H-2A program provided her to improve her housing and living standards and help her daughter go to college. She proudly explained how she had used the earnings accrued working in California.

> When I came back this last time I fixed up my kitchen. I was able to buy my kitchen sink because I didn't use to have a place for washing dishes. Last year I bought my stove, and this year I fixed up my kitchen and bought a washer and dryer. I put flooring in this room, and the little that's left goes to my daughter for her school. And this year, if God allows me to go back, well, I'll fix the roof because this year with the rain all the pieces of cardboard lifted and it leaks. . . . I'll do it little by little, as I can.

Rather than seasonal, however, Celeste's migration as a farmworker to the United States became more regular and prolonged, revealing the structural codependency between employers and immigrant workers that seasonal labor programs often foster (Martin 2001). When her oldest two children reached eligibility, Sierra-Cascade Nursery recruited them to go with her to work in California, allowing the family to increase the savings they brought back home. Then in 2015, Celeste was offered a nine-month contract instead of the ninety days she had had until then. At that point, she relied on her oldest sister who had graduated from college to take care of Marco while she was gone. By 2016, she began her second season with a nine-month contract along with another fifty workers from San Quintín, as Sierra-Cascade was apparently employing around a thousand farmworkers from the region to work in Northern California and Oregon. At that point, she gave her house in Colonia Arbolitos to her oldest daughter who had recently married, and with her additional savings from working longer in the United States, she bought a new parcel nearby and began building a new home for herself, planning for her future retirement.[6] Since then, she has worked in California from March to November, returning the rest of the year to San Quintín with her family and, many years after leaving, visiting her hometown in Oaxaca.

Celeste's story, along with similar ones from other workers I met in San Quintín who are recruited as H-2A laborers, is significant for several reasons. First, the expansion of the H-2A program reflects the institutionalization of seasonal labor programs that imported Mexican workers to the United States in the recent past (Griffith 2014). Under this program, U.S. companies capitalize on the skills and work experience of farmworkers during their most productive years, externalizing the economic and social costs of raising, training, and maintaining them to their communities in Mexico. Second, the growth of this program in San Quintín reveals the close articulation between settlement and migration in workers' lives. Farmworkers' labor experience and acquired skills, along with their determination to improve their living conditions in Baja, make them ideal recruits for U.S. companies. Third, the labor trajectories of farmworkers like Celeste show the shortcomings of Mexico's neoliberal agrarian reforms that promoted export agriculture as a development policy meant to provide jobs for poor rural workers and stop labor migration to the United States. Instead, the low wages paid in the horticultural industry, along with the economic costs settlement involves, push farm laborers to look for migration opportunities to work in the United States to support their families, a common trend among women who engage in this type of labor migration to help their children (Preibisch 2010). Despite workers' increasing skills, work experience, and enhanced productivity, export agriculture has not provided a living wage, forcing them to undertake temporary migration outside the region.

INTERREGIONAL MIGRATION AND CAPTIVE LABOR

Labor migration to the United States is not the only way farmworkers combine settlement with migration in San Quintín. Interregional migration to Baja California Sur to work at agricultural sites like Vizcaíno, Loreto, and La Paz on a temporary basis is another common practice by which farmworkers seek to maintain their families, especially during the winter. The growing U.S. demand for fresh export crops has fostered new production sites in other regions in Baja, such as the Santo Domingo Valley in Comondú and the Vizcaíno Valley in Mulegé (Velasco and Hernández Campos 2018), often by the same companies that operate in San Quintín. This trend gained momentum in the late 1990s when, because of overexploitation of the aquifer for horticultural production, water in the region became scarce. In response, some large companies began developing satellite sites in southern Baja. In the process, a new pattern of interregional labor migration emerged in which growers recruit farmworkers in San Quintín as seasonal laborers at those sites.

Often isolated in remote areas with a captive labor force housed in camps and little or no government oversight, smaller production sites are predicated on the vulnerability of migrant workers, often indigenous people from southern Mexico. In San Quintín, I often heard rumors about southern Baja where allegedly farmworkers were kept against their will in labor camps far away from towns or populated areas for a period of time, often without pay. Yet I had never met anyone who had gone through this ordeal. It was only late during my fieldwork that Ramón Suárez, who had been involved in such a situation, told me about his experience. One evening when talking about his involvement in labor strikes, he told me a story about labor unrest in La Paz in 1997. Before then, Ramón had gone as an undocumented laborer to the United States on several occasions. But he accepted an opportunity to go to La Paz to pick tomatoes, as he figured it was a good way to earn some money during the low season in San Quintín without the risk and costs involved in crossing the border to California.

Ramón's story in Baja California Sur reveals the structural vulnerability farmworkers in these production sites confront and the regime of captive labor on which agricultural companies often rely. The recruiting company offered workers free transportation to La Paz and wages considerably higher than what most of them made in San Quintín. Ramón recalled that two buses full of workers departed from San Quintín, and after arriving in La Paz they were taken on about a five-hour ride on an unpaved desert road until they arrived at a labor camp, as he put it, "in the middle of nowhere." To his surprise and disappointment, the camp had none of the services, like beds, bathrooms, and drinking water, that were promised at the time of recruitment. Once inside he learned that workers, most of them indigenous laborers recruited from the southern state of Guerrero, were not allowed to leave until they finished the harvest, kept there by armed security guards contracted by the company. By then, he said, it was too late for him to leave: "When we arrived there I found lots of people who were being exploited, really exploited, and I couldn't get away. The ranch had its own security guards and was surrounded by a high fence with surveillance, all private security. If you tried to leave they threatened and forced you to get back to the camp; you couldn't escape. . . . . Most workers were from Guerrero."

The work was hard and the days were long, a situation compounded by the fact that the site was isolated and there was no transportation available. Without a town nearby, workers had to buy food and other basic items at the *tienda de raya* (camp store), putting them in debt even before receiving any payment for their work. One day, a group of workers who had grown tired of the exploitation decided to organize a plantón to protest the conditions of their employment and confinement in the camp. Ramón recalled the events that followed.

> We all got united and one night began to spread the word in secret. It wasn't easy to organize a work stoppage because there were lots of armed security guards watching us, so we had to be very careful in spreading the word. We had studied the guards' movements and the times they changed shifts. Around 3:00 A.M. we began organizing. There were ten guards we were watching and three controlling the main entrance, which were the first that got knocked down. They tried to get their guns, but there were many workers, and they threw them on the ground, disarmed them, and removed their clothes and walkie-talkies. At sunrise we all were in our positions, but later in the morning more guards arrived on special motorbikes that run in the sand and began threatening to open fire on us. But there were lots of us, about five hundred workers, men and women, and they didn't fire; instead they surrounded the camp and didn't let anybody out, waiting until the patrón arrived.

Ramón's recollection conveys the risks workers often confront in this type of satellite production site. In an isolated labor camp, farmworkers' structural vulnerability materialized in vivid and painful fashion. Unlike San Quintín since the late 1990s, there were no government agencies overseeing this labor site and camp, leaving workers with no place to go for help. The ordeal they went through after the patrón arrived to put an end to the workers' rebellion reveals how structural violence is deployed in the lives of migratory farmworkers.

> The patrón arrived in a helicopter. Then a bunch of *judiciales* [judicial police] began pouring out of white pickups fully armed and started to fire their arms to threaten us. "Who started this revolt?," they asked. They sorted us and separated the men in groups, bringing us to different parts in the camp. They brought a workmate and me to a corner and asked, "Do you know who started all this? You need to tell us the truth," and I responded, "No, I don't know anything, I just arrived this week." One of my workmates got it worse because they threatened to kill him if he didn't talk. . . .

[Then] they put all the men in two lines and searched us one by one looking for arms. "Why are you organizing this stoppage?," they asked. "Where are the arms?" We didn't have any guns, only a few knives. To be honest, it was harsh. It was very tough because they threatened me: "You know what? We are going to break you if you don't talk."

Fortunately for the workers, the situation did not escalate. After a few hours of interrogation and negotiation, Ramón explained, the company decided to lay them off. Shortly afterward two buses arrived to take workers back to La Paz, where the company said they would get paid, and then continue the trip back to San Quintín. The buses were "escorted" by pickups with security guards and did not stop in La Paz but in an empty field a few miles away from town, where workers were paid in cash. "Why didn't they pay us in La Paz?," Ramón asked rhetorically. "Because if they stopped in La Paz a courageous worker could have gone to denounce them to the Procuraduría [government agency]." The buses were packed with "three or four people per seat," he recalled, as all the workers wanted to escape the labor camp. A few of them got off in Constitución and Loreto, two other sites producing export crops, to look for employment while he and the rest continued back to San Quintín. When he finally arrived home about a week after he had left, hoping to bring some good savings back for his family, Ramón only had 20 pesos ($3) in his pocket.

Many years had passed before Ramón told me about his experience in La Paz. With the passage of time he retold the story with a mixture of fear and humor, the latter referring to the little money he brought back home, a matter about which his wife, Aurelia, liked to tease him. Yet his ordeal reveals the violence and lawlessness farmworkers still confront in labor camps in commercial agriculture in Mexico. Unlike settled workers in San Quintín, migrant workers employed seasonally at smaller production sites and isolated areas lack the social networks of kin and townsfolk, rendering them a highly vulnerable labor force, a contemporary version of unfree labor. In these horticultural enclaves, indigenous people constitute a mobile, unattached, and easily exploitable labor force (Lara Flores 2010).[7] Ramón's story also shows that settlement does not preclude labor migration; instead it has reconfigured farmworkers' migratory circuits. Today there are new forms of international migration to the United States as well as to other horticultural sites in Baja California Sur that have expanded in the recent past in response to the growing demand for conventional and organic vegetables and fruits by consumers in the United States (Lara Flores 2010, 265; Velasco and Hernández Campos 2018).

CONCLUSION

In this chapter, I have discussed the experiences of people who went from being seasonal migrants to settled farm laborers. In so doing, I move beyond farm laborers as workers to examine their lives as settlers in order to capture the social and human dimensions of the globalization of food production in San Quintín. Farmworkers confronted not only the intensive labor regime of export agriculture but also the multiple challenges of moving to their own land lots, building their homes, mobilizing to bring public services to their communities, and setting down roots in this region while earning wages of about $8 a day. The collective struggles they endured, along with the development of diverse forms of social solidarity and support, contributed to a new sense of political agency. Unlike migrant farmworkers in labor camps who in the 1980s mobilized around labor issues, settled farm laborers engaged in collective mobilizations for residential independence and access to public services, infusing the region with new forms of labor and political mobilization and energy. In the process they developed a new sense of political citizenship, claiming full-fledged rights as legitimate residents that challenged the nativist discourse fostered by powerful growers and middle-class government workers that portrayed them as outsiders who do not belong. The historical significance of this settlement endeavor cannot be overstated. After several failed attempts to populate this arid valley, including state-led colonization initiatives in the 1930s and 1940s, it was farmworkers' efforts, determination, and collective struggles that finally succeeded.

The massive settlement of indigenous farmworkers in San Quintín is also significant for the discussion on the labor force renewal of farmworkers employed in export agriculture. Residential independence has allowed farmworkers to diversify their job opportunities and income sources, a trend also noticed in other agroexport enclaves in northern Mexico (Lara Flores and Sánchez Saldaña 2015). Settled workers have options other than working in agriculture, which allows them to retain some degree of autonomy and avoid their complete dependence on poorly paid and exploitative horticultural jobs. Domestic production of food for self-provisioning and barter—what I referred to as the backyard household economy—has been enhanced by farmworkers' access to their own residential lots, opening a new niche that was not available when they were housed in labor camps or cuarterías. The various types of income generated in informal occupations, petty commodity production, and food production for family consumption speak to what Cristóbal Kay (2008) calls "multiple income-generating activities," which is central for the replenishment of the labor force in the fresh-produce industry. With less economic dependence on their home communities in Oaxaca, the labor reproduction costs of workers employed in export agriculture are thus mostly absorbed by workers and their families in Baja.

As a social process, place making and community building are at the heart of the settlement experience of indigenous and mestizo workers. As I have shown, moving to their own parcels, building their homes, and having a place they can claim as their own has brought a sense of accomplishment and pride for many farmworkers. Settlement has also allowed them to reconstruct their social lives, strengthening a sense of belonging and attachment to the land. In the process they have reinvented themselves as a group, engaging in a process of reterritorialization to claim ownership of their communities and actively participating in community politics to advance their labor and civil rights. But settlement does not preclude migration. Rather, settlement and labor migration are deeply intertwined in the lives of many farmworkers in San Quintín, disclosing the structural limitations of the fresh-produce industry to provide adequate wages to their employees.

7

Watercide: Export Agriculture, Water Insecurity, and Social Unrest

There is an inequity in how water is distributed in the valley. I estimate there are around 250,000 boxes of tomatoes being exported to the United States, and I see them as [the equivalent of] 250,000 boxes of water leaving the region without paying taxes. Meanwhile as you could see, there are people who live here who don't get water in their homes.
—JORGE DE LEÓN, AT A COMMUNITY MEETING IN LÁZARO CÁRDENAS, 2009

On a warm evening in June 2009, I attended a community meeting organized by the residents of Lázaro Cárdenas to protest the water problems they were experiencing. Despite having piped water, a privileged status compared to many colonias, residents had grown concerned about the irregularity and unpredictability of water delivery to their homes. To convey their distress and request a solution to the problem, they invited to the meeting Bernardo Gastelum, then head of the Comisión Estatal de Servicios Públicos de Ensenada (CESPE; State Commission of Public Services of Ensenada), the state agency in charge of delivering water for domestic use in the region. Soon after the meeting started, the forty or so residents in attendance began expressing their discontent. One person complained that CESPE shut down piped water from a well in the colonia every day for several hours to divert it to residents in a neighboring colonia. Following up, another neighbor said, "We only get water every third day, but CESPE charges us for the service as if we were getting water every day." "We have to pay our water bills to CESPE every month, but we don't get enough water and have to buy it outside from private vendors," another person stated. "We are the ones suffering the consequences of CESPE's action because there are times when four and five days go by without getting water at home," one man commented. As the meeting continued, more people raised their hands to speak and the tone became angrier and more combative. Then Jorge de León—a neighbor who runs a barbershop who, unlike most of the farmworker residents, is a middle-class mestizo and active in public life in San Quintín—raised his hand to speak: "Lack of access to water has become a major social problem here, and the government tries to address it with Band-Aids instead of long-term solutions. We have an inefficient government that doesn't give solutions to the people's needs.... We cannot continue living as third-class citizens and we aren't gonna sit idly.... We want the government to regulate the water extracted in agricultural wells that are overexploited by large agricultural companies."

By the time Bernardo Gastelum was given the opportunity to respond, the anger and frustration in the audience had escalated. Gastelum expressed sympathy for their complaints and acknowledged there was a problem of water scarcity in the region. He then listed several initiatives his agency was undertaking to address this problem, including the search for potential water sources at different sites to build wells. While listening to him, residents nodded skeptically. When the meeting was over and I walked outside, many residents were still standing around in small groups, and Jorge de León, who had noticed I was taking notes, approached me to talk. While large agribusinesses have their own desalination plants, he stated, the local government had not built a single such plant for residents, although one could be "supported by a state tax for companies exporting tomatoes." Jorge's frustration reflected the view of many of his neighbors who blamed the government for their poor water service and the inequity of water distribution in the valley.

In this chapter, I examine how the production of fresh produce for international consumer markets has affected access to water resources for farmworkers and other residents in San Quintín. Although commercial agriculture has fostered economic growth and employment opportunities for indigenous farm laborers, it has also contributed to the overexploitation of underground water resources and a decline in the quantity and quality of water for local residents. The rise of horticultural production along with the growth of rural settlements put these trends on a collision course. I analyze the connections between the neoliberal economic policies that drive the growth of the global fresh-produce industry and the ways in which they shape regional power and differential access to water along class and ethnic lines. From a political ecology perspective, I discuss the inequalities and hardships that water-extracting technologies used by the agroexport sector have entailed for local residents. As the chapter shows, water insecurity has spurred the development of household coping strategies as well as collective mobilizations to demand access to water as a basic civil and human right. Water, I contend, serves as a powerful heuristic tool to analyze the deep social and ethnic inequalities caused by the regime of export agriculture; it also allows linking people's demand for water with larger issues of equity and social justice in this region.

EXPORT AGRICULTURE AND WATER SCARCITY

The production of fresh produce in developing countries for consumer markets in affluent nations has important consequences for the water resources in the regions where the crops are grown. Anthropologists who specialize in the study of water contend that the commodification of water by policies that favor its privatization and intensive use for commercial agriculture has exacerbated social inequities and consolidated structural violence against the poor (Whiteford and Whiteford 2005, 11). Specifically, the extensive pumping of groundwater for agricultural production has been recognized as a key factor leading to water scarcity in many regions throughout the world (Whiteford and Whiteford 2005). Following the water footprint used in the production of fresh produce for international markets, Arjen Hoekstra and Ashok Chapagain (2008, 138) conceptualize the transfer of large volumes of water embedded in the export of fresh fruits and vegetables as "virtual water flows." Historically, they argue, water was seen as a local rather than a global resource, but with the expansion of international trade it has become a global commodity (Hoekstra and Chapagain 2008, 135). Moreover, they add, the costs of water-intensive agricultural commodities in the exporting country are not generally included in the price of the products consumed in the importing country, and consumers are not generally aware of the water problems in the regions where these crops are grown (138).

At the same time, virtual water flows can exacerbate water scarcity. The concept of water scarcity refers to the lack of sufficient resources to support human needs, estimated at a minimum of 3 to 6 liters per capita daily for drinking and 50 liters for consumption and household use (Wutich and Brewis 2014, 444–45).[1] But water scarcity not only refers to the dynamics of supply and demand; it also includes the economic values and cultural meanings that different social groups ascribe to this resource and their differential power to control its distribution (Johnston 2005, 135–36). The concept allows us to analyze the cultural meanings of water use by different social actors and the ideas and values disempowered groups articulate when mobilizing for water rights. By focusing on the effects of and responses to water scarcity in agroexport enclaves, we can reveal how social struggles over this vital element materialize and shape people's ideas about water and water rights.

WATERSCAPES: WATER CRISIS AND AGRIBUSINESS'S TECHNOLOGICAL FIXES

The development of large-scale agriculture for export markets in the San Quintín Valley in the 1980s radically transformed the political ecology of the region. Unlike other regions along the U.S.–Mexico border that rely on irrigation infrastructure built by the Mexican government since the 1930s or the United States since the early 1900s, in San Quintín commercial agriculture mostly depends on underground water. For several decades, local growers tapped the regional aquifers to water their lands, building wells as horticultural production increased. The main irrigation method consisted of running water through the furrows, a system locally known as *agua corrida*, a rather inefficient and wasteful technique. Over time and as water became scarcer, most growers shifted to drip irrigation, a method that made more efficient use of this scarce resource (Aguirre-Muñoz et al. 2001, 144). But the intensification of export agriculture placed enormous pressure on the watershed. While traditional crops such as wheat and barley were still grown, the expansion of water-intensive crops such as tomatoes and strawberries posed a major ecological stress on a region that has a mean annual rainfall of only about 150 millimeters (mm), compared to a national average of 774 mm (Aguirre-Muñoz et al. 2001).[2] A study of water use in the region showed that commercial agriculture extracted six times more groundwater than the recharge rate of the watersheds (Aguirre-Muñoz et al. 2001, 145). As a result, in the 1990s the water table dropped about one foot per year (Lizárraga 1997, 3). By the late 1990s, overexploitation and saltwater intrusion in the water basins led to a water crisis, drastically reducing the amount of land under cultivation to the point that some experts predicted the end of commercial agriculture in the valley (e.g., Aguirre-Muñoz et al. 2001; Lizárraga 1997).[3]

Despite this prediction, large agricultural companies decided to invest in modern water-extraction technologies to continue the production of lucrative export crops. As mentioned before, only between the early 2000s and 2009, largely relying on direct capital investment from U.S. agribusinesses under the umbrella of NAFTA, twenty-five desalination plants of different sizes were built in the region, and by 2017 sixty-two plants were registered. Usually the desalination technique for horticultural purposes consists of extracting freshwater from oceanic salt water; yet in San Quintín, to reduce costs most companies extract salt from overexploited water wells, further contributing to the mining of the aquifer.[4] And while the shift to indoor agriculture initially reduced the use of water, as cultivation in protected environments expanded and allowed for the production of multiple annual crops, the demand for water also increased.[5] Commenting on the inner logic of this technological fix, an agronomist at the local office of SAGARPA explained how large companies joined the race to invest in production technologies to increase their profits: "Once companies began investing in desalination plants, they had to develop a new cultivation program to recoup the high costs of such investment. To continue producing in open fields wasn't an option because the high salinity of the soil would have required many years before the costs of desalination plants could be recouped. By shifting to production in shadehouses, companies can recoup such costs and make a profit in two years. That's why shadehouses and desalination plants began at the same time in the region."

Talking with growers, I realized that they view water from a utilitarian perspective and reduce it to its economic cost. Water is treated as a factor of production rather than as a precarious ecological resource with intrinsic value for human life and other economic activities. As growers became increasingly efficient in the use of irrigation technologies, maximizing every drop of water, they extracted as much water as needed to increase production. Bernardo Gastelum, at the time head of the state water agency, was openly critical of the exploitation of the aquifer by growers because, in his view, this was the central factor preventing access to water for the local population. He shared his view on growers' utilitarian approach: "I've seen that growers are merciless with nature and the extraction of water and yet extremely careful in the use of water; they don't waste a single drop. . . . They are also merciless with residents in the region. They don't care about their workers; they just care about their crops, not their workers or the population."

Gastelum's perspective speaks to the ecological and social consequences of the virtual water flows embedded in the export of fresh fruits and vegetables. Elaborating on the larger effects of water-extraction technologies, he criticized growers' greed and their disregard for the ecological consequences of those technologies: "You can't produce a tomato without water; you can't export a tomato if you don't have water. Then essentially we have become water exporters. Growers here don't see tomatoes as food but just as an opportunity to earn dollars and make a profit without any care about the water shortage you cause by exporting produce. And yet they don't say they are exporting water; they say, 'I export tomatoes,' but in reality they are exporting water. They are extracting it from the watershed of the nation to the detriment of the ecology and its sustainability."

Gastelum's critique was similar to that of local residents. As more companies built desalination plants, water reservoirs—oases carefully guarded to irrigate export crops—became visible throughout the valley. I use the term "waterscapes" to refer to the assemblage of capital-intensive technologies to mine water for commercial agriculture that transformed the landscape, creating artificial water reservoirs to keep horticultural production going. Waterscapes make it possible for the indirect costs associated with the production of fresh produce for international markets to be externalized to local communities in developing countries where they are produced. Every time I returned to the region, the expansion of water reservoirs struck me as a naked symbol of the waterscapes created by the fresh-produce industry and the inequity of the distribution of water between agribusinesses and the local population of farmworkers who produce their crops.

NEOLIBERAL WATER POLICIES AND THEIR EFFECTS ON SMALL FARMERS

In agroexport enclaves, access to water is not just dictated by agribusiness needs; state policies and power politics play a central role in determining access to and distribution of water resources. Who controls access to water in a given community is the result of political factors such as state water policies, regional structures of power, and the challenges to or reinforcement of such internal power structures by global forces (Pérez Prado 2002; Treitler and Midgett 2007). In Mexico, neoliberal policies have played a pivotal role in advancing the privatization of water as a means to foster economic growth, including by means of export agriculture. Neoliberal water reforms date to 1992, when the National Water Law decentralized the management of urban and agricultural water services and reduced the role of the federal government. In the agricultural sector, the goals of this neoliberal approach were to "enhance efficiency," fairness in water management, and resource sustainability (Whiteford and Melville 2002, 20). Meanwhile water policies for domestic use aimed to decentralize water service management to states, municipalities, or private concessionaires and to "reduce consumption" (Walsh 2011).

In San Quintín, the new water law exacerbated the power inequality between agribusiness and civil society regarding access to local water supplies. The technological fixes and waterscape assemblages manufactured by large companies—desalination plants and greenhouse and shadehouse facilities—not only had the financial support of transnational corporations, but also of the Mexican government, which subsidizes the cost. These subsidies, some direct and others indirect, take different forms. Growers can obtain public funds provided by SAGARPA under a program called Activos Productivos (Productive Assets) to build desalination plants. Since the early 2000s, SAGARPA has channeled several million Mexican pesos into numerous desalination plants for irrigation by fresh-produce companies. The agency subsidizes up to 50 percent of desalination plants and well pumps, or 750,000 pesos of the cost to build a desalination plant for commercial agriculture (López 2017, 193). This program mostly benefits large agribusinesses as they have the capital to finance the remaining costs (and sometimes the political connections to influence the process).[6] A second type of subsidy is through reduced energy costs. As part of the National Water Law, the Mexican government ended subsidies for electricity to operate the water pumps generally used by small farmers (Ennis-McMillan 2001, 379). Electricity from power generation plants that feed desalination plants and greenhouses, however, remains heavily subsidized (Nauman 2007).[7] Thus in San Quintín growers can apply for a subsidy to cover 50 percent of the power costs used for agriculture, an important incentive for agribusinesses that rely on desalination, computer-operated shadehouses, and other electricity-dependent technologies. This subsidy includes water irrigation systems, shadehouses, greenhouses, and desalination plants, among others.[8] As I discovered in the field, even water meters for agricultural wells are subsidized. The cost for well meters is about $292 apiece. Under a national government program called Efficient Use of Water and Electric Power (Uso Eficiente del Agua y Energía Eléctrica), the federal government pays 50 percent, the state government 25 percent, and growers the remaining 25 percent. Together, these three types of subsidies help growers reduce the operating costs of extracting and treating water for the production of fresh crops, reinforcing the incentive to invest in export agriculture.

The political influence of powerful growers and large companies also allows them to evade government regulations to monitor the use of well water for agriculture at the expense of small farmers. The National Water Law created watershed councils (*consejos de cuenca*) to enhance efficiency and fairness in the use and distribution of water, stipulating the formation of technical committees of underground water (so-called COTAS) for each council (Mumme and Brown 2002, 231; Whiteford and Melville 2002, 19–20). These committees are responsible for overseeing the permits and water concessions to local users and resolve water disputes when they arise (Santes-Álvarez 2015, 98–99). In the San Quintín Valley six such councils were formed in 1999, one per aquifer, yet most are inactive as they remain under the control of large growers who have little interest in enforcing water controls.[9] One exception is the committee for the San Quintín aquifer, which was formed by about fifty growers with small and midsized companies who had been severely affected by the overuse of water by large companies contiguous to their farms. In response, the committee installed meters and sensors to monitor the quantity and quality of water in the aquifer. While most of these growers embraced the initiative, large companies refused to comply and resisted providing accurate data on the number of water wells and water extraction on their properties. Ricardo Holgado, a local grower with deep roots in the region, was elected chair of this committee and was in charge of collecting data on water use from all growers operating in the jurisdiction. Every time I visited with him in his office, he complained that the "water crisis"—insufficient and salinized water in the wells operated by regular farmers—was to a large extent the result of intense exploitation by large companies that were often "reluctant to cooperate," either preventing the installation of meters or providing inaccurate data on water extraction.[10] I was particularly surprised by the fact that the Mexican National Water Commission (Comisión Nacional del Agua, or CNA)—the major federal agency that regulates the use of water for agriculture in the country—did not have a single office in the region, despite the fact that it is one of the leading agroexport hubs in Mexico.[11] The invisibility of the CNA undermined the ability of the COTA council committee to perform its job. The committee headed by Holgado received very limited financial support from the CNA; it had a small and rudimentary office in a commercial strip staffed with one part-time worker, Holgado's daughter-in-law, and a phone line that was often out of service because of unpaid bills.

In addition to evading government-mandated reporting on water use, powerful growers often engage in illegal predatory practices, extracting more water than permitted. Some of the largest companies are known for drilling new wells on their properties without a permit despite the fact that since the early 2000s the CNA has not issued licenses for more wells because of the overexploitation of the watersheds. Because the CNA does not allocate enough resources to enforce the law and relies on self-reporting by agricultural companies, there is little control of this illegal practice. Other companies use a more invasive strategy by tapping water in the mountains from springs that feed the aquifers to bring it to their fields, causing a dramatic reduction in the water flowing to the coastal area where most rural colonias are located.[12] The extraction of water from the springs before it takes its natural course down the mountains into the valley is an example of water theft that undermines the availability of water for people in the region. As an agricultural engineer at SAGARPA explained to me, the water-mining practices large companies often use had an adverse consequence for the aquifer, amounting to what I call an "assault on the commons."

> Because the government doesn't allow gathering water from the streams and only permits water wells, companies began to drill wells up in the mountains next to where the streams originate. That is the reason why the water streams coming from the mountains are dry, because large companies are mining water at its source; in the past most of the streams had running water but not anymore. To bring the water to their fields, they pay ranchers up there to buy a strip of their properties to install a pipe. Because of this, urban water wells don't get water anymore. These companies are tapping water from far away; we are talking about 23 kilometers and even 43 kilometers to where they have their fields!

Small growers who cannot afford expensive desalination technologies have been especially affected by the overexploitation of the aquifer. Some farmers who tried to stay in business producing strawberries for large firms, for example, lost their crops before the harvest when the wells supplying water to their fields ran dry (López 2017, 194). Others abandoned farming altogether and began renting their wells to larger producers. In some cases, large companies used "intermediaries" to offer those growers "participatory stock" in exchange for the right to extract water from their lands. Ricardo Holgado—who in addition to being the former president of San Quintín's COTA committee farmed on a small lot following the tradition of his family, which arrived in the region in the 1960s—confronted the consequences of having big companies extract large quantities of water near his lot. Comparing the approach to water use of agribusinesses and small growers like himself, he emphasized the more conservationist and water-sensitive approach used by the latter: "There're companies that, let's say, have three water wells. They run these wells continuously day and night for years. . . . In contrast, small growers follow the seasonal growing cycles and don't run the wells all the time; when the harvest is over we stop the wells in the winter and begin using them again the next production season."

Despite following more sustainable practices, small growers confronting either insufficient or saliferous water or a combination of both were unable to farm. With

FIGURE 22. Waterscapes: A water reservoir at Rancho Las Palmas in Vicente Guerrero.

no means to finance their own desalination plants, many of these growers decided to rent the water wells on their properties to large companies with the ability to treat and use the underground water. Speaking on behalf of the farmers from the San Quintín council he represented and with a mixture of sadness and resignation, Ricardo complained about the effects of the predatory water practices of large companies: "Many growers don't have the option to continue producing because of the salinity of their water wells. Then they either sell or rent their wells to large companies that have desalination plants. Thus a water well that could be resting is being exploited, which further aggravates the problem."

The predicaments growers like Ricardo face embody what Barbara Johnston and John Donahue (1998, 3) call "the politics of water struggles." This approach conceptualizes water as a crucial site of contestation between neoliberal forces of "economic progress" and community-based values associated with subsistence agriculture. In San Quintín, the struggle between large companies and small farmers occurred on an uneven field shaped by the state government's lack of political will to enforce water regulation policies and the resistance of companies to comply with the law. The last time I saw Ricardo, he had built a small desalination plant on his property to irrigate the crops of his little parcel. As he told me, it was the only option left if he wanted to keep his farm, and he was forced to use most of his own savings and take out a loan to finance it. During the numerous conversations I had with him over the years, he often asked if I knew of funding opportunities from the United Nations or other international organizations to help small farmers build desalination plants or to obtain water by other means. The difficulties he confronted speak to the harmful consequences the capital-intensive water-mining technologies of transnational companies have for small-scale producers in the region for whom farming has been the traditional way of life.

ARIDSCAPES: WATER SCARCITY FOR LOCAL RESIDENTS

Unlike agribusinesses, farmworkers and other local residents in San Quintín have limited access to water, no desalination plants, and little help to cope with water scarcity. Because of overextraction of water, by 2009, CESPE had only thirty-two urban wells, several of which were dry, compared to about five hundred wells registered for agricultural irrigation. Moreover, about 40 percent of the colonias in the region do not have running water, and residents have to buy it, if available, from CESPE's mobile trucks or at inflated prices from private vendors. Without access to piped water, many colonias are "aridscapes" of dry, unpaved streets, bare lots, and dust-filled air, an aridity only punctuated by small green patches where farmworkers grow a few vegetables for family consumption and/or plants to beautify the roughness of the land. The landscape in these rural communities sharply contrasts with the waterscapes made up of water reservoirs and green fields that surround the desalination plants and properties of the large companies that grow fresh produce.[13]

Rather than the "natural" result of a dry climate, San Quintín's aridscapes are the result of state policies that privilege access to limited water resources to agribusinesses at the expense of the local population. Responding to the Mexican Water Law, state politicians in Baja increased the cost of piped water to make the agency "financially sustainable." At first, CESPE proposed an increase of about 300 percent to take effect in 2007, but massive protests by residents, merchants, and small business owners derailed the plan. Despite this, local residents who did not have meters and paid a flat fee experienced a 115 percent increase in the cost of water (from 23 to 53 pesos per month). Although most farmworkers did not pay more than 60 pesos per month, the increase in the cost of water had a negative impact on their budgets, as many workers live from paycheck to paycheck.[14] In addition, and to hold residents accountable, CESPE started to install water meters in their homes. While water meters for agrarian wells were heavily subsidized, for households the average cost of installing a meter was 2,500 pesos (around $227), well beyond the limited means of most farm laborer families. Each new contract

FIGURE 23. Aurelia Suárez and a son get water to do laundry.

came with three separate fees for local residents, a connection fee, a piping fee, and the cost of the water meter, presenting a challenge to workers who could barely afford to put food on the table for their families (Zlolniski 2011, 585). Moreover, because of salt intrusion residents can use piped water only for a few household tasks such as cleaning, washing, bathing, or watering their plants and have to buy clean water in the private sector for cooking and drinking. Over time, water scarcity and rising water costs contributed to the expansion of informal markets, the proliferation of water theft, and other illegal practices. Among them was the emergence of a black market for water. Some CESPE employees were caught selling water from an agency truck after business hours for their own profit. In another case, a private vendor was accused of stealing water from a colonia well to sell it in settlements without piped water.

To justify the higher water prices and new policies, CESPE espoused a moralizing public discourse emphasizing the values of responsibility and accountability. The agency often portrays residents as wasting water for superfluous purposes and launched a public campaign to "educate" the citizenry to make rational use of water. The installation of water meters in residents' homes is justified not only to hold "customers" accountable for the amount of water they used but also as a tool to foster "a culture of water use" among indigenous residents in the region (Rojas 2008). This approach embodies the neoliberal philosophy that emphasizes individual responsibility and treats citizens as customers, an approach with particularly negative consequences for the poor. It also shows that when water costs are inadequately subsidized, poverty and water insecurity tend to reinforce each other, disproportionately falling on the shoulders of the most vulnerable populations (Wutich and Brewis 2014, 447).

WATER SCARCITY AND LOCAL RESPONSES IN COLONIA ARBOLITOS

The inequity of water distribution in San Quintín has had clear social and human consequences for its residents. The lack of a reliable source of water especially affects farmworker communities, which do not have enough water to support the basic needs of families and households. The case of Colonia Arbolitos reveals the drudgery of daily life that residents experience when access to water for everyday use is precarious and the ways in which they seek to cope with this situation. Until 2005, residents had to buy water from private water truck vendors who passed by only weekly because of the colonia's small size and difficult access. Facing increasing hardships to fetch water for their households, a group of neighbors in the colonia decided to organize to press the local government to deliver piped water. In summer 2006, they instructed the colonia's committee, composed of four elected members, to place water at the top of their list of collective demands. Rather than a confrontational approach, the committee opted to use negotiation and persuasion to convince public officials and gain their support. Joaquín Aguilar, a Zapotec and former farmworker who was elected president of Arbolito's committee, explained their rationale to me. Joaquín was one of the few Zapotecs in the community who had been able to leave farm labor to go to college in Ensenada, earning a degree in education. After returning to San Quintín, he became a bilingual teacher in a public elementary school and a respected and trusted leader to negotiate with government officials on behalf of the colonia's residents. Joaquín used his visibility as an indigenous leader to press CESPE and other local government offices to secure funding for the installation of a well in the colonia. He articulated to government authorities that access to water is a basic human right, tying the demand for water to the right to good hygiene and health of women and children in his community. He explained his strategy to me:

> We didn't hold protest rallies but negotiated through written memos and petitions in a peaceful manner. We laid out the cost that families in the community had to pay to buy water. We were using about fifteen to twenty water barrels a month for a family of four, each barrel at 15 pesos apiece—we're talking about 300 pesos a month just to bathe and for basic use in the household, not to water our plants.... We told them

FIGURE 24. Aridscapes: A man rides his bike in Colonia Arbolitos.

FIGURE 25. With no sewage system, residents in colonias use latrines.

that children have the right to be clean and healthy. We presented it as a basic right and told them that often women couldn't wash their children's clothes because the piped water trucks didn't come to our colonia.

Collective work and perseverance by the committee finally produced positive results. In 2008, after two years of patient negotiations with CESPE and the CDI, the federal agency that develops and funds projects for indigenous peoples in Mexico and successor to the famous National Indigenist Institute (INI), the committee secured 2.5 million pesos ($238,500) to build a well in the colonia. When the well was inaugurated, people celebrated it as an important political victory won by the persistent and diligent work carried out by the committee. Shortly afterward, the price for water fell dramatically, from about 300 to 40 pesos per month for a family of four. Elisa Robles, for example, recognized the improvement piped water had for her family. Before, she would buy seven water barrels a week for bathing and other basic household needs, paying 105 pesos a week. After having piped water and water meters, her water bill fell to 50 pesos a month, a significant reduction for a farmworker who at the time earned 1,100 pesos a week. Having running water improved the quality of life for her and her family. As she put it, "Things for me got much better; now I have my small plants and can do laundry and clean my house more often."

Despite the improvement, residents in the colonia often have to deal with water disruptions, particularly in the summer. To confront water scarcity, they have developed a series of ingenious water-saving strategies. One of the most common I observed among Zapotec women consists of recycling laundry water to clean their homes and water their gardens, a practice known as "water multitasking" (Webb and Iskandarani 1998, 5). After washing their families' clothes, women pour the used water into separate barrels that they later use for such purposes. Rather than an isolated phenomenon, the use of so-called gray water is a common practice of many people in San Quintín, including indigenous Triquis (López 2017, 195), and a strategy by which the poor cope with water insecurity in other regions in the world (Wutich and Brewis 2014, 448–49). Witnessing the time and patience invested by Zapotec farmworkers in Colonia Arbolitos to optimize the use of water, I could not help but think about public officials' inaccurate and unfair portrayal of indigenous residents as "irresponsible" for "wasting" water. Like growers in the region, residents in San Quintín have learned to use water in a highly efficient fashion. But unlike the former, who extract as much water as possible for irrigation, local residents are very thrifty in its use, as they have to pay for every drop they consume.

The hardships and lived experience of accessing water to meet their most basic needs also transformed people's notions about water itself. While many residents still considered water a public good, others referred to it as a scarce and "limited good" that could not be shared with people living in adjacent colonias. Local residents conveyed ambivalent views about water rights, ranging from water as a universal right that comes from nature to water as a limited and contested resource that needs to be protected. Reflecting the tension between these poles, Celeste Hernández, who acknowledged having participated in a group of neighbors digging up a CESPE pipe to prevent water from being delivered to a neighboring settlement, told me, "When God gives us water it's for everybody; God never deprives anybody of water but gives it out evenly to all people.... My sister, uncles, and other relatives, though, live in Colonia Ampliación [with no piped water], and it hurts to know they do not get water; it's sad. I know what is like not having water at home to wash the dishes, bathe our children and oneself. But the majority of people in Arbolitos don't want water from our well to be taken away."

Celeste's narrative shows that in water-scarce environments, households may refuse requests for water from outsiders and/or engage in social norms of "water sharing" (Wutich and Brewis 2014, 450). Water scarcity thus triggers what Michael Ennis-McMillan (2001) calls "water suffering," a deep emotional experience that reflects people's perceptions of the social and political conditions underpinning their personal anguish when confronting water insecurity.

AGROEXPORTS AND ENVIRONMENTAL DEGRADATION

In a critical assessment of the impact of intensive industrialized farming in Mexico, Humberto González (2012) argues that the economic restructuring of the agricultural sector in the 1980s led to a severe degradation of ecosystems in regions that specialize in this type of agricultural production. One factor behind this trend is the integration of markets on a global scale and the intensification of production that caused the depletion of natural resources and the creation of contaminating residues (González 2012, 484). A second factor is the response by large transnational corporations, which adopted production models to increase productivity without considering their impact "in damaging the environment and in depleting natural resources" (484). The result has been compromising sustainable agricultural systems in regions linked to global markets.

In San Quintín, as the region deepened its integration into the global fresh-produce industry, the impacts on the environment and water resources became increasingly evident. As the production of water-intensive crops for international markets increased, especially after the rapid growth of berry production, water extraction of the aquifer intensified, with the horticultural sector draining the bulk of this natural resource. Of the total water consumed in the region, estimated at 130 cubic hectometers a year, 93 percent is dedicated to agricultural production, with only 6 percent for public use and less than 1 percent for other industries and services (Riemman 2015, 21).[15] This trend has contributed to water overextraction in most of the region's aquifers, generating a deficit that compounded the water scarcity that already affected local residents.[16] This overextraction of water for agricultural production is especially risky given that the San Quintín Valley is one of Mexico's most arid regions. As one of the thirteen administrative hydrologic regions in the country, Baja California North has the lowest annual rainfall (169 mm a year). Within the state, the San Quintín Valley registers a 10 to 20 percent deficit of annual rainfall, compared to the average in Baja (Vázquez León 2015, 61), which begs the question of why this region was chosen for the production of water-intensive crops.

Overextraction of water has also contributed to regional environmental degradation. The increasing salinization of the watershed has left water available in many urban wells unfit for domestic use. A study conducted by the state government in Baja California showed that the water in most of the region's aquifers was not usable due to the saline intrusion caused by several decades of overexploitation of the watershed (Sánchez Munguía 2015, 127). The limited sewer system in the region, almost nonexistent in most colonias where farmworkers live, has been associated with a high risk of water contamination (Sánchez Munguía 2015, 134). Along with the salinization and contamination of the soil and watershed, the discharge of the desalination plants has also had a visible impact on the environment. Mexico's Secretariat of the Environment, Natural Resources, and Fisheries (SEMARNAT) requires desalination plants to discharge the salt and chemicals that result from reverse osmosis into the ocean's interior so that they mix with seawater and minimize their impact on the ecosystem. Yet some companies illegally discharge the salt and chemicals on beaches or in streams, causing severe environmental damage and posing a high risk for local populations (Riemann 2015, 25). These practices, however, did not go uncontested. After the first decade of the 2000s, as the production of water-intensive export crops increased, the demand for water ignited numerous localized protests and large riots across the valley. The protests unleashed powerful emotions among the local people, transforming water into one of the most contentious political issues in the region.

WATER RIOTS AND SOCIAL UNREST

On December 21, 2016, after a closed-door nighttime meeting of a small work committee, the congress of Baja California announced a new law to privatize water services in the state, Ley de Agua para el Estado de Baja California. The law sought to transfer the provision, maintenance, and administration of water to private entities to increase the efficiency of water service and address the chronic water shortages many localities regularly experience. It also allowed the liberalization of water rates and authorized a privatized water agency to cut service to users after ninety days if they had not paid their dues. The public announcement of the law provoked an immediate and massive public reaction. Beginning on January 5, 2017, intense public mobilizations were carried out in some of the largest cities in the state, such as

Mexicali, Tijuana, and Ensenada. In Mexicali, the state capital, more than forty thousand people took to the streets to protest (Corral 2017). Residents of San Quintín also joined the rally. A group of farmworkers from the region traveled hundreds of miles to join the march and express their opposition to the new law. Members of the Coordinadora Nacional de Trabajadores de la Educación, retirees and pensioners from the Mexican Institute for Social Security and Services for State Workers (ISSSTE), and workers from other sectors also joined the farmworkers (Corral 2017). Facing massive discontent, the state government closed state, municipal, and legislative offices. Five days later, the governor of Baja California, Francisco Vega de Lamadrid, announced the rescindment of the law, canceling the announced water price increases but stating he was calling a meeting with academics, water specialists, and representatives of different sectors of civil society to discuss alternatives to resolve the water problems in the state (Corral 2017).[17]

The massive protests prompted by the attempt to privatize water in Baja was not a novel response for the people in San Quintín. After the first rallies in 2008, when CESPE announced the increase in water rates, residents continued to organize public protests to demand access to water in their colonias and homes.[18] On June 3, 2014, for example, hundreds of farmworkers and other local residents gathered in front of CESPE's offices to protest the failure of the agency to deliver water to their communities. When I talked to Enrique Alatorre, president of the new union Sindicato Nacional Independiente de Jornaleros Agrícolas, in summer 2017, he told me that the organizers had asked for a meeting with CESPE's officials to discuss their demands. When the latter did not respond, the participants decided to block the highway to press the government to act. "It's a federal felony to close a federal highway, but it's also a crime that the government fails to provide water to its people," Alatorre said, explaining the rationale for the group's decision. Along with other water protests in the region, this rally galvanized the frustration people experienced about chronic water shortages in their communities and contributed to fueling the labor strike of 2015. Thus, although the initial set of demands by the leaders of the strike revolved around labor issues, they made it clear that the improvement of living conditions in their local communities, especially access to water, was at the heart of the collective revolt. Reflecting the increasing public perception that the production of fresh produce was at the core of the water problems workers experienced, Alatorre complained that many people still did not have access to water two years after the strike. "Companies like BerryMex, Los Pinos, and Agrícola Colonet are stealing the water and taking it to the United States, leaving none here," he told me. Like Alatorre, many residents felt that water scarcity was one of their most pressing concerns. Leocadio Simeon, for example, a resident of Colonia Ampliación Lázaro Cárdenas who I had originally met in 2005, complained that while his colonia finally had piped water after many years of having to buy it from mobile trucks, or *pipas,* water was increasingly more scarce and only available a few hours once or twice a week. "Sometimes we get the monthly water bill even though for periods we didn't receive any water!," he told me when I last saw him in July 2017.

Despite the water riots and people's protests, the view and policies of CESPE in San Quintín did not significantly change; it continued to emphasize the need to "educate the citizenry" as the best tool to make "more rational" use of water in the region. In an interview with Alberto Torres, CESPE's head in 2017, he told me there was a "lack of water culture in the region," especially among indigenous people, who "used water to clean the streets and plant small orchards on their parcels." Collective protests that were regularly organized by residents, he added, reflected misconceptions and "ignorance" by people about water in this arid land. "There is resistance from indigenous groups who don't like to pay for water; they want everything free," Torres observed, reflecting a nativist view according to which indigenous residents only demand rights but do not assume their civic responsibilities.[19] Torres acknowledged, however, that CESPE was unable to provide water to the citizenry. By then the agency had only twenty-eight wells registered for human use, down from thirty-two in 2009, several of which had a diminishing water flow. By 2016, water scarcity had reached such a critical point, he told me, that the state agency had to "rent" a desalination plant operated by a large horticultural company to deliver water to residents in several colonias. At that point growers were buying and renting water as a commodity; while in the past they could only rent water wells, they could now buy and sell water well concessions.

In light of the water scarcity, other companies began providing water from their wells and desalination plants to nearby colonias where their workers live. These actions are aimed at ensuring that workers have minimum access to this vital resource and meet the hygienic conditions to work in the field, as well as preventing the escalation of social unrest (Pinzón Aranda 2016, 72).[20] One of these companies was Driscoll's, which, according to Henry Clark, was "giving water to the people" from its own wells, blaming the state government for not doing its job and having old and decaying water infrastructure insufficient to meet the needs of the citizenry. "If CESPE were efficient and transparent and people would pay, we would be willing to give [more] water to the population," he added, revealing that in addition to dominating berry production in the region, this company controls and can distribute desalinated water from the watershed to the state. This marked a new threshold of water politics in the region, one in which the public sector has to "borrow" water from horticultural companies that extract it from the aquifer, often with little control.[21]

The water insecurity of residents, along with public pressure on the government to provide water to their communities, forced state officials to respond. A few months after the labor strike of 2015, the governor of Baja California announced the construction of the first desalination plant for water for human use in San Quintín. Scheduled to open by late 2019, the plant is expected to desalinate ocean water to provide 5.7 million gallons of water to several communities, such as Lázaro Cárdenas, San Quintín, Camalú, Vicente Guerrero, and Papalote, reaching about 86,000 residents (Sánchez 2018). Rather than a public project, however, the plant was approved under a public-private partnership. In this business venture, about 75 percent of the estimated 875 million pesos ($30 million) for the plant comes from private investment by the Bank for the Development of North America (BDAN) and a consortium made up of RWL Water Group and two Mexican partners (Dibble 2016; San Diego Union Tribune). The remaining 25 percent of its cost is funded by the CNA and Baja state government agencies such as CESPE and the Secretariat of Urban Development (SIDUE) (Sánchez 2018). While the plant will help alleviate the water shortages for local residents, it is also expected that its cost will sharply rise. According to CESPE (pers. comm., July 6, 2017), the real average price of water per household could be 240 pesos a month, compared to the 65 pesos residents without water meters pay. Because of the limited budgets of farmworkers and the potential for social unrest, the government will likely subsidize part of the cost and implement moderate price increases over time. Moreover, because of the semiprivate nature of the project, the water desalinated by the plant will also be used by growers for agricultural irrigation (Pinzón Aranda 2016, 60). Thus it is estimated that 70 percent of the resource will go to the agricultural sector (Santes-Álvarez 2015, 110). Meanwhile, facing water insecurity, Driscoll's also began building its first ocean desalination plant in the region. After years of desalinating underground water, the company's next "technological fix" is to use ocean water, a more expensive and energy-intensive technology that was postponed until well water was unusable. With the same optimism that he described the first desalination plants Driscoll's built in the early 2000s, Henry Clark told me that the new plant would yield 250 liters per second, enough to keep up with the company's business plans for berry production in the region.[22]

CONCLUSION

For many centuries, water scarcity prevented the development of commercial agriculture and large human settlements in the San Quintín Valley. The arrival of a new regime of intensive capitalist agriculture in the 1980s transformed the delicate balance between water, agriculture, and people in this arid region. Facing water shortages, transnational companies with vast financial resources invested in desalination plants, sophisticated irrigation technologies, and shadehouses and greenhouses. I have used the term "waterscapes" to refer to this assemblage of capital-intensive technologies used to mine underground water to sustain and augment agricultural production with no regard for its ecological and social effects. While technological innovations have secured water for year-round production for large growers, access to water for small farmers and for the farmworkers who produce these crops has become more sporadic, unpredictable, and vulnerable to seasonal changes. The result is what I have termed "aridscapes," rural settlements where residents struggle to fetch water to meet even their basic household consumption needs. Aridscapes, I contend, embody the structural violence perpetrated by the production of water-intensive crops by the fresh-produce industry on the commons and the peoples who work and live in the region.

Chronic water shortages for the local population in San Quintín can be conceptualized as "contrived," or manufactured, scarcity, a situation in which the combination of global agricultural forces and regional ecological conditions generates water insecurity at the local level (Whiteford and Cortez-Lara 2005, 233). Rather than a phenomenon of nature, the water crisis is the result of large grower-shippers moving production from California to Baja to deal with water scarcity; salt intrusion in places like Oxnard, Oceanside, and the San Joaquin Valley; and rising production costs. In this process, transnational companies engage in virtual water flows, externalizing the ecological and social costs of water to agroexport regions in Mexico. At this point, water ceases to be a local resource and becomes an externality, a global resource for agricultural production for international markets (Hoekstra and Chapagain 2008). This is the equivalent of "watercide," a process by which the intensification of production of water-intensive crops in San Quintín has caused the decimation of the watershed, the salinization of underground water, and the suffering of thousands of families who live daily with water insecurity.[23]

Market forces alone, however, cannot explain the problems and suffering residents experience when confronting water scarcity. As I have shown, the water policies implemented by the Mexican government in Baja critically shifted the power dynamics in favor of the agroindustry when adopting neoliberal policies to foster agriculture as an avenue for economic and regional development. At the same time, in its zeal to attract foreign and domestic capital investment, the Mexican state has contributed to exacerbating the water crisis in the region, while the lack of enforcement of the nation's water laws has increased the inequity of water access that its own nationals confront. Like in other developing countries where local governments seek to transform the fiscal relationship between citizens and the state regarding the provision of water (von Schnitzler 2010), government water conservation regulations in Baja are aimed at the citizenry rather than agribusiness, despite the fact that about 85 percent of the water is consumed by commercial agriculture (Walsh 2011, 55). This shows that in the era of neoliberal trade and water policies indigenous people on the frontiers of capitalist expansion bear the burden of insufficient access to water (Nash 2007).[24]

Rather than passive victims, however, residents of San Quintín have used access to water as an arena for collective resistance and mobilization. Articulating their demands as a basic civil and human right, they have learned to openly contest the exploitation of water by agribusiness and the government policies behind the unequal use and pricing of water for agriculture versus the citizenry. Collective social protests over water represent the notion of "suprahousehold water riots" (Wutich and Brewis 2014, 457), a form of political activism for mobilizing against public policies and the ecological impacts of water-intensive practices by agribusinesses that underpin water insecurity. When engaging in water protests, I have argued, indigenous workers engage in political citizenship, demanding the right to be treated as full-fledged residents, a political development at the heart of the process of settlement. Along with labor demands, water rights are a central arena of class struggle that arises from the local tensions and contradictions elicited by export agriculture as a model of economic and regional development.

Conclusion

The Labor Regime of Transnational Agriculture

In his classic book, *The Death of Ramón Sánchez,* Angus Wright depicted in graphic detail the lethal effects that pesticides and herbicides had on migrant indigenous farmworkers in northwestern Mexico. Wright exposed the major collateral effects that the expansion of commercial agriculture in the 1990s was causing in Sinaloa and Baja California and the laborers employed in this sector. By the second decade of the twenty-first century, the growing appetite for healthy green vegetables and fruits by consumers in the United States has pushed even farther the expansion of export agriculture in Baja and many other regions in northern and central Mexico. In this book, I have examined the complex ecological, economic, and social effects that the production of fresh crops in Baja destined for consumer markets in the United States has had on the lives of growers and workers associated with this industry in the San Quintín Valley. As a bourgeoning agricultural frontier, the fresh-produce industry, I have argued, has brought profound economic, ecological, and social consequences that have radically transformed this arid region and the people who populate it today. Through a grounded ethnographic approach, I have tried to unveil the basic pillars of the production regime of export agriculture in Baja and the new social and class configurations it has entailed. In this analytical endeavor I am indebted to pioneers such as Eric Wolf, Sidney Mintz, and William Roseberry who examined the social transformations that emerge across time and space as capitalist agriculture continues its relentless pursuit of new production zones, consumption markets, and greater profits. The stories I have portrayed reflect the long history of asymmetrical and uneven economic and social processes that define Baja California as a transborder region whose fate has long been deeply intertwined with capitalist interests in the United States (Heyman 2017, 2010; Weaver 2001).

The expansion of export agriculture in Baja rests on technological changes in the production of the vegetables and fruits we consume. As I have shown, in Baja, this technological transformation has entailed, among others, a shift from production in open fields to protected environments, reflecting the old capitalist dream of "liberating agriculture" from the constraints of soil, climate, and water to replicate industrial production to its fullest possible extent. The result is a heightened contemporary version of what Carey McWilliams called "factories in the fields" in California, namely, horticultural technoscapes of greenhouses and shadehouses covering hundreds of hectares that have profoundly transformed the landscape. I have referred to this agricultural model as agro-dystopia, predicated on the standardization of fresh produce along size, shape, and aesthetic appearance to meet the requirements of U.S. consumer markets at the expense of local ecological and social effects, with multiple but still poorly understood consequences for the health of farmworkers laboring in these facilities.

While reflecting regional and transnational features of Baja's geopolitical positioning in the Mexico-U.S. economy, export agriculture in San Quintín speaks to the neoliberal governance in the global fresh-produce industry. Since the 1990s, control of the production and distribution of food has steadily shifted away from state and government agencies to the international system and large agribusiness corporations (Muller 2010; McMichael 1994). In the process, the United States has been gaining greater prerogatives to regulate the terms of the production of export crops, including rules for certifying their safety and quality. Norms of good agricultural practices, I have argued, are an integral part of this regime, heightening labor discipline and control in the workplace. Codified in the "neutral" technical language of "product safety and quality," GAP norms convey the neoliberal values and language of individuality, loyalty, excellence, and productivity that are the new mantra that companies use to indoctrinate their workers. This culture of certification penetrates all the way down to the growing fields and workplace, enabling the extraterritorialization of labor disciplining across the U.S.-Mexico border in what is, as Robert Álvarez (2006) calls it, an "ethos of control" by the United States as a transnational state. While for farmworkers in Baja this workplace regime has improved sanitary conditions in the fields, it has also led to the reintensification of labor and the augmentation of the workload in which speed and mechanical scripted and repetitive tasks have become the new normal. Norms for "food safety and quality" have not been accompanied by socially responsible standards for wages, labor benefits, and working conditions, revealing the inner contradiction of a labor system predicated on professionalizing farmworkers but treating them as perpetual temporary or casual labor. As a global production system, the fresh-produce industry re-creates class and ethnic inequalities, as shown in other regions in the world where the production of fresh produce relies on vulnerable migrant labor (e.g., Gertel and Sippel 2014b).

The growth of export agriculture in Baja reflects a structural change in power relations among growers in the fresh-produce sector. Transnational companies have grown in size and influence, gradually but inexorably displacing small-scale farmers and relegating medium-size growers to the category of second-class players. In this process ejidatarios and small producers have been dispossessed from their land and water resources, often having to rent them to growers and companies with more capital, a phenomenon of "reverse tenancy" that characterizes class relations in modern capitalist agriculture (Narotzky 2016, 305). A new generation of growers eager to embrace the rules and competitive ethos of export agriculture has emerged, many of whom inherited farms from their parents. This cohort of young growers has more education, professional training, and nuanced understandings of the global marketplace than the pioneers who first started production for export markets. Their identity as "independent producers," however, should not obscure the power inequalities at the heart of the global fresh-produce industry. Growers' discourse about individualism, autonomy, and choice veils their vertical integration and economic dependence on the global commodity chain of horticultural production. Younger growers in Baja are increasingly integrated in a large "agro-maquila" system that leaves less room to decide what crops to grow, when, and how, reducing them to the function of recruiting, managing, and disciplining the labor force employed in this sector.

TECHNOLOGICAL PROGRESS OR ECOLOGICAL ARROGANCE?

An important argument of this book is that the production of water-intensive crops in the arid lands of the San Quintín Valley exposes the ecological and social costs of export agriculture as a model for economic and regional growth. As I have documented, export agriculture unleashed fierce competition for scarce water resources between agribusinesses and the people who settled in these lands. The growth of commercial agriculture rests on what Lucero Radonic and Thomas Sheridan (2017, 288) call "speculative mentality," the conviction that water shortages can always be "engineered" by technological artifacts on the supply side. Rather than empirical givens, environment and technology are "socially constructed outcomes" reflecting production relations between actors with different power (Oliver-Smith 2010, 74). What I have called waterscapes, desalination technologies to irrigate export crops, and aridscapes, the fragile ecological conditions in the colonias where farm laborers seek to make a livelihood, constitute the two sides of the same production regime.

From a political ecology viewpoint, the production of water-intensive crops for export markets using capital-intensive technologies rests on a utilitarian view of nature that reduces water to a cost of production void of ecological and social context. To understand the ecological violence that occurs when local water resources are extracted at higher rates than the watershed's natural capacity to replenish itself, the concept of capitalist "predatory formations" proposed by Saskia Sassen (2014, 220) is quite helpful. By this concept, she refers to regimes of extraction of natural resources in advanced capitalist economies that show little regard for their environmental consequences and that denote "dangerously narrow conceptions of economic growth" led by corporations seeking to liberate themselves from ecological, social, and juridical constraints in their pursuit of profit (Sassen 2014, 213). In Baja, the formation of an agroexport enclave driven by large economic players has led to a production system decoupled from the historical ecological constraints that prevented the expansion of commercial agriculture beyond its natural sustainability limits. The overextraction of water resources for horticultural production has caused the salinization and degradation of the soil, leaving large extents of land unfit for production. The exploitation of limited water resources for the production of export crops is not a phenomenon confined to northern Mexico but part of a global geography of water extraction by commercial agriculture selling fresh crops in international markets. The rapid growth of export agriculture in Mexico and other countries in Latin America over the past few decades has introduced intense competition for water between global players and local communities, raising questions about its long-term ecological and social sustainability. In Chilascó, Guatemala, for example, development policies have promoted the production of water-intensive crops such as broccoli for export to the United States and Europe, while cultivation of traditional crops such as corn and beans has been relegated to marginal lands (Fisher and Benson 2006; Holder 2006). The introduction of irrigation to support the production of broccoli has resulted in conflicts over water, as many people feel their rights have been usurped by neighboring communities, giving rise to a dispute between communal and state control over water resources (Holder 2006, 279).[1]

The ecological and social consequences of growing export crops have important implications for the discussion of the "ecological agrarian question" in the twenty-first century (Akram-Lodhi and Kay 2010). This question refers to the ecological degradation caused by intensive capitalist agricultural practices, especially the production of fresh vegetables for international markets (Akram-Lodhi and Kay 2010, 269). In Baja, I have argued, export agriculture has intensified regional power disparities along class and ethnic lines, whereby unequal access to water embodies and reproduces inequity and uneven power relations. This outcome and the power struggles over water raise important ethical questions that are often ignored when proposing the export of fresh produce as a model of economic development. While organizations such as the World Bank and the Inter-American Development Bank support export agriculture for economic growth, ethnographic-based studies indicate that this model often generates water insecurity for the poorest and more marginalized local populations, threatening the UN resolution to ensure access to clean water as a universal human right. Raising this issue for public discussion is an important moral imperative for scholars studying local communities engulfed by the global fresh-produce sector.

SETTLEMENT AND CLASS TRANSFORMATION

The social and class transformation indigenous farm laborers from southern Mexico have experienced after settling in Baja is an important focus in this book. The production of fresh produce along the U.S.-Mexico border, I have argued, has generated a new class of transnational farmworkers trained in the work skills and requirements of modern capitalist agriculture. Displaced by neoliberal agrarian policies and land competition and scarcity in their rural communities, thousands of peasant-workers migrated to San Quintín, attracted by employment opportunities that would allow them to start a new life. While the transformation into wage workers is shaped by a particular set of regional and political forces, it mirrors the global trend of agrarian systems that has deepened the process of labor commodification in developing countries with the expansion of capitalist agriculture (Akram-Lodhi and Kay 2010, 267). This trend has important theoretical implications for the classic debate among anthropologists and social historians about the class transformation of peasants throughout the world as they became engulfed in capitalist commercial agriculture. Current processes of de-agrarianization, a product of neoliberal economic policies, have further undermined peasant economies and livelihoods, leading to different outcomes and social formations such as proletarianization, semi-proletarianization, or a hybrid class of worker-peasants, among others (Narotzky 2016, 304).

In the case of farm laborers in Baja, rather than a linear transformation from peasant-workers into wage workers, the picture that emerges is a social hybrid that combines elements of semi-proletarianization with social and cultural features of peasant background and knowledge. It is clear that settlement has consolidated the transition from migrant peasant-workers into wage laborers employed in commercial agriculture on a year-round basis. At the same time, however, most farmworkers engage in different types of creative informal occupations to earn extra income that combine traditional knowledge from their home communities with skills they have learned in their jobs in San Quintín. They are also invested in domestic production of food for self-provisioning and barter, a backyard household economy and subsistence economic strategy that expanded when they moved from labor camps and rented rooms to homes on their own parcels. Growing vegetables and raising small animals for family consumption on their parcels and engaging in social and cultural practices of barter has allowed them to re-create the subsistence economy of their home communities by incorporating new irrigation skills learned at their current jobs in Baja. The set of "nonmarket labor processes" (Griffith 1987) I have documented are indispensable for the reproduction of labor, subsidizing low wages for a large pool of workers employed in capitalist horticultural production in Baja and the United States. Peasant subsistence practices also provide some respite from the exploitative conditions they face as wage laborers, allowing them to re-create a sense of autonomy, dignity, and pride. These simultaneous processes reveal that nonmarket peasant economies and social practices are still articulated in advanced capitalist agriculture, attesting not only to the persistence of the peasantry in contemporary circuits of capital accumulation (Palerm 2014; Narotzky 2016) but also to the active social-cultural creative forms by which they adapt and resist these capitalist forces in their lives.

At the same time, settlement has also contributed to occupational diversity and internal socioeconomic differentiation among the local farmworking population. As I have shown, the technological restructuring of the fresh-produce industry opened the doors for a segment of field workers to move up to more specialized occupations such as irrigators, machine operators, fumigators, quality checkers, maintenance technicians, and others, a step up on the employment ladder of this sector. The regime of labor flexibility has also opened a space for former field workers and mayordomos to become labor contractors, supplying growers with a continuous pool of flexible labor. In addition, the incursion of some farmworkers into nonagricultural occupations as a means of livelihood or to supplement agricultural wage labor has further contributed to internal occupational diversification as well as the emergence of petty capitalists such as store owners and other small business owners. Rather than a unique regional phenomenon, this occupational and class diversity mirrors a larger trend of socioeconomic differentiation in rural communities that have been incorporated into the global circuits of contemporary capitalist agriculture (Akram-Lodhi and Kay 2010; Palerm 2014). This social differentiation represents an important but still understudied dimension of class transformation in regions that have fallen within the orbit of the fresh-produce industry. Whether and to what extent economic activities outside of agriculture may provide avenues for upward mobility for farmworkers in modern agroexport regions remains an important empirical question with significant implications for the discussion on social diversification and stratification.

COLONIZATION AND PLACE MAKING

A key argument presented in this book is that the class transformation of farmworkers in Baja cannot be fully understood without examining the social and cultural practices by which they have established roots in the region. From an ethnographic perspective, I have emphasized the central importance of place making in farmworkers' lives and the determined and creative ways in which they have appropriated, transformed, and adopted the San Quintín Valley as their new home. The individual and collective ways by which they have reshaped the territory and social topography of the region constitutes a central dimension of the larger process of class transformation into settled workers. Examining farm laborers' lives not only as workers but also as settlers is thus a key analytical endeavor to understand the social consequences of the production regime of export agriculture in Baja.

From this perspective, farmworkers' settlement can be best conceptualized as a process of colonization. In this endeavor, they have constructed a new sense of place and belonging and forged strong social ties locally and transnationally with kin and indigenous organizations across the Mexico-U.S. border. Place making is at the heart of this process by which indigenous farmworkers appropriate the land, beautify their colonias, and develop social and cultural organizations to consolidate their roots in their adopted land. As such, settlement is a contested political project, one created through the concrete initiatives of specific individuals and groups invested economically and emotionally in transforming the land (Oliver-Smith 2010, 165). Their success in populating this young valley is one of the most important chapters in the recent social history of Baja, one that has gone largely ignored by a theoretical approach that reduces them to the unidimensional category of farmworkers. Settlement thus is "social change writ small" (Guggenheim and Cernea 1993, 10), involving issues of power, community, and the struggle for equity and social justice.

Settlement and place making, however, are rarely gender-neutral endeavors. As Anthony Oliver-Smith (2010, 90) argues, when peoples and communities are displaced by development projects or policies that undermine their livelihoods and force them to resettle in distant lands, women's economic and social roles are more profoundly transformed than those of men. In San Quintín, I have shown that women shouldered a significant majority of the costs entailed in settlement, building new homes and communities and playing a key role in the "multiple livelihoods" that often characterize the subsistence economic strategies of farmworker households (Griffith, Preibisch, and Contreras 2018, 3; Kay 2008, 921). In fact, settlement has been a double-edged sword for women workers in Baja. On the one hand, it has opened new spaces and power in the decision-making process in their households, provided an opportunity to forge social links of solidarity and mutual support, and re-created their social lives. It has also allowed them to regain some control over their social reproduction activities, particularly the care of their children, an important and culturally valued form of affective labor (Griffith, Preibisch, and Contreras 2018). On the other hand, women are disproportionately burdened with additional responsibilities and expectations to generate additional income for their families, participate in community projects, and serve as community brokers for government-sponsored social and community projects. The burden of community work reflects the broader feminization of the labor force in the fresh-produce industry in Mexico, which has placed added pressure and responsibilities on women.

Settlement and labor migration, however, are not mutually exclusive processes. On the contrary, as I have documented, they are deeply integrated in the lives of male and female farmworkers in Baja. Low wages in the horticultural industry continue to push them to look for work opportunities in the United States to support their families. The militarization of the U.S.-Mexico border and the criminalization of undocumented laborers in the United States have generated new forms of labor migration, especially of contract workers under the H-2A program. This program capitalizes on Mexican farmworkers' skills and experience during their most productive years, externalizing the economic and social costs of raising, training, and maintaining them to San Quintín and other communities in Mexico. Rather than an isolated phenomenon, the expansion of the H-2A program in the United States mirrors the reemergence of contract labor migration programs in capitalist agriculture across the world, for example, in Mediterranean countries that specialize in the production of fresh produce (Griffith 2014; Gertel and Sippel 2014a). The expansion of new modalities of contract labor in an era defined by strong anti-immigrant political rhetoric and nativist exclusionary policies in countries that depend on immigrant labor will likely remain an important arena for future research, with significant political implications.

NEW FORMS OF POLITICAL MOBILIZATION

The economic and social changes farmworkers have experienced as they settle in San Quintín raise the issue of their impact on the ways in which workers organize for their labor and civil rights. The regimented workplace of the fresh-produce industry in Baja has not gone uncontested but has elicited novel forms of labor and community mobilization and politics. As transnational companies developed new forms of labor intensification, workers came up with a variety of forms of labor resistance, providing an analytical window into political agency and class politics in today's capitalist agriculture. Everyday forms of resistance, from work stoppages and foot-dragging to absenteeism, litigation, and labor strikes, speak to what Oliver-Smith (2010, 33), following Foucault, calls "plurality of resistances," namely, diverse and often spontaneous collective responses that tend to arise in a context of labor migration and resettlement. As I have shown, settlement is a major source of farmworker activism; feeding off each other, labor and community politics are not mobilized in an orderly fashion but follow an irregular and volatile "fractal" pattern (Oliver-Smith 2010, 49), which varies in strength and intensity according to the historical moment and the issue at stake.

The irregular and variegated forms of labor resistance expose the decline of traditional forms of labor union representation for farmworkers in regions dominated by export agriculture. As in other Latin American countries where centralized trade unions were an important part of the structure of the government (Lazar 2017, 10), in Mexico corporatist unions have become largely obsolete for representing the interests of workers. Alienated from these organizations and critical of their collusion with employers, farmworkers have pushed to form independent unions to mobilize for higher wages, benefits, and a voice in the process. Yet, rather than being focused on labor issues alone, independent unions articulate a public discourse that combines labor demands with community-based demands to improve living conditions in colonias. This approach mirrors the social movement unionism that has gained momentum in different countries as precarious workers seek more responsive forms of labor representation. The collective desire for new unions with a more democratic and transparent structure denotes the "external challenges" that conventional unions face at a time when the old alignment between traditional political parties and labor unions has weakened and workers search for alternative forms of labor organizing (Lazar 2017, 12). Yet the route and future of new independent unions is still uncertain as they confront powerful forces from the corporate world and the state that undermine the potential and expectations many workers and other social and political actors have placed on them.

Regardless of what new forms of labor organizing may bring, compared to migrant workers who are more vulnerable, settled farmworkers can be more demanding about wages and labor conditions as they have wider family and kinship support networks. Community organizing allows them to address their demands as residents and focus on "the politics of the living space" (Lazar 2017), which is crucial for their social integration in the local society. In the process, they develop a new sense of political citizenship that challenges nativist discourses that portray them as seasonal migrants who do not belong. The book shows the importance of paying attention to the bonds of sentiment and affect that community organizing and place making entail when farmworkers mobilize for their labor and citizen rights. While the majority of those employed in commercial agriculture are indigenous workers from different ethnic backgrounds, they share a common class identity as farm laborers that shapes their political subjectivities. Coming from many different regions in Mexico, speaking diverse indigenous languages and dialects, and possessing a rich history of farmworker labor migration in Mexico and the United States, they are united in common goals in Baja by the shared experience of working as poor laborers in the fresh-produce industry.

Capitalizing on their public visibility as employees of large agribusinesses along the Mexico-U.S. border, farm laborers in Baja have also learned to mobilize their transnational networks with kin and indigenous organizations in the United States while also appealing for support from consumers north of the border. Facilitated by the expansion of information technologies, the morphology of labor resistance increasingly resembles a decentralized network made up of dynamic multiple local and transnational linkages, a phenomenon noted by Michael Kearney (1996) in the study of indigenous Mixtecs in the Mexico-U.S. borderlands. The latest ingredient in this model is the use of social media activism as a political tool to build new networks to denounce and mobilize against violations by local employers, transnational companies, and government authorities. These resemble what June Nash (2007, 140–50) calls "activist networks," those consisting of new actors such as indigenous workers that emerge in export-oriented zones as a way of organizing by disenfranchised groups. In so doing, farmworkers in Baja are infusing labor and community politics with novel tools, strategies, and actors, which today include a new generation of young people raised in the region who are pushing to bring about social and political change.

APPENDIX

Policy Recommendations
Moving the Needle

According to *Migration Dialogue,* about half of the fresh fruit and a quarter of the fresh vegetables consumed in the United States are imported, and half of fresh fruit imports and three-fourths of fresh vegetable imports come from Mexico (https://migration.ucdavis.edu/farm-labor). Growing demand for fresh vegetables and fruits has also translated into growing labor demand in Mexico. While Oaxaca and Guerrero were the preferred regions for labor recruitment, today it is impoverished indigenous communities in Chiapas that are being tapped by horticultural companies as new "greenfields" for the recruitment of migrant labor. In this context the question arises as to what changes are needed to improve the working and living conditions of the workers who grow the fresh produce we consume. What does the experience of the San Quintín Valley teach us about the predicaments of farm laborers employed in the fresh-produce industry? What issues need more attention and offer the best potential to bring about effective change? And who are the actors and institutions that should be responsible and involved in making those public policies changes?

This book rests on the premise that despite the specific features of its geographic location, the San Quintín Valley offers a unique opportunity to understand the long-term ecological and social effects that U.S. consumers' appetite for fresh food has on growers and farmworkers who produce those crops in Mexico. From a critical applied anthropology approach, below I outline a series of proposals to address some of the most important challenges that farmworkers and small-scale growers in the export agricultural sector face based on the major findings discussed in the book. Underlying these recommendations is the need for a new social pact that brings all social actors to the table to voice their needs in an inclusive fashion, including farmworkers who for many decades were ignored by government authorities and the agribusiness sector.

LABOR AND WORK STANDARDS

Enhancing farmworkers' labor benefits and working conditions is central to ameliorating many of the problems identified in the previous chapters. Along with the Good Agricultural Practices (GAP), companies and growers exporting produce to the United States should be required to implement a set of Good Labor and Social Practices (GLSP) for their employees. A code of socially responsible practices should focus on labor benefits, work standards, and workers' rights. This proposal is not new. In 2015, a group of fresh-produce-industry leaders from Mexico and the United States founded the International Fruit and Vegetable Alliance for Social Responsibility (AHIFORES) with the stated purpose of promoting "industry-wide awareness and consistency in the implementation of socially responsible business practices" in Mexico's expanding fresh-produce industry (www.andnowuknow.com/whats-store/mexican-and-us-fresh-produce-associations-form-alliance-social/christofer-oberst/44495). A good model to enforce strict labor standards is the Fair Food Program created by an Immokalee group of farmworkers to persuade large companies like Walmart and McDonald's to buy their tomatoes from growers who comply with such standards, an initiative that it is estimated has benefited about 35,000 laborers, mostly in Florida (Scheiber 2019). Also in Baja, some companies launched their own social programs after the labor strike in 2015. In 2017, for example, BerryMex—Driscoll's largest grower in Mexico—launched the "Fair Trade Program" to implement a series of community projects for its workers in education, health, and housing with funds generated through Driscoll's Fair Trade Certified organic program (www.berry.net/mex/driscolls-fair-trade-program-helps-schools-san-quintín-mexico). While this was a step in the right direction, the certification of responsible labor and social practices cannot be left to companies or growers' associations to "monitor" themselves; certification should be in the hands of independent third parties, as in the case of GAP. Company-based "community programs" can help but should not be a substitute for GLSP; in fact, these initiatives are often formulated under the assumption that farmworker poverty and suffering are "community problems" resulting from bad government rather than labor issues.

To be effective, participation in GLSP should be required not only for large companies but also for the satellite of contract growers who produce fresh crops in partnership with those grower-shippers. Too often, contract farming is a business strategy to externalize the labor costs and legal responsibilities to midsized companies, leaving the name and logo of transnational corporations as a public relations front for labor and working conditions. Farmworkers employed by contract farmers often have fewer labor benefits and higher workloads and are subjected to more arbitrary rules; GLSP certification should also apply to subcontractors.

A central issue that needs to be addressed regarding basic labor standards are rules for piece rate. Piece rate is a scheme to keep daily wages low and to intensify the work process. As I have shown, piece rate—either individual or crew based—is the predominant system of remuneration in Baja's fresh-produce industry, a system often used unilaterally by employers to increase the workload associated with each task. Labor agreements should include basic guidelines to limit the maximum amount of work allowed for different work tasks and a formula by which workers earn more than the minimum wage when paid piece rate. Likewise, when produce is rejected in second- and third-quality inspection points after passing quality inspection in the field, workers should be paid for the time invested in harvesting and repacking additional fruits in order to avoid unpaid work time, a common practice in the industry. The use of the *salario integrado* (compacted salary) also needs to be regulated. Companies use this modality to avoid paying workers windfall benefits and Christmas bonuses, instead slightly raising their weekly checks by a few pesos (a light version of wage theft). Workers and independent unions have contested this practice, which deprives them of a small but much-needed income at the end of the year when employment slows down and their expenses rise. A code of fair labor practices should ensure that farmworkers benefit from their employers' earnings as stipulated by the law. This code should also regulate the use of third-party temporary agencies that some horticultural companies contract to avoid paying benefits to their workers.

To enhance the well-being of farmworkers in Mexico, the Mexican government needs to exert more pressure on agricultural companies to register their workers with the IMSS, which provides basic health and pension benefits. While some large companies in Baja are complying, others continue to resist, including recalcitrant employers who use their regional and national political connections to avoid penalties. This creates an uneven field for companies and growers who register their workers, creating a disincentive to comply. Attention to occupational hazards and health issues is more important than ever at a time when work in enclosed structures such as greenhouses and shadehouses has become common in many agroexport enclaves. In these environments, workers are subjected to high temperatures and humidity, which combined with the pressure to work fast under the piece rate often leads to high blood pressure, fainting, dehydration, and other health issues. Companies growing produce in indoor agriculture should implement safety guidelines for mandatory rest breaks, access to drinking water, and other measures to protect workers' health, just as they have phytosanitary rules to ensure the safety of the produce grown there.

Attention to sexual harassment in the workplace is also part of the policy changes needed to improve workers' labor and human rights. Among the twelve key demands presented by the leaders of the Alianza in San Quintín in 2015 was an end to the sexual harassment of female field workers by mayordomos and supervisors in the fields. Companies should include clear guidelines to protect women from physical and verbal abuse in the workplace and require mandatory training for all supervising employees. Workers should be provided with an avenue to present complaints about sexual harassment without fear of retribution by their supervisors and/or employers. Growers should also implement policies to recruit women workers as mayordomas and supervisors to better reflect the gender makeup of the farm labor force. Breaking the extreme gender division of labor that still predominates in the industry is an important step to address the structural problem of sexual abuse and harassment.

INDEPENDENT UNIONS

The persistence of traditional corporatist unions in Mexico is a major obstacle to workers' ability to speak for themselves and formulate their demands. Government-controlled unions have become outdated and are unable to respond to the challenges farmworkers confront in the fresh-produce industry in the twenty-first century. Independent unions and new leaders who can represent workers' claims offer the best option to move forward. New unions need to establish democratic and transparent procedures to elect leaders, have representatives in the major companies elected by the rank and file, and set term limits to avoid the concentration of power in a few hands. Farmworkers with experience in the industry can provide much-needed new blood to rejuvenate unions in this sector along the lines of the dynamic, network-based social movement unionism that has emerged in the twenty-first century. Women, who constitute a large segment of the workforce, need to be given more representation in the leadership of these unions, which still are dominated by men.

Independent unions can serve to negotiate bargaining agreements with employers. The contracts should stipulate wages that set a living wage below which companies cannot go regardless of the form of payment. They should also establish grievance procedures and binding arbitration to settle disputes between employers and workers when they cannot come to an agreement. Unions should push for the recognition of seniority when companies make decisions about hiring, layoffs, and bringing employees back to work. A good model for a fair labor contract with workers employed in the fresh-produce sector is that signed in Washington State in June 2017 by the independent union Familias Unidas por la Justicia and Sakuma Bros. Berry Farm, a company that employs large numbers of Mixtec and Triqui workers (http://familiasunidasjusticia.org/en/2017/06/17/historic-union-contract-ratified-by-members-of-familias-unidas-por-la-justicia).[1]

To be effective, farmworker unions in Mexico need to strengthen collaboration with sister organizations in the United States. As I have shown, today's fresh-produce industry is truly transnational in nature, with large corporations operating on both sides of the border; yet transnational collaboration among labor unions has not kept pace, placing organized labor at a structural disadvantage. While wages in Mexico will most likely remain lower for the near future, collaboration among U.S. and Mexican unions can help to homogenize some basic labor benefits and standards. U.S. unions should particularly reach out and support independent unions recently founded to represent jornaleros in Mexico's most important agroexport regions, as they compete on an uneven field with old-fashioned unions.

At the same time, consumer boycotts in the United States in support of farmworkers in Mexico can be an effective vehicle. Yet boycotts need to be responsibly planned and executed to truly represent workers' interests. In the past, some of these boycotts have responded to the political interests of labor leaders in California, targeting companies in Baja that have the best records for registering their workers in the IMSS at the expense of less-known but powerful companies with much bleaker labor records. While capitalizing on multinational companies with "brand recognition" as a strategy to "lift all boats," blanket boycotts that focus on a single company often let some of the more ruthless employers off the hook, including powerful Mexican companies that use their political connections to break the law and benefit from operating in global markets. Labor unions should carefully listen to what workers say about which companies should be held accountable.

GOVERNMENT POLICIES AND PROGRAMS

Market forces alone do not account for the problems and suffering of farmworkers in Mexico. Government policies and institutions have historically played a central role in keeping this sector of the labor force in a precarious state. In Baja, the Mexican government followed a laissez-faire policy of "free market" capitalism to attract foreign investment and create jobs. For decades, powerful agricultural barons monopolized economic and political power, and when government institutions and programs arrived in the 1990s, they followed policies sympathetic to large growers' interests at the expense of small-scale producers, ejidatarios, and farmworkers. To correct this historical bias, several changes are needed.

To that end, first, the federal and state governments in Baja should support the production of less water-intensive crops, which can ameliorate damage to San Quintín's water table and regional ecology. The state and municipal governments should develop a strategy for sustainable regional resource management that can guarantee the sustainability of local natural resources. Government institutions need to take a more robust role in enforcing water regulations for agricultural production, including the rules and use of quotas for underground water extraction. The Comisión Nacional del Agua has no presence in the region, which has allowed large companies to engage in illegal water grabs and extract much more water than their assigned quotas allow. To that end, it is imperative to strengthen the local COTA committees in charge of measuring and controlling the extraction of water for agricultural production. Local COTA committees can help create a more balanced and fair distribution of water resources among large companies and small farmers who have been displaced from agriculture and who often follow more sustainable practices.

Second, the state should promote alternative and sustainable types of agricultural production in the region better fitted to its ecological features and constraints. One is to revamp the *agricultura de humedales* (wetland agriculture) now in existence with one that requires less water, allows the natural recharge of the aquifer, and protects the biodiversity of the region (Rangel 2015, 51). An additional path is to promote small-scale agriculture by independent farmers. A tested model for this alternative is the experience of the Sustainable Iowa Land Trust project (SILT) as an alternative to large-scale corporate agriculture (https://silt.org/). The goal of this project is to provide access to land to young farmers who want to produce crops that fit the ecology of the region and are sustainable over time (Durrenberger 2018). Adapting it to the environmental and social conditions of the San Quintín region, sustainable small farming would provide opportunities to young people with knowledge about farming methods in the region, including mestizo and indigenous students who have graduated as agronomists from local higher education institutions, who could harness the expertise, entrepreneurial spirit, and commitment to the future of the region. These and other alternatives fall under the umbrella of what Humberto González (2012, 485) calls "agroecological reconfiguration alternatives (AERA)," namely, programs developed by local and regional actors and organizations to reverse the environmental degradation produced by intensive industrialized agriculture. This model integrates ecological, economic, and social dimensions into the design and management of agricultural production and has been implemented with different degrees of success in several regions in Mexico that suffered the negative environmental effects of large-scale intensive agriculture.

Third, to level the field between large transnational corporations and smaller-scale local producers, local SAGARPA offices need to be better supported. Since the neoliberal agrarian reform in Mexico, the personnel and funding for local SAGARPA offices have been drastically reduced, including for agronomists who in the past assisted small-scale farmers. In San Quintín, funding for the office has dwindled over the years despite the rapid growth of this region as a major transnational agroexport enclave. As a result, the agency is no longer able to fulfill its mission and does not have even the basic funding to pay for the automobiles and gas for the few agronomists left to gather the most basic data on crops produced by the region's companies. In addition, funding from this agency destined to help growers build basic infrastructure should be given to midsized and small producers rather than large transnational companies.

Fourth, the state and municipal governments need to bring basic infrastructure and public services to the colonias where local workers live, especially piped water, sewage, and paved roads. The need to improve this infrastructure is recognized by the state government in Baja California in its Program 2015–2019 for the San Quintín region (COPLADE 2017). Yet, the current administrative structure the San Quintín Valley depends on—which is based in the city of Ensenada hundreds of miles away and often shows little knowledge and interest in the problems people in this region confront—aggravates the situation. The political will expressed by many residents in San Quintín to make the region an independent municipality can be a step in the right direction. The so-called *proyecto de municipalización* (municipalization project) could break long decades of government neglect of this region and its citizenry. This political project, however, needs to be inclusive and democratically conducted, allowing all social and political actors to express their needs and be involved in the decision-making process. The state and municipal governments should also adjust the taxes and penalties it imposes on local residents who seek to regularize their property titles. Low-income farmworker families, who are often required to pay retroactive fees well above their means, are left in a highly vulnerable status regarding the lots that they earned with the sweat of their labor.

Government programs designed to provide economic support for low-income families to strengthen community building are essential as well to protect farmworkers from the vagaries of the labor regime in export agriculture. Many families depend on economic aid from programs like Prospera to put food on the table and keep their children in school. These programs, however, should not continue operating under the premise that women are "free labor" for community initiatives and that community work is a natural extension of their family tasks. Women involved in government-sponsored programs should be compensated for their time and labor and given the necessary training and support to carry out their assignments.

The government should also invest resources to enhance the educational opportunities of children and youth. An ample second generation of young people born and raised in the region by farmworker parents are well positioned to take advantage of educational opportunities that will allow them to find employment in sectors other than agriculture. Unlike their parents, a significant proportion of young adults have completed *prepa* (high school) and would like to go to college, but their families' limited economic means and the lack of funding opportunities prevent them from pursuing that path. Providing fellowships and other funding opportunities for teens and young adults can enhance their prospects of upward occupational and socioeconomic mobility, help lift their families out of poverty, and diversify employment opportunities beyond wage work in agriculture. To attend to the needs of indigenous communities, the federal government should increase funding for the Comisión para el Desarrollo de los Pueblos Indígenas. This agency has the mission to generate and fund public policies for the betterment of indigenous communities in Mexico. Currently the CDI in Baja is severely underfunded for the size of the indigenous population and the geographic extent of its jurisdiction. Numerous infrastructure and productive projects for indigenous peoples and local colonias in San Quintín and other regions in Baja depend on funding from this agency, including some to bring water to these communities. In recent years, funding for the CDI in Baja has declined, critically undermining its ability to meet even its most basic goals. This has not only affected indigenous groups in San Quintín, but it has also made it impossible for the agency to reach out to other sites south of this region such as Vizcaíno, where horticultural companies are producing fresh crops for export with indigenous migrant laborers housed in labor camps.

WATER MANAGEMENT

At the heart of many problems affecting the local population in the San Quintín region is water. The overexploitation of the aquifer for horticultural production has contributed to water scarcity and salinization, causing deep social inequities. While desalination technology may help to alleviate this problem, the long-term sustainability of producing water-intensive crops in one of the most arid regions in Mexico remains questionable. As several experts have argued, the government of Baja California needs to develop a new water governance approach to ensure the long-term sustainability of water and economic enterprises and population in the region.

First, the state must develop an integrated approach that takes into account not only the economic but also the environmental and social factors of water distribution and use (Santes-Álvarez 2015, 111). In this endeavor, it is imperative to include not only government agencies like CESPE, federal agencies like the Mexican National Water Commission, and growers associations but also the region's citizenry, which until now has had limited means to express their demands and grievances. Rather than cast them as the source of the problem, residents and business owners who have been negatively impacted by water scarcity need to be brought to the negotiation table to discuss a fair and sustainable model for water access and use in the region.

Second, the state should consider a water tax levied on the water content of commercial crops produced in the region. Revenue accrued via the tax could help finance government-funded projects to enhance water-capture projects. A water tax would function like the carbon tax levied on the carbon content of fuels as an incentive to develop alternative sources of green energy. As in the case of the carbon tax, the overexploitation of underground water for commercial crops represents a negative externality on the local ecology and the citizenry. A water tax will offer environmental, economic, and social benefits while promoting a more diversified economy.

Third, the CNA needs to ensure that the local COTA committees are working properly as intended in the National Water Law. This means that each of the committees overseeing the aquifers of the San Quintín Valley should be properly constituted and functional, as well as ensure genuine representation of small and medium-size growers. To that end, the CNA needs to have a visible presence in the region to support the local COTA councils in the performance of their duties.

Fourth, desalination technologies should only be allowed for the treatment of ocean water; the extraction of underground water that has been severely decimated should be banned. In addition, the SEMARNAT should have a more robust presence and role in the region overseeing that all regulations regarding the discharge of salt and chemicals used in desalination are properly followed to avoid further damage to the delicate ecosystem.

Far from comprehensive, this list of policy suggestions indicates that the problems farmworkers and other workers and residents face are multifaceted and that there is not a single policy that can fully address them. From an applied anthropological perspective, what is needed is a holistic approach that involves the diversity of economic, social, and political actors with whom agricultural laborers are articulated as a subordinated group. As consumers of fresh produce, we wield an important but unrealized potential to shape the discussion and move the needle in pursuit of economic and social justice that is long overdue. In this endeavor and under the guise of global citizenship, it is our responsibility to respectfully listen to the demands and claims farmworkers themselves convey and to incorporate their diverse voices in the decision-making process to address them.

NOTES

INTRODUCTION

1. The San Quintín Valley belongs to the *municipio* (municipality) of Ensenada, a city on the Pacific coast located about 110 miles to the north. The largest of the region's four districts is San Quintín, with about 41,000 inhabitants, followed by Vicente Guerrero, Camalú, and Punta Colonet, with approximately 21,000, 14,000, and 10,000 residents, respectively, according to the latest census (2010). These districts include five main towns named after them and Lázaro Cárdenas located in the San Quintín District. The population in the region is spread among these towns and about 50 rural settlements that range in population from 4,000 inhabitants (Colonia Lomas de San Ramón) to a few with less than 100 residents each (INEGI 2010).

2. The Agrarian Reform officially ended the state's obligation to redistribute land to the peasantry and indigenous populations, launching about half of agricultural lands into the market (Pechlaner and Otero 2010, 194). For a critical account of the impact of Mexico's ejido reform and its impact on peasants and small farmers, see Grindle 1995.

3. The growth of export agriculture in Mexico is part of what scholars of agrarian political economy call the "third food regime," which expanded globally from the early 1980s (Bernstein 2016, 624–25). From this macro and historical perspective, this third stage is characterized by deeper integration of transnational agrifood capital whereby "global sourcing is the norm," a regime in which transnational corporations along with international trade liberalization agreements undermine national regulation of agriculture (Pechlaner and Otero 2010, 183).

4. In the case of the citrus industry, Mexican workers provided a key source of labor in Southern California since the early twentieth century, where they developed full-fledged rural communities until their decline in the 1960s (González 1994).

5. The region has a troubled past that included violence and repression of indigenous leaders (Velasco, Zlolniski, and Coubes 2014, 231–49). Old-time growers familiar with

critical accounts by outside observers about the agricultural industry and the treatment of indigenous farmworkers (e.g., Garduño, García, and Morán 1989; Clark 1985) were reserved, sometimes unwelcoming to outsiders.

6. For a detailed discussion about the need for an engaged activist anthropology in the United States, see Hale 2007.

CHAPTER ONE. THE BIRTH AND DEVELOPMENT OF EXPORT AGRICULTURE

1. The archaeological and ethnohistorical records of the San Quintín region (like the rest of Baja California) are sketchy at best and open to discussion (Laylander 2006). The form of early human adaptation is an example of this discussion. While the archaeological record seems to indicate a simple type of foraging, ethnohistorical accounts recorded by Spanish expeditions in the early seventeenth century suggest a well-developed maritime economy with interregional exchange links (Moore 2006, 189–91). Likewise, while archaeologists indicate there were only small and transient human settlements, ethnohistorical records based on a short expedition in 1602 by the Spanish explorer Sebastián Vizcaíno reveals the presence of three ranchería settlements in the vicinity of Bahía de San Quintín (Moore 2006, 192).

2. Dominicans started building missions in northern Baja in 1774, including Nuestra Señora del Rosario (1774), Santo Domingo de la Frontera (1775), San Vicente Ferrer (1780), San Miguel Arcángel (1787), Santo Tomás Aquino (1791), and San Pedro Mártir (1794). Yet settlements in these missions remained small because of the harsh environmental constraints on agriculture (Rodríguez Tomp 2002, 213).

3. For a detailed discussion of the extent of demographic decline of native populations in Baja California and the different factors involved, see Rodríguez Tomp 2002, 195–228.

4. The Baja California Land Company amassed properties amounting to about 18 million acres in Baja. While British citizens held a majority of the stock in that company, U.S. banks and financial investors such as J. P. Morgan of the Morgan Bank of New York were also deeply involved, as the historian John Mason Hart (2000, 512) has documented.

5. Interview with Vicente Guerrero Herrera (first president of the Municipalization Project), San Quintín, Baja California, April 16, 2005.

6. Until 1946, most lands in the San Quintín Valley were held by of only two owners who had received them by concession from the Mexican federal government (Velasco, Zlolniski, and Coubes 2014, 248). At the time of the ejido land distribution, there were only a few groups of peasants that received land, as the government gave them mostly to farmers from central and western Mexico to compensate them for lands lost in their home communities during the land reforms of the time (Velasco, Zolniski, and Coubes 2014, 248).

7. The increase in tomato production in northwestern Mexico began in the late 1960s. Dietary habit changes in the United States prompted a demand for fresh vegetables and fruits at a time when Florida growers' ability to produce tomatoes suffered a set of environmental and political crises (Lizárraga 1993, 24). Moreover, with the termination of the Bracero program in 1964, many California growers were afraid they would run short of labor and saw investment in northwestern Mexico, especially Sinaloa, as an attractive option for labor-intensive crops, leading to an influx of American capital and technological expertise in Mexico (15).

8. The "golden age" of tomato production in Sinaloa was the 1920s, only interrupted by the Great Depression of 1929 (Lara Flores and de Grammont 2011,: 37). By the 1940s, Sinaloa became the primary source of export vegetables, accounting for about 80 percent of the total national output (Goodmand and Lizárraga 1998, 14). For a detailed history of U.S. growers' investment in fresh-produce production in Sinaloa, see Lizárraga 1985; Wright 2005.

9. Cooling technology allows the lowering of the temperature of fresh crops after harvest in the summer from about 80° to 55° Fahrenheit and keeps it constant until the produce arrives in the United States. A.B.C. shipped the produce to its distribution center in Chula Vista, California, where it was stored in a cool room at the same temperature. This procedure also revolutionized packinghouses in the valley, marking a transition to modern facilities equipped with cooling technologies.

10. Luis Ávalos recalled that at the time there were only a few midsized growers, including families such as the Rodríguez in Los Pinos, Valladolid, Castañeda, Librado Heredia, González Mota, and Diego Rojas, among others.

11. Migration of *jornaleros* (seasonal farm laborers) to northwestern Mexico has a long tradition that resulted from government policies to make this region the most important source of export agriculture in the country. These policies set in motion large rural-to-rural migratory flows from depressed peasant communities in southern Mexico to the north, particularly to Sonora, Sinaloa, and Baja California (C. de Grammont, Lara Flores, and Sánchez Gómez 2004, 363).

12. For a description of the conditions indigenous farmworkers endured in the labor camps in San Quintín in the 1980s, see Garduño, García, and Morán 1989.

13. During this phase, horticultural production declined from about 12,000 hectares in 1998 to 6,000 in 2005 and 3,500 by 2009 (SAGARPA, pers. comm., June 14, 2005). The production of fresh crops is concentrated along the coastal zone with a width of about 15 kilometers and covering about 2,400 square kilometers (Riemann 2015, 15).

14. For example, for tomatoes cultivated in open fields, there are three main production seasons (March–April, August–September, and fall), while with shadehouses and greenhouses companies can extend production through the end of November and attain higher market value in the United States.

15. Strawberry production in the valley began to increase in the late 1980s. By 1988, there were about 1,200 hectares cultivated, a significant jump compared to only 40 hectares in 1985 (Lizárraga 1993, 86). Strawberry cultivation received a boost in the late 1990s at the peak of the tomato war between Florida and Mexican growers, which led to a temporary boycott of tomatoes imported from Mexico based on the claim of Mexican dumping. In response, local tomato growers affected by the boycott turned to strawberries as an alternative crop to boost their revenues (Lizárraga 1985).

16. The growth of blackberries was more modest, increasing from 10 hectares in 2012 to 55 hectares in 2018 (SAGARPA, pers. comm., March 6, 2019).

17. Large Mexican farm production companies such as Los Pinos and San Vicente Camalú SPR established U.S.-registered firms associated with their home farms to market their produce in the United States and often that of other smaller Mexican growers as well (Mines 2010, 21).

CHAPTER TWO. TRANSNATIONAL AGRIBUSINESS, LOCAL GROWERS, AND DISCONTENTS

1. Agricultural trade liberalization in Mexico caused a big shift to high market value fruit and vegetable production for export at the expense of lower-value grains for domestic consumption. Export of fresh fruits and vegetables, as González and Macías note, is a highly concentrated sector with only three hundred companies accounting for 80 percent of all exports in the country (cited in Pechlaner and Otero 2010, 201).

2. Growers in San Quintín started to experiment with strawberry production in the 1980s as a seasonal option instead of tomatoes, their main cash crop that often suffered difficulties in the market because of "tomato wars" between the United States and Mexico. While productivity in the 1980s was rather low, by the mid-1990s it exceeded Michoacán's productivity. Later, between 1990 and 2000, San Quintín's small group of strawberry growers doubled their total acreage in production from 739 to 1,574 while increasing productivity per acre from 10 to 21 tons annually (López 2011, 63). While in the past most strawberries produced in Mexico came from the central-western agricultural basin in El Bajío, by 2010 there had been a significant "geographical reconfiguration of strawberry production" in which U.S. firms heavily invested in the San Quintín Valley to expand their seasonal production, especially during the winter (44–45).

3. As Teresa Figueroa Sánchez (2002, 25) shows in her ethnographic study of strawberry farmworkers in Santa María, the electronic card symbolizes the power of farmers to control and punish workers who do not follow specific labor and phytosanitary practices on the farm.

4. Fresh fruits and vegetables are increasingly produced using industrial procedures that are not familiar to regular consumers, including the use of this technology (Coff, Korthals, and Barling 2008, 2). In Mexico, traceability has been a widely used tool in the export fresh-produce industry since the late 1990s as part of a larger process of standardization and to respond to food safety and quality market requirements (C de Grammont and Lara Flores 2010, 237).

5. BerryMex launched a program for strawberry growers in Mexico in 1994, and since then it has experienced rapid growth, with production in Jalisco, Michoacán, and Baja California.

6. In Mexico the growth of contract farming, known as *agricultura de contrato*, expanded in the 1980s and was supported by the government for the production of grains and fueled by private agribusinesses in the fresh-produce sector (Echánove and Steffen 2005, 172–74). The expansion of contract agriculture is due to increased demand and national agrarian policies that have led to the severe reduction of subsidies from the government for production, trading, and services, increasing growers' dependence on the food industry for financing, technical assistance, and access to markets (Echánove and Streffen 2005).

7. While it first started with a handful of local growers, by 2010, after developing competence in producing strawberries to Driscoll's standards, the company brought a larger number of experienced local growers under its umbrella (López 2011, 108).

8. For a detailed analysis of the types and ideologies of nativism espoused by the economic and political elites in San Quintín and other regions in northern Mexico, see Martínez Novo 2006.

CHAPTER THREE. LABOR RECRUITMENT

1. In Argentina, for example, large companies use labor contractors to minimize payroll taxes and health insurance payments, insulating them from legal responsibilities to their workers (Quaranta and Fabio 2011, 204).

2. The dual-wage system has a long history in the employment of Mexican workers in the United States, especially in the Southwest. In this system, as documented by Chicano historians, lower wages were paid to Mexican-origin workers compared to those paid to Anglo employees (Camarillo 1979, García 1981, Romo 1983). More recently, Christine Marin and Luis F. B. Plascencia (2018), examining the employment of Mexican Americans in the copper mining industry during World War II in Arizona, argue that wage hierarchies have played a key role in developing an "elastic supply of labor" on which the copper mines relied.

3. By 2005, about a dozen such associations, each with twenty to forty members, were founded, including several cooperatives formed by indigenous workers who used their savings and loans from kin to leave their jobs as farmworkers to become independent labor contractors.

4. CROM defines two types of union members: permanent workers, who have stable contracts with their employers and receive all labor benefits such as health, pension, and seniority; and temporary or casual workers, who are hired by growers for specific tasks and periods and have limited benefits while employed. A large majority of the union members, according to CROM's president, Arnulfo Quintanilla, have temporary contracts and considerably fewer benefits and rights than the small core of permanent workers with stable, year-round work contracts.

5. As I later learned, Sierra-Cascade had gotten into legal trouble for violating numerous contract obligations and rights of farmworkers recruited from Mexico through the H-2A program. In 2012, the U.S. Department of Labor issued a $290,000 fine to the company to pay back wages to 430 temporary workers who were recruited under the H-2A program in the 2006–7 season. The investigation by the Labor Department's Wage and Hour Division found Sierra-Cascade had changed the conditions of employment originally promised, did not pay workers their wages when due, and cheated them of payment for the time spent waiting to board buses to and from the work sites. Sierra-Cascade also failed to keep records of the hours laborers worked, did not comply with housing and health provisions that are part of the program, and discriminated against twenty-three workers at its Tule Lake facility for asserting their rights afforded under the Immigration and Nationality Act (U.S. Department of Labor 2012).

6. In 2007, 87,316 workers were approved to receive an H-2A visa to work in the United States, compared to 46,432 in 2006. By 2017, the number of workers jumped to 412,820, a staggering 789 percent increase.

7. In July 2017 when I interviewed the vice president of BerryMex in Baja, he told me the H-2A program was taking a toll on the company, pressing it to raise wages and causing a shortage of experienced workers.

CHAPTER FOUR. "THEY WANT FIRST-CLASS WORKERS WITH THIRD WORLD WAGES"

1. From a similar theoretical perspective, Kerry Preibisch (2014, 86) used the concept of workplace regime to refer to the labor arrangements used in the production process and the

negotiations that shape them and the series of actors involved in the context of capitalist agriculture. Analyzing the experience of Mexican immigrants contracted as seasonal workers in Canada's fresh-produce industry, she showed how the combination of local, regional, and global factors produce a highly flexible and vulnerable labor force in which the Canadian state contributes to the weakening of workers' bargaining power.

2. Over time, the cost of sheltered facilities decreased, and by 2010, it was estimated that one hectare of shadehouse required an initial investment of 1,200,000 pesos ($92,307). While large companies such as Los Pinos, Agrícola San Simón, and Agrícola Colonet were pioneers in the introduction of sheltered production, in 2005 midsized companies also started to invest in indoor agriculture, as it was the only path to stay in business. As indoor agriculture increased, more workers went from laboring in open fields to shade- and greenhouses, yet SAGARPA does not provide figures for the number of employees in these facilities.

3. For a discussion of the primary forms of payment in California's berry industries, including hourly wages and *contrato* (number of cases picked), see López 2007, 120–23; Hernández-Romero 2012.

4. The culture of certification also affected Mexican agronomists in San Quintín. In the field, I witnessed how when certification inspectors from U.S. companies were scheduled to arrive at the local ranchos, the field agronomists were often frantic to make sure everything was in order in the fields, greenhouses and shadehouses, packing plants, and cooling facilities, often with their jobs on the line if problems emerged.

5. Describing rural peasants in Ecuador, Syring (2009) observed a struggle between a balanced model of work and life and the more rigid model of clock time of industrial agriculture. Reflecting on similar struggles in other regions in Latin America, he stated, "An increasing number of people from Latin America who have lived largely as rural peasants with one sense of how work should be ordered and how their everyday lives should be lived, are being incorporated into a system of labor and time that is fundamentally different than the rhythms of work and daily life that they have previously lived" (128). Other anthropologists have similarly pointed out that "learning the capitalist work discipline of industrial time" is an essential ingredient of the training of Mexican immigrant workers in California (e.g., Figueroa Sánchez 2013, 23).

6. In Morelos, Mexico, farmworkers employed in export agriculture have capitalized on the lack of work contracts and labor benefits to quit working when they find better job opportunities and to take time away from work to travel to their hometowns to tend to their families, *milpas* (corn fields), and social and ceremonial obligations (Sánchez Saldaña 2006).

CHAPTER FIVE. RESISTING THE *CARRILLA* IN THE WORKPLACE

1. About 76 percent of indigenous workers in San Quintín are employed in agriculture, compared to only 43 percent of mestizo and white workers. Indigenous women are especially trapped in low-income horticultural jobs; about 80 percent are relegated to employment in this sector, compared to 46 percent of nonindigenous women (Velasco, Zlolniski, and Coubes 2014, 107).

2. Not surprisingly, 22 percent of people employed in commerce are at least forty-five years old, and 35 percent of women workers older than forty-five are concentrated in this sector (Velasco, Zlolniski, and Coubes 2014, 108–9).

3. White unions are part of a corporatist political structure established by the PRI (Partido Revolucionario Institucional (Institutional Revolutionary Party), which held power from 1929 to 2000, when the right-wing Partido de Acción National (PAN; National Action Party) won the general election. This structure was originally developed by the Mexican government as a political-economic institutional framework to control labor unrest and support the model of import-substitution industrialization that characterized Mexico's economy until the shift to neoliberal economic policies in the 1980s (Samstad and Collier 1995). In this context, government-supported unions worked closely with the state to maintain the political power of the PRI and support the interest of employers (De la O 2015).

4. For a further account of the revealing history of the CTM in San Quintín, see Velasco, Zlolniski, and Coubes 2014, 237–39.

5. For an in-depth account of growers' violations of health, pension, and other labor benefits of farmworkers in San Quintín and their lobbying efforts to circumvent the law, see Pérez Hernández 2012.

6. For a description and analysis of this important chapter of San Quintin's labor conflict history, see Velasco's account (Velasco, Zlolniski, and Coubes 2014, 239–49).

7. For a detailed history and analysis of the transborder economic and social nature of these organizations, their members, and their political demands, see Stephen 2007; Velasco 2005.

8. Ethnic leaders, however, are often criticized by growers and many workers as "corrupt" for taking advantage of their position to "collect money" from negotiating parties. For a history of conflicts among indigenous leaders in San Quintín and accusations of corruption, see Velasco's discussion (Velasco, Zlolniski, and Coubes 2014, 239–49).

9. For a detailed account of this important episode in the labor and political struggle of Triqui workers in San Quintín, see Velasco, Zlolniski, and Coubes 2014, 254–62.

10. These institutions included the Autoridad Tradicional (Traditional Authority Council) to legislate and mediate internal affairs in the community; the Consejo de Ancianos (Council of Elders), composed of elderly men with the experience to guide people in civil, religious, and community issues; and the Mayordomía, a traditional institution in charge of organizing the patron saint festivities every June in the colonia (Camargo Martínez 2014, 327–34).

11. According to Ramón Torres, president of Familias Unidas por la Justicia, the social network indigenous farmworkers have built across the Mexico-U.S. border makes building a union in Washington easier as they rely on the experience of some of the leaders in San Quintín who now work as farmworkers under the H-2A program in Washington (Bacon 2018).

12. The focus on Driscoll's caused some divisions among leaders in the Alianza. Some leaders, like Justino Herrera, did not support using the company as a public target because of its international brand recognition as they considered Driscoll's one of the best in the region because it paid higher wages and was one of the few employers that registered its workers in the IMSS. In Justino's view, "political interests prevailed" when labor leaders in the United States who supported the Baja strike pushed to focus on Driscoll's. I too was surprised as I followed the news about the strike. Companies like Los Pinos—the largest regional exporter of tomatoes to the United States, with corporate clients like Walmart, and regarded by many workers as one of the worst employers in the valley—did not receive much attention in the media along with other companies with a long history of labor violations. For a critical perspective of Los Pinos, see Gallegos 2018.

13. Shortly after the strike, Driscoll's began publicizing these programs on its website in an effort to defend its public image. Some of these initiatives were described in www.driscolls.com/about/worker-welfare/fair-trade; www.unitedfresh.org/a-letter-to-our-members-joint-committee-on-responsible-labor-practices/; www.driscolls.com/about/worker-welfare/baja.

14. For a suggestive proposal to the "anthropologists of capitalism" to develop a more nuanced analysis of how large corporations seek to navigate the complicated relationship between economics and morality in response to consumers' pressure, see Arciniega 2018.

CHAPTER SIX. COLONIZING AND ESTABLISHING ROOTS IN ARID LANDS

1. The amount workers had to pay for a lot varied depending on the colonia chosen for settlement: older and more established colonias with some basic services were more expensive than newer and unregulated ones. The year of settlement was also an important factor; in the early 1990s, for instance, a 20 by 10 square meter lot in Colonia Santa Fe cost between 1,500 and 5,000 pesos ($490–$1,600), while families who settled in the same colonia in the 2000s paid 15,000 to 25,000 pesos ($1,450–$2,400) for a lot of the same size.

2. Farmworkers' struggles in San Quintín resemble the experiences of Mexican Americans and Mexican immigrants in colonias in California, Arizona, New Mexico, and Texas. As Vélez-Ibáñez (2017, 32) puts it, in rural communities through the Southwest, these populations seek "a livelihood in subecologies characterized by a combination of fragile desert environments and unprepared areas for human habitation" that lack basic infrastructure such as potable water, sewage, and roads, helping to subsidize an agricultural labor system.

3. For an early account of indigenous political mobilizations for their rights as citizens in San Quintín in the 1990s, see Reth-Mariscal 1998.

4. In 2005, for example, when some old camps were still in place, they were mostly composed of active workers and small children, with a dependency ratio of 43.2 percent of working-age people. In contrast, the dependency ratio in colonias was 72 percent, meaning that for every 100 working-age people (ages 15 to 64), there were 72 individuals who depended on them (Velasco, Zlolniski, and Coubes 2014, 163).

5. Oportunidades also sought to decentralize decision making on food subsidies, creating local "solidarity" committees, a change that marked the first stage in converting subsidized food to cash transfers as the main currency of social programs to alleviate poverty (Ansell and Mitchel 2011, 303). The program has been criticized on several fronts. As Tamar Diana Wilson (2015, 213) insightfully argues, the program rests on the neoliberal assumption of "merocratic individualism, whereby the poor rather than the system in which they are embedded are responsible for their fate."

6. Her two children also continued to participate in the program. With their savings they bought two land lots valued at 50,000 pesos (about $3,800) each, planning for the future when they get married.

7. The Comisión Nacional para el Desarrollo de los Pueblos Indígenas, a federal agency established to defend and promote the rights of indigenous peoples in Mexico, has an office in San Quintín with jurisdiction over some agricultural sites in Baja that have a significant

indigenous population. Budget cuts, however, prevent its staff from fulfilling its mission, and by 2017, they were not able to visit any such sites.

CHAPTER SEVEN. WATERCIDE

1. It is estimated that 783 million people lack access to safe drinking water. For an in-depth discussion of the concept of water scarcity and its twin notion of water insecurity, see Hadley and Wutich 2009.

2. About 30 percent of the water used in agriculture takes place in northern Mexico. During the winter season, nearly half of the fresh produce sold in the United States and Canada comes from regions like Sinaloa and Baja California (Lizárraga 1997), putting pressure on the water resources in the region (Walsh 2004, 2009).

3. Water overextraction continued well into the first decade of the 2000s. For example, Camalú's aquifer has a water quota of 11.25 cubic millimeters (mm^3), with an annual recharge of 3.90 mm^3, a deficit of −7.35 mm^3. Likewise, the aquifer of Vicente Guerrero has an approved concession of 36 mm^3, with an annual recharge of 19.50 mm^3, resulting in a −16 mm^3 deficit; and the San Quintín aquifer approved 27.63 mm^3 with a 19 mm^3 annual recharge and a resulting deficit of −8.63 (Pinzón Aranda 2016, 25).

4. Only after 2013, when many water wells had gone dry, did some of the largest agricultural companies begin using reverse osmosis to remove salt from ocean water to irrigate their crops (López 2017, 188).

5. By 2012, for example, when most large companies were producing in sheltered environments, horticultural production of fresh produce extracted 47 million cubic meters of groundwater, while the annual recharge was estimated at 35 million cubic meters (López 2017, 194).

6. In 2009, for example, Los Pinos, the largest fresh-produce company in the region, was awarded Mex$2,800,000 to build its second desalination plant, even though its first one was built only a few years before and was the largest in the valley. According to local rumors, the company's political connections—one of the brothers who own the company was at the time head of the Secretariat of Agricultural Development (SEFOA) in Baja California—"played a hand," helping to win this generous subsidy.

7. The Ley de Energía para el Campo (Rural Energy Law) approved by the Mexican government in 2002 established a subsidy for electricity. Known as Tarifa 09, it covers energy used by irrigation water pumps as well as electricity to illuminate the facilities where water pumps operate. This subsidy is considered one of the leading factors in the overexploitation of the Mexican aquifers (Pombo López 2015, 89).

8. This subsidy has a limit of Mex$700,000 per grower. Growers receive 0.33 peso per kilowatt to reduce the electrical costs of operating their desalination plants and well water pumps (López 2017, 1930).

9. There are six underground watersheds in the region (from north to south, Camalú, Santo Domingo, San Quintín, San Simón, San Rafael, and San Telmo). Of the 736 wells registered in 1994, 436 were abandoned or destroyed because of overexploitation (Aguirre-Muñoz et al. 2001, 146).

10. The lack of a consolidated COTA structure has led to the inequity with which the volume of water is distributed throughout the valley, the absence of "water justice," and the

accumulation of "water capital," defined as the concentration of economic and technological power by privileged actors to benefit from access to water (Pinzón Aranda 2016, 87).

11. The closest CNA office is located in the city of Mexicali, about eight hours' drive from San Quintín (Pinzón Aranda 2016, 68).

12. In so doing, some companies transfer water from one basin to another—a practice explicitly prohibited by the National Water Law—as in the case of a transnational tomato-export company that diverts water from the San Telmo to the Camalú water basin.

13. The proliferation of irregular farmworker settlements throughout the valley—colonias built on open lands at the margin of state regulations—has also contributed to the difficulty of providing water to residents. For example, in Vicente Guerrero, there are 47 colonias, of which 17 are labeled by the government "irregular" (Pinzón Aranda 2016, 28).

14. For example, a nonrandom survey on household budgets (income and expenses) I conducted in Colonias Santa Fe and Arbolitos in the summer of 2009 showed that a family of four used an average of 20 water barrels per month at 15 pesos apiece (about 300 pesos per month), a high price for farm laborers making 90 pesos per day at the time (about 2,160 pesos per month). This means that farmworkers spent about 15 percent of their income on water for bathing, cleaning, and washing—plus the additional cost of buying water for drinking and cooking in the local grocery stores.

15. About 98 percent of the underground water in the San Telmo aquifer is used for agriculture; 92 percent, in the Camalú aquifer; and 90 percent, in the Vicente Guerrero and San Quintín aquifers (Vázquez León 2015, 64).

16. For example, Camalú's aquifer has a water quota of 11.25 mm^3, with an annual recharge of 3.90 mm^3, thus resulting in an annual deficit of -7.35 mm^3). Likewise, the aquifer of Vicente Guerrero has an approved concession of 36 mm^3, with an annual recharge of 19.50 mm^3, leaving it with a -16.5 mm^3 deficit; and the San Quintín aquifer's quota of 27.63 mm^3, with a 19 mm^3 annual recharge, results in a -8.63 deficit (Pinzón Aranda 2016, 25).

17. Water rates had gone up on January 1, 2017, by 20 percent in Mexicali and 30 percent in Tijuana (Corral 2017).

18. Public protests about either lack of water or insufficient water as well as about the poor quality of water for domestic use and raises in price occurred on a regular basis in San Quintín. The newspaper *El Vigia* in its local edition *El Valle* published dozens of news reports on the topic. See www.elvigia.net/el-valle/.

19. For an extended discussion of nativism among the ruling class in San Quintín, see Velasco, Zlolniski, and Coubes 2014, 292–305.

20. Other growers are in the business of selling water, often through obscure agreements or under the table. According to a public officer in San Quintín, for example, a well-known grower in Vicente Guerrero owns about 65 water wells in this locality, despite the fact that his company has only about 100 hectares registered for production, which probably indicates the company sells water not used for production.

21. For instance, confronted with the complaint that Los Pinos was illegally extracting water from the San Simón basin, an officer from the CNA in Mexicali stated that "there are economic and political interests" in the region about which he did not want to elaborate (Pinzón Aranda 2016, 69–70).

22. In the meantime, the intensification of horticultural production since the arrival of berries in the early 2000s further contributed to the increasing aridity of soil and salinity of water and soil. The salinity of water increased from 3,000 to about 5,000 parts per million in 2017, leading to a reduction in production in open fields and increasing dependency on greenhouse, shadehouse, and, more recently, hydroponic production, a system of growing plants without using soil that relies on mineral nutrient solution in a water solvent.

23. The overexploitation of water for agricultural production in San Quintín is not an isolated phenomenon in Mexico. The number of overexploited aquifers in the country increased from 32 in 1975 to 96 in 2000, while the quality of water due to saline intrusion affects 16 coastal aquifers like San Quintín's (Sánchez Munguía 2015, 126).

24. Not surprisingly, the United Nations Special Rapporteur on the Human Rights to Safe Drinking Water stated at the Human Rights Council in 2017 that Mexico lagged behind in the provision of water to its citizenry. The report also stated that there were deep inequities in access to this basic resource along class and ethnic lines, with indigenous populations in rural areas experiencing the most problems and the most vulnerable populations paying the highest prices to access water (United Nations General Assembly 2017).

CONCLUSION

1. This trend is not confined to Latin America but has spread to many other world regions. This is the case, for example, of the semiarid tropics in India's agricultural sector, where the capitalist "modernizing zeal" has exacerbated environmental degradation, including water stress, salinization, and soil erosion (Harriss-White 2008, 556–58).

APPENDIX

1. For a complete account of indigenous farmworkers' organizing in Washington, see Tomás Madrigal 2017.

REFERENCES

Aguirre-Muñoz, Alfonso, et al. 2001. "Sustainability of Coastal Resource Use in San Quintín, Mexico." *Ambio* 30 (3): 142–49.
Akram-Lodhi, A. H., and Cristóbal Kay. 2010. "Surveying the Agrarian Question (Part 1): Unearthing Foundations, Exploring Diversity." *Journal of Peasant Studies* 37 (1): 177–202.
Alonso-Fradejas, Alberto. 2015. "Anything but a Story Foretold: Multiple Politics of Resistance to the Agrarian Extractivist Project in Guatemala." *Journal of Peasant Studies* 42 (3–4): 489–515.
Álvarez, Robert. 1998. "*La Maroma*: Chile, Credit and Chance: An Ethnographic Case of Global Finance and Middlemen Entrepreneurs." *Human Organization* 57 (1): 63–73.
———. 2005. *Mangos, Chiles, and Truckers: The Business of Transnationalism*. Minneapolis: University of Minnesota Press.
———. 2006. "The Transnational State and Empire: U.S. Certification in the Mexican Mango and Persian Lime Industries." *Human Organization* 65 (1): 35–45.
Ansell, Aaron M., and Kenneth Mitchell. 2011. "Models of Clientelism and Policy Change: The Case of Conditional Cash Transfer Programs in Mexico and Brazil." *Bulletin of Latin American Research* 30 (3): 298–312.
Appadurai, Arjun. 1990. "Disjuncture and Difference in the Global Cultural Economy." *Public Culture* 2 (2): 1–24.
Arciniega, Luzilda Carrillo. 2018. "Starbucks, Racism, and the Anthropological Imagination." *Anthropology News* website, May 24.
Arcury, Thomas A., and Sara A. Quandt. 1998. "Occupational and Environmental Health Risks in Farm Labor." *Human Organization* 57 (3): 331–34.
Aznar-Sánchez, José A., et al. 2014. "The Industrial Agriculture: A 'Model for Modernization' from Almería?" In *Seasonal Workers in Mediterranean Agriculture: The Social Costs of Eating Fresh*, ed. Jörg Gertel and Sarah Ruth Sippel, 112–20. London: Routledge.

Bacon, David. 2018. "The Cross-Border Farmworkers Rebellion." *American Prospect*, October 31. http://davidbaconrealitycheck.blogspot.com/2018/11/the-cross-border-farmworker-rebellion.html.

Barrón, Antonieta. 1999. "Las migraciones en los mercados de trabajo de cultivos intensivos en fuerza de trabajo: Un estudio comparativo." In *Agricultura de exportación en tiempos de globalización: El caso de las hortalizas, frutas y flores*, ed. Hubert C. de Grammont, Manuel Ángel Gómez Cruz, Humberto González, and Rita Schwentesius Rindermann, 255–84. Mexico City: CIESTAAM / UACH / UNAM / CIESAS / Juan Pablos Editor.

Benson, Peter. 2008. "El Campo: Faciality and Structural Violence in Farm Labor Camps." *Cultural Anthropology* 23 (4): 589–629.

Bernstein, Henry. 2016. "Agrarian Political Economy and Modern World-Capitalism: The Contributions of Food Regime Analysis." *Journal of Peasant Studies* 43 (3): 611–47.

Bonanno, Alessandro, and Douglas H. Constance. 2001. "Globalization, Fordism, and Post-Fordism in Agriculture and Food: A Critical Review of the Literature." *Culture and Agriculture* 23 (2): 1–18.

Camargo Martínez, Abbdel. 2014. "Asentamiento y organización comunitaria: Los Triquis de Nuevo San Juan Copala." In *De jornaleros a colonos: Residencia, trabajo e identidad en el Valle de San Quintín*, ed. Laura Velasco, Christian Zlolniski, and Marie-Laure Coubes, 309–42. Mexico City: El Colegio de la Frontera Norte.

———. 2015. "Migración y cambio religioso: La construcción de 'nuevas comunidades' de indígenas migrantes en la frontera noroeste del país." PhD dissertation, Universidad Nacional Autónoma de México.

Camarillo, Albert. 1979. *Chicanos in a Changing Society: From Mexican Pueblos to American Barrios in Santa Barbara and Southern California*. Cambridge, MA: Harvard University Press.

Cavanaugh, Jillian R., and Shalini Shankar. 2014. "Producing Authenticity in Global Capitalism: Language, Materiality, and Value." *American Anthropologist* 116 (1): 51–64.

C. de Grammont, Hubert, and Sara Lara Flores. 2010. "Productive Restructuring and 'Standardization' in Mexican Horticulture: Consequences for Labour." *Journal of Agrarian Change* 10 (2): 228–50.

C. de Grammont, Hubert, Sara Lara Flores, and M. Sánchez Gómez. 2004. "Migración rural temporal y configuraciones familiares (los casos de Sinaloa, México; Mapa y Sonoma, EEUU)." In *Imágenes de la familia en el cambio de siglo*, ed. Marina Ariza and O. de Oliveira, 357–86. Mexico City: Instituto de Investigaciones Sociales, UNAM.

Chayanov, Alexander V. 1966. *Theory of Peasant Economy*. New York: Random House.

Chibnik, Michael. 2011. *Anthropology, Economics, and Choice*. Austin: University of Texas Press.

Clark, Víctor. 1985. "Los mixtecos de la costa de Baja California: Prisioneros de su miseria y su destino." *Zeta*, May 17, 17–19.

Coff, Christian, Michiel Korthals, and David Barling. 2008. "Ethical Traceability and Informed Food Choice." In *Ethical Traceability and Communicating Food*, ed. Christian Coff et al. New York: Springer.

Cohen, Jeffrey H. 2011. "Migration, Remittances, and Household Strategies." *Annual Review of Anthropology* 40: 103–14.

Collins, Jane. 2003. *Threads: Gender, Labor, and Power in the Global Apparel Industry*. Chicago: University of Chicago Press.

COPLADE. 2017. "Programa para la Atención de la Región de San Quintín (2015–2019). Comité de Planación para el Desarrollo del Estado, Baja California." www.coplade.bc.gob.mx/Programa%20para%20la%20Atencion%20de%20la%20Region%20de20San%20Quintin%202015-2019.pdf.

Corral, César. 2017. "Marcha contra el gasolinazo y contra la nueva ley estatal de aguas reúne a miles en Mexicali." *Animal Político*, January 12. www.animalpolitico.com/2017/01/marcha-gasolinazo-mexicali/.

De la O, María Eugenia. 2015. "The Struggle for Labor Rights in Mexican Maquiladoras in Northern Mexico." In *Uncertain Times: Anthropological Approaches to Labor in a Neoliberal World*, ed. Paul E. Durrenberger, 185–208. Boulder: University Press of Colorado.

DeWalt, Kathleen M., and Billie R. DeWalt. 2011. *Participant Observation: A Guide for Fieldworkers*. Plymouth, MA: Altamira Press.

Dibble, Sandra. 2016. "Second Desalination Plant for Baja California." *San Diego Union Tribune*, March 7. www.sandiegouniontribune.com/news/border-baja-california/sdut-san-quintin-desalination-plant-2016mar07-story.html.

Domínguez, Juan Carlos. 2015. "Rebelión en San Quintín." *Proceso*, March 21. www.proceso.com.mx/399069/399069-rebelion-en-san-quintin.

Du Bry, Travis A. 2007. *Immigrants, Settlers, and Laborers: The Socioeconomic Transformation of a Farming Community*. New York: LFB Scholarly Publishing.

Durrenberger, Paul E. 2017. "Introduction: Hope for Labor in a Neoliberal World." In *Uncertain Times: Anthropological Approaches to Labor in a Neoliberal World*, ed. Paul E. Durrenberger, 3–31. Boulder: University Press of Colorado.

———. 2018. "A Role for Anthropologists in the Local Food Movement." *Anthropology Now* 10 (1): 1–12.

Echánove, Flavia H. 2001. "Working under Contract for the Vegetable Agroindustry in Mexico: A Means of Survival." *Culture and Agriculture* 23 (3): 13–23.

Echánove, Flavia, and Cristina Steffen. 2005. "Agribusiness and Farmers in Mexico: The Importance of Contractual Relationships." *Geographical Journal* 171 (2): 166–76.

Ennis-McMillan, Michael C. 2001. "Suffering from Water: Social Origins of Bodily Distress in a Mexican Community." *Medical Anthropology Quarterly* 15 (3): 368–90.

Figueroa Sánchez, Teresa. 2002. "Mexican Immigrant Family Farmers in the California Strawberry Industry." PhD dissertation, University of California, Santa Barbara.

———. 2013. "California Strawberries: Mexican Immigrant Women Sharecroppers, Labor, and Discipline." *Anthropology of Work Review* 34 (1): 15–26.

Fischer, E., and P. Benson. 2006. *Broccoli and Desire: Global Connections and Maya Struggles in Postwar Guatemala*. Stanford, CA: Stanford University Press.

Fregoso, Juliana. 2016 "En San Quintín quieren cambiar el modelo sindical agrícola." *Forbes*, June 23. www.forbes.com.mx/san-quintin-quieren-cambiar-modelo-sindical-agricola/#gs.et7x8Sc.

Friedemann-Sánchez, G. 2012. "Paid Agroindustrial Work and Unpaid Caregiving for Dependents: The Gendered Dialectics between Structure and Agency in Colombia." *Anthropology of Work Review* 33 (1): 34–46.

Friedland, William H. 1994. "The New Globalization: The Case of Fresh Produce." In *From Columbus to ConAgra: The Globalization of Agriculture and Food*, ed. Alessandro Bonanno et al., 210–30. Lawrence: University of Kansas Press.

Gallardo, Magdaleno. 2010. "Restructuración productiva en la horticultura del Valle de San Quintín, Baja California y su impacto en la generación de empleo de 1994 a 2008." Master's thesis, El Colegio de la Frontera Norte, Mexico City.

Gallegos, Zorayda. 2018. "Campo mexicano: Mujer y jornalera. El acoso y las condiciones dentro de San Quintín." *El País*. https://elpais.com/especiales/2018/campo-mexicano/baja-california/mujer-y-jornalera.html.

García, Mario T. 1981. *Desert Immigrants: The Mexicans of El Paso, Texas, 1880–1920*. New Haven, CT: Yale University Press.

Garduño, Everardo, Efraín García, and Patricia Morán. 1989. *Mixtecos en Baja California: El caso de San Quintín*. Mexicali: Universidad Autónoma de Baja California.

Gertel, Jörg, and Sarah Ruth Sippel. 2014a. "Epilogue: The Social Costs of Eating Fresh." In *Seasonal Workers in Mediterranean Agriculture: The Social Costs of Eating Fresh*, ed. Jörg Gertel and Sarah Ruth Sippel, 246–52. London: Routledge.

———. 2014b. "Seasonality and Temporality in Intensive Agriculture." In *Seasonal Workers in Mediterranean Agriculture: The Social Costs of Eating Fresh*, ed. Jörg Gertel and Sarah Ruth Sippel, 3–22. London: Routledge.

González, Gilbert G. 1994. *Labor and Community: Mexican Citrus Worker Villages in a Southern California County, 1900–1950*. Champaign: University of Illinois Press.

González, Humberto. 2012. "Agroecological Reconfiguration: Local Alternatives to Environmental Degradation in Mexico." *Journal of Agrarian Change* 12 (4): 484–502.

———. 2014. "Specialization on a Global Scale and Agrifood Vulnerability: 30 Years of Export Agriculture in Mexico." *Development Studies Research* 1 (1): 295–310.

González de la Rocha, Mercedes. 2001. "From the Resources of Poverty to the Poverty of Resources." *Latin American Perspectives* 119 (4): 72–100.

Goodman, David, and Jorge G. Lizárraga. 1998. "NAFTA and Regional Agricultural Integration: North-West Mexico and California." Working Paper 18. Chicano/Latino Research Center, University of California, Santa Cruz.

Griffith, David. 1987. "Nonmarket Labor Processes in an Advanced Capitalist Economy." *American Anthropologist* 89: 838–52.

———. 2014. "Managing and Mismanaging Migration: An Introduction." In *(Mis)Managing Migration: Guestworkers' Experiences with North American Labor Markets*, ed. David Griffith, xi–xxxii. Santa Fe, NM: School for Advanced Research Press.

———. 2016. "Labor Contractors, Coyotes, and Travelers: The Migration Industry in Latin America and the U.S. South." *Eutopía* 9: 115–25.

Griffith, David, Kerry Preibisch, and Ricardo Contreras. 2018. "The Value of Reproductive Labor." *American Anthropologist* 120 (2): 224–36.

Grindle, Merilee S. 1995. "Reforming Land Tenure in Mexico: Peasants, the Market, and the State." In *The Challenge of Institutional Reform*, ed. Riordan Roett, 39–56. Boulder, CO: Lynne Rienner.

Guggenheim, Scott E., and Michael M. Cernea. 1993. "Anthropological Approaches to Involuntary Ressetlement: Policy, Practice, and Theory." In *Anthropological Approaches to Ressetlement: Policy, Practice, and Theory*, 1–13. Boulder, CO: Westview Press.

Hale, Charles R. 2007. "In Praise of 'Reckless Minds': Making a Case for Activist Anthropology." In *Anthropology Put to Work*, ed. Les Field and Richard G. Fox, 103–28. New York: Berg.

Harriss-White, Barbara. 2008. "Introduction: India: Rainfed Agricultural Dystopia." *European Journal of Development Research* 20 (4): 549–61.
Harvey, David. 2005. *A Brief History of Neoliberalism*. Oxford: Oxford University Press.
———. 2010. *A Companion to Marx's "Capital."* London: Verso.
Hernández-Romero, Manuel Adrián. 2012. "Nothing to Learn? Labor Learning in California's Farmwork." *Anthropology of Work Review* 33 (2): 73–88.
Heyman, Josiah. 2010. "U.S.-Mexico Border Cultures and the Challenge of Asymmetrical Interpenetration." In *Borderlands: Ethnographic Approaches to Security, Power, and Identity*, ed. Hastings Donnan and Thomas M. Wilson, 21–34. Lanham, MD: University Press of America.
———. 2017. "Contributions of U.S.-Mexico Border Studies to Social Science Theory." In *The U.S.-Mexico Transborder Region: Cultural Dynamics and Historical Interactions*, ed. Carlos G. Vélez-Ibáñez and Josia Heyman, 44–64. Tucson: University of Arizona Press.
Hoekstra, Arjen Y., and Ashok K. Chapagain. 2008. *Globalization of Water: Sharing the Planet's Freshwater Resources*. Malden, MA: Blackwell.
Holder, Curtis. 2006. "Contested Visions: Technology Transfer, Water Resources, and Social Capital in Chilasco, Guatemala." *Comparative Technology Transfer and Society* 4 (3): 269–86.
Holmes, Seth M. 2013. *Fresh Fruits, Broken Bodies*. Berkeley: University of California Press.
Horton, Sarah. 2016. *They Leave Their Kidneys in the Fields: Illness, Injury, and Illegality among U.S. Farmworkers*. Berkeley: University of California Press.
Hoy. 2016. "Sindicato de jornaleros en San Quintín es reconocido por el gobierno de Baja California." *Hoy Los Angeles,* January 12. www.hoylosangeles.com/noticias/mexico/hoyla-mex-sindicato-de-jornaleros-en-san-quintn-es-reconocido-por-el-gobierno-de-baja-california-20160112-story.html.
Hsien-Tang, Tsai, et al. 2014. "Consumers' Acceptance Model for Taiwan Agriculture and Food Traceability System." *Anthropologist* 17 (3): 845–56.
INEGI. 2010. "Censo de población y vivienda." www.inegi.org.mx/est/contenidos/proyectos/ccpv/cpv2010/iter_2010.aspx.
Instituto Nacional de Estadística y Geografía (INEGI). 2017. "Municipios de la Cartografía Geoestadística Urbana y Rural Amanzanada." https://www.inegi.org.mx/temas/mg/.
Johnston, Barbara Rose. 2005. "The Commodification of Water and the Human Dimensions of Manufactured Scarcity." In *Globalization, Water, and Health,* ed. Linda Whiteford and Scott Whiteford, 133–52. Santa Fe, NM: School for American Research Press.
Johnston, Barbara Rose, and John M. Donahue. 1998. Introduction to *Water, Culture, and Power: Local Struggles in a Global Context,* ed. John M. Donahue and Barbara Rose Johnston, 1–5. Washington, DC: Island Press.
Karst, Tom. 2018. "H-2A Program Experiences Rapid Growth." *The Packer,* May 31. www.thepacker.com/article/h-2a-program-experiences-rapid-growth.
Kay, Cristóbal. 2008. "Reflections on Latin American Rural Studies in the Neoliberal Globalization Period: A New Rurality?" *Development and Change* 39 (6): 915–43.
Kearney, Michael. 1996. *Reconceptualizing The Peasantry: Anthropology In Global Perspective*. Boulder, CO: Westview Press.

Krissman, Fred. 2000. "Immigrant Labor Recruitment: U.S. Agribusiness and Undocumented Migration from Mexico." In *Immigration Research for a New Century,* ed. Nancy Foner, Rubén Rumbaut, and Steven Gold, 277–300. New York: Russell Sage Foundation.

Lara Flores, Sara M. 1995. "La feminización del trabajo asalariado en los cultivos de exportación no tradicionales en America Latina: efectos de una flexibilidad 'salvaje.'" In *Jornaleras, temporeras y bóras-frias: El rostro femenino del mercado de trabajo rural en América Latina,* ed. Sara María Lara Flores, 15–34. Caracas: Editorial Nueva Sociedad.

———. 1996. "Mercado de trabajo rural y organización laboral en el campo mexicano." In *Neoliberalismo y organización social en el campo mexicano,* ed. Hubert C. de Grammont, 69–112. Mexico City: Plaza y Valdes.

———. 2010. "Los 'encadenamientos' migratorios en regiones de agricultura intensiva de exportación en México." In *Migraciones de trabajo y movilidad territorial,* ed. Sara María Lara Flores, 251–79. Mexico City: CONAYCT / Porrúa.

Lara Flores, Sara M., and Hubert C. de Grammont. 2011, "Reestructuraciones productivas y encadenamientos migratorios en las hortalizas sinaloenses." In *Los encadenamientos migratorios en espacios de agricultura intensiva,* ed. Sara María Lara Flores, 33–78. Mexico City: El Colegio Mexiquense y Miguel Ángel Porrúa.

Lara Flores, Sara M., and Kim Sánchez Saldaña. 2015. "En búsqueda del control: Enganche e industria de la migración en una zona productora de uva de mesa en México." In *Asalariados rurales en América Latina,* ed. Alberto Riella and Paola Mascheroni, 73–94. Montevideo, Uruguay: CLACSO.

Laylander, Don. 2006. "Issues in Baja California Prehistory." In *The Prehistory of Baja California: Advances in the Archaeology of the Forgotten Peninsula,* ed. Don Laylander and Jerry D. Moore, 1–13. Tallahassee: University Press of Florida.

Lazar, Sian. 2017. Introduction to *Where Are the Unions? Workers and Social Movements in Latin America, the Middle East and Europe,* ed. Sian Lazar, 1–22. London: Zed Books.

Little, Peter D., and Catherine S. Dolan. 2000. "What It Means to Be Restructured: Nontraditional Commodities and Structural Adjustments in Sub-Saharan Africa." In *Commodities and Globalization: Anthropological Perspectives,* ed. Angelique Haugerud et al., 59–78. Lanham, MD: Rowman & Littlefield.

Lizárraga, Jorge G. 1985. "Binational Agroindustry in Northwest Mexico: A Geography of the Mexico-US Fresh Produce Trade." Master's thesis, University of California, Berkeley.

———. 1993. "Binational Agroindustry in Northwest Mexico: A Geography of the Mexico-U.S. Fresh Produce Trade." PhD dissertation, University of California, Berkeley.

———. 1997. "Mexican Agribusiness and the U.S. Food System." *Urban Ecology* 2. http://sustainablecity.org/articles/mexican.htm.

Llambi, Luís. 1994. "Comparative Advantages and Disadvantages in Latin American Nontraditional Fruit and Vegetable Exports." In *The Global Restructuring of Agro-Food Systems,* ed. Philip McMichael, 190–213. Ithaca, NY: Cornell University Press.

López, Ann Aurelia. 2007. *The Farmworkers' Journey.* Berkeley: University of California Press.

López, Marcos. 2011. "Places in Production: Nature, Farm Work, and Farm Worker Resistance in U.S. and Mexican Strawberry Growing Regions." PhD dissertation, University of California, Santa Cruz.

———. 2017. "In Hidden View: How Water Became a Catalyst for Indigenous Farmworker Resistance in Baja California, Mexico." In *The Politics of Fresh Water: Access,*

Conflict, and identity, ed. Catherine M. Ashcraft and Tamar Mayer, 188–202. London: Routledge.

Madrigal, Tomás. 2017. "We Are Human!": Farmworker Organizing across the Food Chain in Washington." In *Mexican-Origin Foods, Foodways, and Social Movements*. ed. Devon G. Peña et al., 251–90. Fayetteville: University of Arkansas Press.

Marin, Christine, and Luis F. B. Plascencia. 2018. "Mexicano Miners, Dual Wage, and the Pursuit of Wage Equality in Miami, Arizona." In *Mexican Workers and the Making of Arizona*, ed. Luis F. B. Plascencia and Gloria H. Cuádraz, 203–26. Tucson: University of Arizona Press.

Marosi, Richard. 2015. "Farmworkers in Baja California Protest Low Pay, Poor Conditions." *Los Angeles Times*, March 18. www.latimes.com/world/mexico-americas/la-fg-baja-farmworkers-20150318-story.html.

Martin, Philip. 2001. "Guest Workers, Amnesty and U.S. Agriculture." *Defense of the Alien* 24: 87–100.

———. 2014. "The H-2A Program: Evolution, Impacts, and Outlook." In *(Mis)Managing Migration: Guestworkers' Experiences with North American Labor Markets*, ed. David Griffith, 33–62. Santa Fe, NM: School for Advanced Research Press.

Martínez Novo, Carmen. 2006. *Who Defines Indigenous? Identities, Development, Intellectuals and the State in Northern Mexico*. New Brunswick, NJ: Rutgers University Press.

Martínez Veiga, Ubaldo. 2001. *El Ejido: Discriminación, exclusión social y racismo*. Madrid: Los Libros de la Catarata.

———. 2014. "The Political Economy of El Ejido: Genealogy of the 2000 Conflict." In *Seasonal Workers in Mediterranean Agriculture: The Social Costs of Eating Fresh*, ed. Jörg Gertel and Sarah Ruth Sippel, 103–11. London: Routledge.

Mason Hart, J. 2002. *Empire and Revolution: The Americans in Mexico since the Civil War*. Berkeley: University of California Press.

McGuire, Thomas R. 2005. "The Domain of the Environment." In *Applied Anthropology: Domains of Application*, ed. Satish Kedia and John van Willigen, 87–118. Westport, CT: Praeger.

McMichael, Philip. 1994. "Introduction: Agro-Food System Restructuring—Unity in Diversity." In *The Global Restructuring of Agro-Food Systems*, ed. Philip McMichael, 1–18. Ithaca, NY: Cornell University Press.

Mines, Rick. 2010. "Jornaleros in Mexico's Agro-Export Industry: Changes and Challenges." https://rickmines.files.wordpress.com/2011/12/jornaleros-in-mexicos-agro-export-industry-unpublished-2010.pdf.

Moore, Jerry D. 2006. "The San Quintín-El Rosario Region." In *The Prehistory of Baja California: Advances in the Archaeology of the Forgotten Peninsula*, ed. Don Laylander and Jerry D. Moore, 179–95. Tallahassee: University Press of Florida.

Muller, Birgit. 2010. "My Own Boss? Strategies of Resistance and Accommodation of Rural Producers to Neoliberal Governance." *Antropologica* 52: 233–36.

Mumme, Stephen P., and Christopher Brown. 2002. "Decentralizing Water Policy on the U.S.-Mexico Border." In *Water, Culture, and Power: Local Struggles in a Global Context*, ed. John M. Donahue and Barbara Rose Johnston, 231–52. Washington, DC: Island Press.

Myhre, David. 1998. "The Achilles' Heel of the Reforms: The Rural Finance System." In *The Transformation of Rural Mexico: Reforming the Ejido Sector*, ed. Wayne A. Cornelius and

David Myhre, 39–65. La Jolla: Center for U.S.-Mexican Studies, University of California, San Diego.

Narotzky, Susana. 2016. "Where Have All the Peasants Gone?" *Annual Review of Anthropology* 45: 301–18.

Nash, June. 2007. "Consuming Interests: Water, Rum, and Coca-Cola from Ritual Propitiation to Corporate Expropriation in Highland Chiapas." *Cultural Anthropology* 22 (4): 621–39.

Nauman, Talli. 2007. "A Future Compromised: Agriculture and Aquaculture Compete for Water." Americas Program Investigative Series, February 28. http://americas.irc.online.org/am/4035.

Oliver-Smith, Anthony. 2010. *Defying Displacement: Grassroots Resistance and the Critique of Development*. Austin: University of Texas Press.

Ong, Aihwa, and Stephen J. Collier. 2005. "Global Assemblages, Anthropological Problems." In *Global Assemblages: Technology, Politics, and Ethics as Anthropological Problems*, ed. Aihwa Ong and Stephen J. Collier, 3–21. Malden, MA: Wiley-Blackwell.

Ortiz, Sutti. 2002. "Laboring in the Factories and in the Fields." *Annual Review of Anthropology* 31: 395–417.

Ortiz, Sutti, Susana Aparicio, and Nidia Tadeo. 2013. "Dynamics of Harvest Subcontracting: The Roles Played by Labour Contractors." *Journal of Agrarian Change* 13 (4): 488–519.

Paciulan, Melissa, and Kerry Preibisch. 2013. "Navigating the Productive/Reproductive Split: Latin American Transnational Mothers and Fathers in Canada's Temporary Migration Programs." *Transnational Social Review* 3 (2): 173–92.

Palerm, Juan Vicente. 1989. "Latino Settlements in California." In *The Challenge: Latinos in a Changing California*, 125–71. Report of UC SCR 43 Task Force. Riverside: University of California Consortium on Mexico and the United States.

———. 1995. "Policy Implications of Community Studies." Paper presented at the conference, "Changing Face of Rural California," Pacific Grove, CA.

———. 2002. "Immigrant and Migrant Farmworkers in the Santa Maria Valley." In *Transnational Latina/o Communities: Politics, Processes and Cultures*, ed. Carlos Vélez-Ibáñez and Anna Sampaio, 221–50. Lanham, MD: Rowman & Littlefield.

———. 2010. "De colonias a comunidades: La evolución de los asentamientos mexicanos en la California rural." In *Migraciones de trabajo y movilidad territorial*, ed. Sara María Lara Flores, 221–50. Mexico City: CONACYT/Porrúa.

———. 2014. "An Inconvenient Persistence: Agribusiness and Awkward Workers in the United States and California." In *Hidden Lives and Human Rights in the United States: Understanding the Controversies and Tragedies of Undocumented Immigration*, vol. 3, ed. Lois A. Lorentzen, 55–119. Santa Barbara, CA: Praeger.

Pechlaner, Gabriela, and Gerardo Otero. 2010. "The Neoliberal Food Regime: Neoregulation and the New Division of Labor in North America." *Rural Sociology* 75 (2): 179–208.

Pérez Hernández, Isidro. 2012. "La eficacia de las normas laborales y de seguridad social: Trabajadores agrícolas del Valle de San Quintín, Baja California." Master's thesis, Universidad Iberoamericana, Puebla.

Pérez Prado, Luz Nereida. 2002. "Managing Social Relations under the Transfer of Irrigation Management in the Michoacán Lowlands." In *Protecting a Sacred Gift: Water and Social Change in Mexico*, ed. Scott Whiteford and Roberto Melville, 107–24. La Jolla: Center for U.S.-Mexican Studies, University of California, San Diego.

Phillips, Lynne. 2006. "Food and Globalization." *Annual Review of Anthropology* 35: 37–57.

Pinzón Aranda, José F. 2016. "Procesos de organización social y acceso al agua: El caso de las colonias rural-urbanas del Valle de San Quintín, Baja California, México, 2010–2016." Master's thesis, El Colegio de la Frontera Norte, Monterrey, Mexico.

Pombo López, Óscar A. 2015. "Adaptaciones tecnológicas en el manejo del agua y sus consecuencias en la población de la zona agrícola de San Quintín." In *El agua en la región agrícola Camalú–El Rosario, Baja California*, ed. Hugo Riemann, 81–94. Puebla: Editorial de la Red Nacional de Investigación Urbana (RNIU).

Preibisch, Kerry. 2010. "The Other Side of *El Otro Lado:* Mexican Migrant Women and Labor Flexibility in Canadian Agriculture." *Signs* 35 (2): 289–316.

———. 2014. "Managed Migration and Changing Workplace Regimes in Canadian Agriculture." In *(Mis)Managing Migration: Guestworkers' Experiences with North American Labor Markets*, ed. David Griffith, 83–106. Santa Fe, NM: School for Advanced Research Press.

Quaranta, G., and F. Fabio. 2011. "Intermediación laboral y mercados de trabajo en agriculturas restructuradas: El caso del Valle de Uco, Mendoza, Argentina." *Región y Sociedad* 23 (51): 193–225.

Radonic, Lucero, and Thomas E. Sheridan. 2017. "Co-producing Waterscapes: Urban Growth and Indigenous Water Rights in the Sonoran Desert." In *The U.S.-Mexico Transborder Region: Cultural Dynamics and Historical Interactions*, ed. Carlos G. Vélez-Ibáñez and Josia Heyman, 287–304. Tucson: University of Arizona Press.

Rangel, Norma, and Hugo Riemann. 2015. "Los humedales en la region Camalú–El Rosario: De las misiones a la agricultura en el valle de San Quintín." In *El agua en la región agrícola Camalu–El Rosario, Baja California*, ed. Hugo Riemann, 29–56. Puebla: Editorial de la Red Nacional de Investigación Urbana (RNIU).

Raynolds, Laura T. 1994. "Institutionalizing Flexibility: A Comparative Analysis of Fordist and Post-Fordist Models of Third-World Agro-Export Production." In *Commodity Chains and Global Capitalism*, ed. Gary Gereffi and Miguel Korzeniewicz, 143–62. Westport, CT: Greenwood Press.

———. 2000. "Negotiating Contract Farming in the Dominican Republic." *Human Organization* 59 (4): 441–51.

Reth-Mariscal, William. 1998. "Settling In: Indian Communities and the Transformation of Citizenship in Mexico." PhD dissertation, University of Califonia, San Diego.

Riemann, Hugo. 2015. "La región agrícola Camalú–El Rosario y sus recursos hídricos." In *El agua en la región agrícola Camalú–El Rosario, Baja California*, ed. Hugo Riemann, 11–28. Puebla: Editorial de la Red Nacional de Investigación Urbana (RNIU).

Rodríguez Tomp, Rosa E. 2002. *Cautivos de Dios: Los cazadores-recolectores de Baja California durante el periodo colonial*. Historia de los Pueblos Indígenas de México. Mexico City: CIESAS.

Rogaly, B. 2008. "Intensification of Workplace Regimes in British Horticulture: The Role of Migrant Workers." *Population, Space, and Place* 14: 497–510.

Rojas, Enrique. 2008. "Invita Cespe a exponer quejas por nuevas tarifas." *El Vigia*, February 28.

Romo, Ricardo. 1983. *East Los Angeles: History of a Barrio*. Austin: University of Texas Press.

Roseberry, William. 1996. "The Rise of Yuppie Coffees and the Reimagination of Class in the United States." *American Anthropologist* 98 (4): 762–75.

Saldaña Ramírez, Adriana. 2017. "Territorio, asentamientos residenciales y migración: El caso de jornaleros indígenas de La Montaña de Guerrero en Morelos." *Nueva Antropología* 30 (86): 120–38.

Samstad, James G., and Ruth Berins Collier. 1995. "Mexican Labor and Structural Reform under Salinas: New Unionism or Old Stalemate?" in *The Challenge of Institutional Reform in Mexico*, ed. Riordan Roett, 9–38. Boulder, CO: Lynne Rienner.

Sánchez, Gerardo. 2018. "Crédito por 665 mdp para desaladora de SQ." *El Vigia*, December 5. www.elvigia.net/general/2018/3/29/crdito-para-desaladora-299659.html.

Sánchez Munguía, Vicente. 2015. "San Quintín: La gestión del agua bajo un modelo agotado e insostenible." In *El agua en la región agrícola Camalú–El Rosario, Baja California*, ed. Hugo Riemann, 117–40. Puebla: Editorial de la Red Nacional de Investigación Urbana (RNIU).

Sánchez Saldaña, Kim. 2006. *Los capitanes de Tenextepango: Un estudio sobre intermediación cultural, México*. Mexico City: Universidad Autónoma del Estado de Morelos / Porrúa.

———. 2016. "Los intermediarios laborales tradicionales como brokers culturales." *Eutopia* 9: 13–27.

Sanderson, Steven E. 1986. *The Transformation of Mexican Agriculture: International Structure and the Politics of Rural Change*. Princeton, NJ: Princeton University Press.

Santes-Álvarez, Ricardo. 2015. "Aspectos que definen la gobernación del uso de agua en la región San Quintín." In *El agua en la región agrícola Camalú–El Rosario, Baja California*, ed. Hugo Riemann, 95–115. Puebla: Editorial de la Red Nacional de Investigación Urbana (RNIU).

Santos-Gómez, Hugo. 2014. *Immigrant Farmworkers and Citizenship in Rural California: Playing Soccer in the San Joaquin Valley*. New York: LFB Scholarly Publishing.

Sassen, Saskia. 2014. *Expulsions: Brutality and Complexity in the Global Economy*. Cambridge, MA: Belknap Press of Harvard University Press.

Scheiber, Noam. 2019. "Why Wendy's Is Facing Campus Protests (It's about the Tomatoes)." *New York Times*, March 7. www.nytimes.com/2019/03/07/business/economy/wendys-farm-workers-tomatoes.html.

Schneider, Sergio, and Paulo Niederle. 2010. "Resistance Strategies and Diversification of Rural Livelihoods: The Construction of Autonomy among Brazilian Family Farmers." *Journal of Peasant Studies* 37 (2): 379–405.

Scudder, Thayer. 1985. "A Sociological Framework for the Analysis of Newland Settlements." In *Putting People First: Sociological Variables in Rural Development*, ed. Michael Cernea, 148–87. Oxford: Oxford University Press.

Silverman, Stephanie J., and Amrita Hari. 2016. "Troubling the Fields: Choice, Consent, and Coercion of Canada's Seasonal Agricultural Workers." *International Migration* 54 (5): 91–104.

Stanford, Lois. 2002. "Constructing 'Quality': The Political Economy of Standards in Mexico's Avocado Industry." *Agriculture and Human Values* 19: 293–310.

Stephen, Lynn. 2007. *Transborder Lives: Indigenous Oaxacans in Mexico, California, and Oregon*. Durham, NC: Duke University Press.

Stuesse, Angela. 2016. *Scratching Out a Living: Latinos, Race, and Work in the Deep South*. Berkeley: University of California Press.

Syring, David. 2009. "La Vida Matizada: Time Sense, Everyday Rhythms, and Globalized Ideas of Work." *Anthropology and Humanism* 43 (2): 119–42.
Thomas, Kedron. 2013. "Brand 'Piracy' and Postwar Statecraft in Guatemala." *Cultural Anthropology* 28 (1): 144–60.
Thompson, E. P. 1967. "Time, Work-Discipline, and Industrial Capitalism." *Past & Present* 38: 56-97.
Treitler, Inga, and Douglas Midgett. 2007. "It's about Water: Anthropological Perspectives on Water and Policy." *Human Organization* 66 (2): 140–49.
United Nations General Assembly. 2017. "Report of the Special Rapporteur on the Human Rights to Safe Drinking Water and Sanitation on His Mission to Mexico." https://documents-dds-ny.un.org/doc/UNDOC/GEN/G17/229/49/PDF/G1722949.pdf?OpenElement.
United States Census Bureau. 2017. TIGER/Line Shapefiles (machine-readable data files). https://www.census.gov/geographies/mapping-files/time-series/geo/tiger-line-file.html.
United States Department of Labor. 2012. "California Agricultural Employer Agrees to Pay $457,000 in Back Wages and Penalties Following US Labor Department Investigation." News Release. www.dol.gov/opa/media/press/whd/whd20120234.
Vázquez León, Carlos Israel. 2015. "El contexto socioeconómico de la escasez de agua en la región de San Quintín, Baja California." In *El agua en la región agrícola Camalú–El Rosario, Baja California*, ed. Hugo Riemann, 57–80. Puebla: Editorial de la Red Nacional de Investigación Urbana (RNIU).
Velasco, Laura, Christian Zlolniski, and Marie-Laure Coubes, eds. 2014. *De jornaleros a colonos: Residencia, trabajo e identidad en el Valle de San Quintín*. Mexico City: El Colegio de la Frontera Norte.
Velasco Ortiz, Laura. 2002. *El regreso de la comunidad: Migración indígena y agentes étnicos. Los mixtecos en la frontera México–Estados Unidos*. Mexico City: El Colegio de México and El Colegio de la Frontera Norte.
———. 2005. *Mixtec Transnational Identity*. Tucson: University of Arizona Press.
Velasco Ortiz, Laura, and Carlos Hernández Campos. 2018. *Migración, trabajo y asentamiento en enclaves globales: Indígenas en Baja California Sur*. Mexico City: El Colegio de la Frontera Norte and Comisión Nacional para el Desarrollo de los Pueblos Indígenas.
Vélez-Ibáñez, Carlos G. 2010. *An Impossible Living in a Transborder World: Culture, Confianza, and Economy of Mexican-Origin Populations*. Tucson: University of Arizona Press.
———. 2017. "Continuity and Contiguity of the Southwest North American Region." In *The U.S.-Mexico Transborder Region: Cultural Dynamics and Historical Interactions*, ed. Carlos G. Vélez-Ibáñez and Josia Heyman, 11–43. Tucson: University of Arizona Press.
von Schnitzler, Antina. 2010. "Gauging Politics: Water, Commensuration and Citizenship in Post-Apartheid South Africa." *Anthropology News* 51 (1).
Walsh, Casey. 2004. "'Aguas Broncas': The Regional Political Ecology of Water Conflict in the Mexico-U.S. Borderlands." *Journal of Political Ecology* 11: 43–58.
———. 2009. "'To Come of Age in a Dry Place': Infrastructures of Irrigated Agriculture in the Mexico-U.S. Borderlands." *Southern Rural Sociology* 24 (1): 21–43.
———. 2011. "Managing Urban Water Demand in Neoliberal Northern Mexico." *Human Organization* 70 (1): 54–62.

Weaver, Thomas. 2001. "Time, Space, and Articulation in the Economic Development of the U.S.-Mexico Border Region from 1940 to 2000." *Human Organization* 60 (2): 105–20.

Webb, Patrick, and Maria Iskandarani. 1998. "Water Insecurity and the Poor: Issues and Research Needs." Center for Development Research, Discussion Papers on Development Policy, Bonn, October.

Wehncke, Elisabet, and Xavier López-Medellín. 2015. "Historical Water Pulses in the Central Desert Region: Following the Paths of the Missionaries' First Explorations of Northern Baja California." *Journal of the Southwest* 57: 145–62.

Wells, Miriam J. 1996. *Strawberry Fields: Politics, Class, and Work in California Agriculture*. Ithaca, NY: Cornell University Press.

Whiteford, Linda, and Scott Whiteford. 2005. "Paradigm Change." In *Globalization, Water, and Health*, ed. Linda Whiteford and Scott Whiteford, 3–15. Santa Fe, NM: School for American Research Press.

Whiteford, Scott, and Alfonso Cortez-Lara. 2005. "Good to the Last Drop: The Political Ecology of Water and Health on the Border." In *Globalization, Water, and Health*, ed. Linda Whiteford and Scott Whiteford, 231–54. Santa Fe, NM: School for American Research Press.

Whiteford, Scott, and Roberto Melville. 2002. "Water and Social Change in Mexico: An Introduction." In *Protecting a Sacred Gift: Water and Social Change in Mexico*, ed. Scott Whiteford and Roberto Melville, 1–28. La Jolla: Center for U.S.-Mexican Studies, University of California, San Diego.

Wilson, Tamar Diana. 2015. "Mexico's Rural Poor and Targeted Educational and Health Programs." *Human Organization* 74 (3): 207–16.

Wright, Angus. 2005. *The Death of Ramón González. The Modern Agricultural Dilemma*. Rev. ed. Austin: University of Texas Pres.

Wutich, Amber, and Alexandra Brewis. 2014. "Food, Water, and Scarcity. Toward a Broader Anthropology of Resource Insecurity." *Current Anthropology* 55 (4): 444–68.

Zabin, Carol. 1997. "U.S.-Mexico Economic Integration: Labor Relations and the Organization of Work in California and Baja California Agriculture." *Economic Geography* 73 (3): 337–55.

Zlolniski, Christian. 2011. "Water Flowing North of the Border: Export Agriculture and Water Politics in a Rural Community in Baja California." *Cultural Anthropology* 26 (4): 565–88.

———. 2015. "The Social Costs of Export Agriculture in San Quintin, Baja California." *Savage Minds: Notes and Queries in Anthropology*. https://savageminds.org/2015/08/23/the-social-costs-of-export-agriculture-in-san-quintin-baja-california-an-interview-with-christian-zlolniski/.

———. 2016. "Sistemas de intermediación laboral en una región agroexportadora del noroeste mexicano." *Eutopía* 9: 101–12.

———. 2017. "Growers, Unions, and Farm Laborers in Mexico's Baja California." In *Uncertain Times: Anthropological Approaches to Labor in a Neoliberal World*, ed. Paul E. Durrenberger, 209–32. Boulder: University Press of Colorado.

———. 2018. "Export Agriculture, Transnational Farmworkers, and Labor Resistance in the Mexico-US Borderlands." *Dialectical Anthropology* 42: 163–77.

Zlolniski, Christian, and Laura Velasco. 2015. "Resurgimiento de movilizaciones laborales." *Jornada del Campo*, no. 94: 5.

INDEX

A.B.C. Farm, 23–24, 32–42, 46, 50, 140, 156–57; collapse of, 40–42; Mendoza, Julio, 23–24, 33–35, 39–42; transformation of agricultural production, 24, 32–37; worker protest at, 41–42. *See also* agribusiness; export agriculture; greenhouse and shadehouse production

agrarian reform (Mexico), 8, 26, 31, 35, 38, 44, 47, 61, 67, 87, 103, 154, 180, 195, 211, 222, 227n2, 230n6; and de-agrarianization, 21; Agrarian Reform Law, 4. *See also* neoliberalism

agribusiness: and displacement of small-scale farmers, 3, 209, 222; and impact on medium-size growers, 209; as industrialized production, 12, 44, 61, 200, 208, 222, 230n4, 232n5; and U.S. consumer demands, 2–3, 8, 29, 31, 37, 49, 62, 75–77, 82, 119, 183, 207–8, 215, 217; employer failure to register workers in IMSS, 13, 60; externalizing labor and social costs, 6, 46, 62, 67, 82, 105–6, 121, 180, 214, 218; Mexico as second-class market, 52, 73. *See also* Agrícola Colonet; Agrícola San Simón; contract farming; Del Monte Foods; Dole Food Company; Driscoll's; export agriculture; greenhouse and shadehouse production; Monsanto; labor and workplace regime

Agrícola Colonet, 13, 44, 91, 202, 232n2. *See also* agribusiness

Agrícola San Simón, 1, 2, 3, 9, 88, 90, 92–94, 110, 116, 129, 232n2; access to capital, 3; from higher volume to lower volume, but higher "quality," 2; need for more skilled workers, 2; partnerships with U.S. corporations, 3; Peña, Jesús, xi, 1–3, 9; reduction in total labor needed, 2; transformation of production from field to greenhouses and shadehouses, 2. *See also* agribusiness; Montes, Rafael; Román, Arcadio

agricultural workers: and labor flexibility, 87–88, 90, 96–99, 105, 125, 212; and surveillance regime, 156; and transnational political links, 11, 141, 145, 148, 152, 213, 215–16, 233n11; and transportation; 39, 85, 87–90, 92, 105, 181–182; as indentured labor, 39–40, 88, 104, 158, 181; as transnational farmworkers, 7, 22, 70, 86, 106, 130, 141, 145, 178, 211; contestation to external view as "migrants," 9; digital production card, 58, 59, 230n3; disciplining of, 3, 60–61, 105, 123, 208; transporting associations, 85, 88, 90, 231n.3; wages, day rate, 21, 57, 114–117, 129; wages, piece rate, 21, 56–57, 79, 86, 93–94, 102–103, 111, 114–17, 119, 122, 125, 128–29, 132, 149, 151, 219. *See also* agribusiness; *carrilla*; export agriculture

Aguilar, Joaquín, 197. *See also* water

Alianza de Organizaciones Nacional, Estatal y Municipal por la Justicia Social, 11, 144–47, 149, 151, 220, 233n12; and internal divisions, 149

Alonso-Fradejas, Alberto, 12, 128, 151
Álvarez, Robert, 3, 51, 75, 208.

Baja California: gateway for U.S. contract labor, 106; history of, 24–27; map, xiv
Barrón, Antonieta, 10
BerryMex, 48, 53–54, 61–62, 64, 65, 98, 103, 118, 150, 202, 218, 230n5, 231n7; and contract growers, 62–69; control of labor and costs, 67; Cuenca, Joaquín, ix, xi, 61, 62, 64, 70–71, 73, 82; permanent workers, 68; seasonal workers, 68. *See also* Driscoll's

C. de Grammont, Hubert, xiii, 7, 10, 30, 33, 82, 119–20, 163, 185, 229nn8,11, 230n4
Camargo Martínez, Abbdel, 18, 40, 84–85, 89, 146, 158, 233n10
carrilla, 127–152; defined 129. *See also* agricultural workers
certification of crops by U.S., 5, 7, 62, 72, 81–82, 87, 94, 119, 208, 218–19; and "quality" euphemism, 3, 7, 21, 75, 108, 119, 120, 125; as culture of certification, 7, 208, 232n4; as extraterritorialized "ethos of control," 208; as neoliberal governance tool of control, 82. *See also* Good Agricultural Practices (GAP)
Chávez, Esther, xi, 84, 85, 85fig, 86, 120, 146, 159, 161, 168, 173
class transformation, 6–7, 12–13, 22, 37, 105, 146, 151, 166, 207–8, 210; and settlement, 211–14
colonias in San Quintín Valley: as squatter settlements, 1; demographic growth, 3; indigenous communities in, 17; Nuevo San Juan Copala, 9, 11; Santa Fe, 17, 19, 84–85, 115, 134, 136, 146, 153–54, 159, 161, 163, 165, 167–68, 171, 173–74, 177, 234, 236; Tress Arbolitos, x, 17, 19, 28, 102, 107–8, 116, 124, 131, 144, 163, 170–71, 175, 177, 180, 197–98, 200, 236n14
colonization. *See* settlement
Comisión Estatal de Servicios Públicos de Ensenada (CESPE), 186, 195–97, 199–200, 202–4, 224. *See also* water
Comisión Nacional del Agua (CNA), 192, 193, 204, 221, 225, 236n11, 236n21. *See also* water
Comisión Nacional para el Desarrollo de los Pueblos Indígenas (CDI), xi–xii, 223, 234n7
compañias golondrinas, 38
Confederación de Trabajadores Mexicanos (CTM), 137, 138–40, 142–43, 145–46, 148, 231n4; Espinoza, Jesús, delegate of, 138–39, 142. *See also* labor unions

Confederación Regional Obrera Mexicana (CROM), 97–98, 106, 137, 142–43, 145–46, 148, 231n4; Rodríguez, Josefina, representative & labor recruiter, xi, 97–99, 164. *See also* labor unions
Confederación Revolucionaria de Obreros Campesinos (CROC), 137
Consejo Agrícola, 137. *See also* agribusiness
contract farming, 16, 61–62, 65, 67, 69–70, 75–76, 82, 230n6; and links to national and international markets, 61; as mechanism to externalize risks and production costs, 62, 82. *See also* agribusiness; export agriculture
cuarterías, 134, 153–55, 157–58, 163–64, 170, 184; advantages over labor camps 157; defined 134. *See also* labor camps; settlement

Del Monte Foods, 23, 37
Dole Food Company, 32–33, 37
DIF (Sistema Nacional para el Desarrollo Integral de la Familia), 146, 173, 175
Driscoll's, 17, 20, 44, 48–53, 55, 57, 58, 60–69, 72–74, 81–82, 117–19, 135, 148, 150, 203–4, 218, 230n7, 233n12, 234n13; and desalination technology, 55; Clark, Henry, xi, 48–51, 53, 55, 57, 61, 63, 82, 150, 203–4; consumer boycott in U.S., 150; quasi-monopoly in strawberry production, 53; registers workers in IMSS, 60; viewed positively by workers, 60. *See also* BerryMex; water
Du Bry, 10, 156, 165

ecological/environmental degradation: aridscapes, 195–97, 205, 209; as agro-dystopia, 24; as "predatory formations," 210; ecological consequences, 3; ecological logic, 7; export agriculture and water, 186–206; externalizing environmental costs, 6, 46, 190, 205; overexploitation of aquifer, 14; social and human consequences, 3, 5, 7, 24, 186–88, 190–97. *See also* export agriculture; water
export agriculture, xiii, 3–8, 10, 12, 16, 21–47, 50, 55, 65, 67, 70, 75, 78, 87, 92, 96, 108, 115, 119–20, 125, 128, 137, 139, 151, 168, 175, 180, 184, 186–89, 191–92, 206–10, 213, 215, 217, 223, 227n3, 229n11, 232n6; and globalization, 2–3, 6, 12, 16, 20–21, 31–32, 39, 44, 46, 50, 61, 69–70, 76, 82, 96, 105–106, 123, 127, 151–52, 184, 187–88, 191, 200, 205, 208–12, 221, 227n3, 231–2n1; and NAFTA/TLC, 82;

as agroexport/agrofood industry, 3, 6, 8, 10, 16, 21, 23–24, 42–43, 46, 81, 83, 86, 88, 92, 96, 99, 105–6, 137, 149, 152, 156, 184, 187, 188, 190, 192, 200, 205, 210, 212, 219, 221–22; as global fresh-produce industry, 6–8, 11–12, 16, 21, 31–32, 46, 61, 69, 82, 86, 106, 127, 151, 154–55, 187, 200, 208–9, 211; as technological fetishism, 46; as transnational agriculture, 5, 6, 13, 20, 24, 32–33, 107, 207; as water exporters, 190; government subsidies of, 191–92, 195, 212, 230n6, 234n2, 235nn6,7,8. *See also* agribusiness; water

farmworkers. *See* agricultural workers
Fernández, Anayeli, xi, 102–104, 106, 110–11
Fernández, Martín, xi, 104, 144, 149, 170
Figueroa Sánchez, Teresa, xii, 58–59, 230n3, 232n5
Flores, Laura, xi, 123, 159, 177
Flores, Luis, xi, 112, 120, 123, 177–78
Frente Indígena de Organizaciones Binacionales (FIOB), 141
Frente Indígena de Lucha Triqui (FILT), 9, 146
Friedemann-Sánchez, Greta, 124, 152

Global Outsource Group 96–98, 105–6. *See also* Confederación Regional Obrera Mexicana; Monsanto; Rodríguez, Josefina
González, Humberto, xii, xiii, 109, 200, 222
Good Agricultural Practices (GAP), 21, 120–23, 125, 208, 218
Goodman, David, 8, 29, 31–33, 229n8
greenhouse and shadehouse production, ix, 1, 2, 7, 14–15, 43–46, 63, 84, 93, 98, 107–15, 121, 125, 189, 191, 204, 208, 219, 229n14, 232nn2,4, 237n22; and health hazards, 112; and increased productivity, 43, 109; cost of, 109; reduced wages, 111; working conditions in, 107, 110–14. *See also* agribusiness; export agriculture
Griffith, David, 86–87, 99, 101, 180, 212–14
growers and farmers: and associations, 137, 143, 218, 224; fieldwork methodology, 15–16; power differences and/or relations 16, 20, 50, 81–82, 192–93, 209. *See also* Consejo Agrícola; Unión Agrícola
Guerrero: preferred labor recruitment area, 3, 12, 47, 157, 172, 182, 217. *See also* Oaxaca

H-2A temporary agricultural visa (U.S.), 21, 100–4, 106, 178, 180, 214, 231nn5,6,7, 233n11; as extraterritorialization of labor control 106; as transnational labor, 11, 99–104; U.S. federal agencies that manage 100. *See also* Sierra-Cascade Nursery
Harvey, David, 24, 42, 122–23
Hernández, Celeste, xi, 124, 129–31, 162–63, 169–70, 178–80, 200
Herrera, Justino, x, 127–28, 141–43, 143fig, 145, 147, 149, 233n12. *See also* Sindicato Nacional Independiente de Jornaleros Agrícolas y Similares
Heyman, Josiah, xii, 207
Holmes, Seth, 18–19, 113, 126, 156
Horton, Sarah, 19, 113, 126
housing. *See cuarterías;* labor camps; settlement

Immigration Reform and Control Act (IRCA), 169; and legalization/amnesty, 169
indigenous workers: Mixtec 3, 17, 20, 30, 39, 47, 92, 105, 115, 117, 127, 130, 140, 146, 148, 173, 220; Triqui, 3, 9–11, 17, 39, 47, 105, 130, 140, 143, 146, 148, 173, 199, 220, 233n9; Zapotec, 3, 17, 20, 28, 39, 47, 102, 105, 107–108, 116, 124, 130–131, 146, 162, 175, 197, 199, 220. *See also* agricultural workers
informal economy, 57, 134, 154, 168–72, 175
Instituto Mexicano del Seguro Social (IMSS), 11, 79, 139, 142, 145, 219, 221, 233n12; Oportunidades, 154, 173–175, 177, 234n5

Johnston, Barbara Rose, 188, 194

Kay, Cristóbal, 6, 175, 184, 210–13,
Kearney, Michael, 216

labor and workplace regime, vii, 6–7, 11–13, 21, 46–47, 50, 69, 79, 82, 86, 92, 104–5; 107–8, 123, 125–26, 128, 137, 150–151, 184, 187, 204, 207–9, 213, 223, 231n1[chap. 4]; regimentation of (regimented flexibility), 7, 21, 108, 125, 156, 214; surveillance of, 3, 39, 95, 110–11, 116, 120, 126, 129, 156, 182. *See also* agricultural workers
labor camps, 3, 6, 10, 13–14, 25, 30, 39–40, 42, 57, 80, 86, 88–89, 97, 99, 105, 107–8, 114, 130, 139–40, 146, 154–58, 160, 163, 164, 169, 170, 172, 181, 183–84, 211, 224, 229n12, 234n4; A.B.C. Farm introduction of, 39; as "controlled residency," 39; demise of, 80, 105, 114; *tienda de raya* in, 182. *See also cuarterías;* settlement

labor resistance: labor strikes/protests, 11–12, 19, 21, 41, 104, 128, 141, 143–50, 152, 202–3, 218, 233n12, 234n13; legal mobilization, 128, 133; labor turnover: 55–57, 79, 122, 124; political mobilization, 10–16, 18, 21–22, 104, 131, 141, 145–147, 149, 150–152, 155, 165, 167–68, 176, 184, 199, 206, 213–16, 233n9, 234n3; resistance to production card, 58–59; silent resistance, 128, 133–137

labor unions, xii, 11–12, 19, 21, 61, 86, 89, 97, 106, 128; Central Independiente de Obreros Agricolas y Campesinos (CIOAC), 89, 139–41, 144, 147, 160; challenge to white unions by CIOAC, 140; Familias Unidas por la Justicia (FUJ), 148, 220, 233n11; independent unions: 139–52, 202, 215, 219–21; white unions, 98, 137–39, 140–42, 145, 147–49, 150–52, 233n3; white union definition 233n3. *See also* Confederación de Trabajadores Mexicanos (CTM); Confederación Regional Obrera Mexicana (CROM); Confederación Revolucionaria de Obreros Campesinos (CROC)

Lara Flores, Sara M., 3, 7, 10, 12, 30, 33, 82, 87, 119–20, 128, 130, 151, 163, 175, 183–85, 229nn8,11, 230n4

Lazar, Sian, xii, 148, 152, 215

Lizárraga, Jorge G., 8, 29, 31–33, 189, 228n7, 229nn8,15, 235n2

maquiladores, 67; and agricultural production as parallel to offshore assembly plants, 67

Martínez Novo, Carmen, 57, 80–81, 140, 230n8

Mexico-U.S. border: 1, 3, 5, 8, 10–11, 20–21, 24, 26, 29–31, 34, 46, 48, 50–51, 53, 66, 69, 70–71, 75, 77, 82, 100–102, 114, 145, 152, 177–79, 181, 188, 211–16, 221, 233n11; as borderlands, 53, 114, 216; and labor circuits, 19, 39; as transborder region, 8, 207, 233n7; crossing, 100–101, 116, 177–79, 181; militarization of, 11, 21, 102, 177–78, 214; U.S. capital flows/links, 3–4, 6, 8–9, 16, 23–24, 29, 31, 37–38, 43–44, 46, 51, 55, 65, 67, 70–71, 81–82, 109, 189, 228n7. *See also* agricultural worker; H-2A temporary agricultural visa

Monsanto, 17, 44, 84–86, 96–99, 105, 112, 120–23, 164, 168; conversion to temporary workers, 105–6; and Rancho el Milagro, 99; use of temporary contract agencies, 99. *See also* Global Outsource Group; Rodríguez, Josefina

Montes, Rafael, xi, 88–92. *See also* Agrícola San Simón

Moreno, Adelina, xi, 107–108, 163, 175, 177
Moreno, Rodolfo, xi, 107–108, 163, 177–78

Narotsky, Susana, 61, 82, 209, 211–12
nativism, 79–83, 166–67; 230n8, 236n19,
neoliberalism, 3, 42, 87, 103, 122, 125, 173, 180, 187, 190–91, 194, 197, 205, 208, 211, 222, 233n3, 234n5; and Mexico's reduction of consumer subsidies, 3; emphasis on export crops, 6; "neoliberal agricultural export bias," 6; privatization emphasis, 188, 191, 201; rise in capital accumulation, 6. *See also* export agribusiness; export agriculture; water

North American Free Trade Agreement (NAFTA)/Tratado de Libre Comercio In (TLC), 4, 8; and access to land, lower-cost labor, and lax governmental regulations, 4; and expansion of U.S. agribusiness in Mexico, 4; impacts of, 4, 8, 44, 63, 67, 82, 189

Oaxaca: preferred labor recruitment area, 2–3, 9, 12–13, 28, 30, 39–40, 47, 79–80, 88, 92, 97, 102, 107, 111, 115, 134, 141, 146, 153, 156–57, 161, 164, 172; and Oaxaca-Sinaloa-San Quintín labor circuit, 164–66, 170–72, 180, 184, 217. *See also* Guerrero

Oliver-Smith, Anthony, 18, 165, 209, 213–14
Oportunidades. *See* Instituto Mexicano del Seguro Social

Ortiz, Sutti, 57, 86–87, 114

Palerm, Juan Vicente, xii, 10, 156, 212
Palma, Andrés, xi, 70–79, 82; and Rancho Las Palmas, 70–79, 82, 194fig; and Las Palmas Strawberries, 76–77. *See also* contract farming

Partido de Acción Nacional (PAN), 140, 173, 233n3

Partido Revolucionario Institucional (PRI), 137–39, 147, 233n3

peasants, 12, 27, 78, 107, 123, 172, 211, 227n2, 228n6, 232n5. *See also* class transformation

Pérez Vaca, Miguel, 27–28
Preibisch, Kerry, 109, 114, 180, 213, 231n1
Programa Nacional con Jornaleros Agrícolas (PRONJAG), 14, 153, 160–61, 173

racism, 9, 79–83, 165–68
Radio XEQUIN, xii, 130, 179
Radonic, Lucero, 8, 209
Robles, Elisa, xi, 116, 129, 131, 148, 199

Robles, Nicolás, xi, 131–33
Rodríguez, Josefina, xi, 97–99, 164. *See also* Confederación Regional Obrera Mexicana; Monsanto
Rogaly, Ben, 7, 12, 108, 111, 119, 128, 151
Román, Arcadio: labor contracting, ix, xi, 92, 93, 94, 95, 96, 105
Roseberry, William, 76, 207

Sánchez, Justina, x–xi, 134, 136fig
Sánchez Saldaña, Kim, xiii, 10, 12, 87, 120, 128, 130, 151, 184, 232n6
Scudder, Thayer, 18, 158–59
Secretaría de Agricultura, Ganadería, Desarrollo Rural, Pesca y Alimentación (SAGARPA), xi, 15, 38, 43–44, 53, 61, 70, 122, 189, 191, 193, 222, 229nn13,16, 232n2; and subsidies for agribusiness, 191
settlement, 10, 153–185; as contested political process, 10–11, 15, 155, 165, 168; as new territorialization, 10, 155, 185; as socio-cultural practice, 164, 168; benefit to workers (residential autonomy), 154–58; claiming land and citizenship, 10, 184, 206, 215; claiming place and belonging, 163–72; costs of settlement, 168–72; settlement and U.S. migration, 176–80; workers as settlers, 13, 154–56, 158–67. *See also* Central Independiente de Obreros Agricolas y Campesinos *(CIOAC);* women
Sheridan, Thomas E., 8, 209
Sierra-Cascade Nursery, 99–103, 178–80, 231n5; and H-2A recruiting office, 100–101; and transnational recruiting (U.S.), 178–80; García, Jorge, 100; U.S. Department of Labor fine for violations, 231n5; virtual test for workers, 102–103
Sinaloa, 10, 23, 29–37, 39–41, 107, 109, 128, 134, 139, 141, 146, 157, 164, 207, 228n7, 229nn8,11, 235n2,
Sindicato Independiente Nacional y Democrático de Jornaleros Agrícolas (SINDJA), 146–47, 149, 202
Sindicato Nacional Independiente de Jornaleros Agrícolas y Similares, 145. *See also* Alianza de Organizaciones Nacional, Estatal y Municipal por la Justicia Social; Herrera, Justino
strawberries: ecological stress of, 189; export production, 6, 10, 44, 46, 48–51, 53, 55, 58, 63–66, 68, 69–77, 79, 91, 98–100, 102–03, 112, 115, 117–18, 134–35, 179, 193, 229n15, 230n2,5,7; link to Florida-Mexico tomato war, 229n15, 230n2; needing skilled harvest labor, 55; switch from tomatoes to strawberry production, 64, 117; water intensive crop, 6, 7, 44, 46, 50, 55, 81, 189. *See also* agribusiness; agricultural workers; Driscoll's; Palma, Andrés; Sierra-Cascade Nursery
Suárez, Aurelia, x, xi, 147–48, 155fig, 161, 167, 171, 174, 196fig
Suárez, Ramón, x, xi, 115, 147, 153, 155fig, 161, 181
Syring, David, 123, 232n5

Thompson, E. P., 122
tomatoes: ecological stress of, 189; export production 1, 2, 6, 15, 28–37, 43–44, 62, 71, 75, 88, 91, 94, 99, 107, 109, 115, 120–21, 135, 153, 181, 186–87, 189, 190, 218, 228n7, 229n14, 233n12; Florida-Mexico tomato war, 229, 230n2;, switch from tomatoes to strawberry production, 64, 117; water intensive crop, 7, 81, 189. *See also* A.B.C. Farms; Agrícola San Simón; Dole Food Company; water
Trans-Peninsular Highway, 28, 49, 84, 143, 145, 153

Unión Agricola, 137–38. *See also* grower associations
U.S. capital: importance of, 3–4, 8, 16, 23, 29, 37–38, 43–44, 46, 55, 65, 67, 81–82, 189, 228n7

Velasco, Laura, 10, 14, 19, 23, 25–27, 39–40, 43 134, 139–41, 157–158, 160, 163, 169, 181, 183, 227n5, 228n6, 232nn1,2, 233nn4,6,7,8,9, 234n4, 236n19
Vélez-Ibáñez, Carlos G., 162, 234n2

Walsh, Casey, 8, 27, 191, 205, 235n2
water: agribusiness providing minimum access and preventing social unrest, 203; and agribusiness transfer of cost to local communities, 190; as civil and human right, 187; desalination, 9, 14, 43, 44–46, 53–55, 66, 72, 76, 78, 81, 109, 187, 189, 190–91, 193–95, 203–4, 209, 224–25, 235n6; desalination as technoscape, 44; Driscoll's desalination of ocean water 204; illegal discharge by growers, 201; Mexican state's role in watercide, 186–206; number of desalination plants, 43, 189; Mexican government subsidy of, 187, 191, 235n8; local multitasking, 199; overexploitation/overextraction, 187, 201; political ecology of, 8, 16, 54–55; resistance/unrest,

16, 200–206; state government construction of desalination plant, 203; state government rental of desalination plant, 203; watercide, 186–206; water insecurity/scarcity, 186–206; waterscapes, 188, 190–191, 195, 204, 209; "water suffering," 200. *See also* ecological degradation

Wells, Miriam, 12, 50, 55, 69, 73, 78, 127, 151

Whiteford, Linda, 188

Whiteford, Scott, 8, 188, 191, 192, 205

Wolf, Eric, 16, 207

women: community work, 146, 175, 176, 176fig, 213, 223; recruited as ideal workers 30; gender cost in settlement, 172–76, 213; workplace sexual abuse and harassment, 9, 11, 99, 143, 219–20

Wright, Angus, 6, 32, 37, 113, 207, 229n8

Zlolniski, Christian, 19, 23, 25–27, 39–40, 43, 86–87, 106, 109, 134, 137, 140, 157–158, 160, 163, 169, 196, 227n5, 228n6, 231–2n1, 232n2, 233nn4,6,8,9, 234n4, 236n19